IMAGES
of America

WAGONER

On the Cover: Wagoner's streets were lined with people and their wagons or cars on most Saturdays, but even more came to town for the Saturday afternoon drawings promoted as trade days by the chamber of commerce. The drawings were held in the late 1940s in front of the H.F. Jones Mercantile at Church and Main Streets. The Wagoner Hotel can be seen at far right. (Courtesy of the Cradow Smith collection.)

IMAGES
of America

WAGONER

Liz McMahan

ARCADIA
PUBLISHING

ISBN 978-1-4671-1427-1

Published by Arcadia Publishing
Charleston, South Carolina

Printed in the United States of America

Library of Congress Control Number: 2015930364

For all general information, please contact Arcadia Publishing:
Telephone 843-853-2070
Fax 843-853-0044
E-mail sales@arcadiapublishing.com
For customer service and orders:
Toll-Free 1-888-313-2665

Visit us on the Internet at www.arcadiapublishing.com

This work is dedicated to my husband, Larry, and all those who have shared their pictures with me over the years.

Contents

ACKNOWLEDGMENTS

The author would like to acknowledge all those who have shared their photographs and memories of Wagoner over the years. My thanks also go to the family of professional photographer Cradow Smith, who shared his collection of negatives, and to my good friend Jerry Hickman, who allowed me to copy many of the postcards and photos from his extensive collection.

It was difficult to remember the source of every photograph. I have tried my best to acknowledge in the captions the origins of pictures and do apologize if I do not give proper credit in some instances.

Finally, to my husband, Larry, who tolerated my many hours in front of the computer while organizing this book, thank you.

INTRODUCTION

Wagoner began as a railroad stop. But from the earliest time of civilization on this continent, people traveled through the area that would become Wagoner. The Caddoan Indians left as evidence of their presence here the small island just north of Highway 51 at Taylor Ferry. Today called the Norman Site, it is one of the most prominent Indian mounds in the state, dating to about AD 600.

The Osage Indians trapped and traded in this area in the early 19th century but were forced out when the Creek Indians were removed from their homes in Mississippi and Alabama and resettled in Indian Territory. Wagoner was in the new Creek Nation.

Confederate and Union soldiers were stationed throughout this region during the Civil War and met in a skirmish just north of Wagoner on September 15, 1864. Just after the war, huge herds of cattle were driven north from Texas up the Texas Road—the East Shawnee Trail—right through the heart of this area on their way to markets in Kansas and Missouri.

And then the railroad came in 1871. The Missouri-Kansas-Texas Railroad (MKT or Katy) built its way south from Kansas to Gibson Station, just south of the future Wagoner, and beyond. About 12 years later, Henry Samuel "Bigfoot" Wagoner, who was stationed at Parsons, Kansas, with the Katy Railroad, decided a switch was needed to load cattle and lumber from the area between Gibson Station and Flat Rock Creek. When the switch was completed, Katy roadmaster Perry telegraphed company officials that "Wagoner's Switch is ready." The spot on the prairie had its name. The Kansas and Arkansas Valley Railroad's announcement in 1883 that it too would be running tracks through this area put Wagoner in a unique position: it would be a crossroads of rail service.

Wagoner got its first permanent residents on June 5, 1887, when William H. and Sallie H. McAnally moved their family to Wagoner's Switch. He had been an MKT employee who had worked at Wagoner's Switch. Eventually, McAnally quit his job with the Katy and built a wooden structure that railroad employees called the Cottonwood Hotel.

In less than a year, a number of enterprises had sprung up in the prairie community. On February 25, 1888, the town's request for a post office was granted and William W. Teague, a native of Indiana, was named the city's first postmaster. Cattlemen, hay dealers, business- and professional men flocked to the new community from surrounding states, seeing the possibility that the Indian Territory soon would be divided and available for private ownership. The people who came here brought in fine lumber to construct business buildings and beautiful homes. While the original businesses were destroyed by fire, many of the original homes still stand as the pride of Wagoner citizens and the delight of city visitors.

Businessmen were not the only ones to visit Wagoner in its earliest days. So did some of the most infamous bandits of the day. On September 15, 1891, members of the Dalton Gang robbed a train at Leliaetta, just north of Wagoner.

By 1892, Wagoner's population had grown to 400. It boasted five general mercantile stores, two drugstores, a cotton gin, gristmill, two blacksmith shops, a livery stable, a newspaper, a church, and four hotels.

In 1895, a group of Wagoner citizens met in the office of Capt. William Jackson, an Englishman married to a Creek woman, to discuss the possibility of establishing a city government. On December 3, 1895, a petition signed by 283 heads of families was filed in the federal court in Muskogee. A hearing was set for January 4, 1896. Later that month, Judge Springer granted the petition, making Wagoner the first town in Indian Territory to incorporate. The city's population that year was reported at 1,500. The new city quickly established the first free public schools for white children.

Wagoner is described in an 1899 *Twin Territories* magazine as "having more and finer buildings than any other town in the Indian Territory. The residences of Wagoner are the handsomest in the Indian Territory while the society is refined and cultivated." The editor of the *Wagoner Record* would have disagreed. In 1901, that newspaper charged that "two gambling halls have been running 'wide open' in Wagoner for the past year."

In its earliest years, Wagoner was surrounded by a fence, according to a history by longtime Wagoner librarian Kate Hersman. She writes in a 1957 *Record-Democrat* article that when her father, Dr. S.D. Lyles, first came to Wagoner in 1898, the town was enclosed by wire fences on all four sides to keep cattle from the huge herds on area ranches out of town. There were four or five gates leading out of town, but many residents carried wire cutters and did not even bother to hunt a gate. This situation was vexing to the cattlemen, she notes.

By the time her father arrived here, Wagoner boosters already were claiming the crown of "Queen City of the Prairies" for Wagoner. The young city had a population of 3,372, the fourth-largest in Indian Territory.

Wagoner was developing its first tourism business—germicidal baths. The mineral waters were said to have "almost a magical character" and were reported to cure even the most stubborn diseases. Bathhouses capable of serving 500 people a day and several hotels offered patrons an opportunity to soak in the miraculous waters.

In the fall of 1900, nearly 100 Wagoner business- and professional men had signed a petition calling for a public meeting at city hall to organize a league to promote the cause of single statehood. Instead, Congress passed an act enabling Oklahoma and Indian Territories to prepare for admission to the union as a single state. In April 1908, an election was held and Wagoner was named the county seat of the new Wagoner County. Porter and Coweta had also vied to become the county seat.

By 1905, Wagoner had its third railroad going through the city. The Missouri, Oklahoma and Gulf ran from Henryetta to Joplin, Missouri. A couple of years later, there were 14 passenger trains a day serving the town's 5,000 residents and the surrounding rural area.

Cultural activities had started to evolve in the community at about the same time Oklahoma was being granted statehood. The Calumet Dance Club met for formal dances at Cobb's Hall, the ballroom area of the S.S. Cobb Building. A library was constructed with local support and funds from Andrew Carnegie's foundation, the Carnegie Corporation.

Churches offered most of the social activities of the community. By the time of statehood, there were several—First Baptist, First Methodist, First Christian, Holy Cross Catholic, St. James Episcopal, First Presbyterian, and others.

Wagoner schools also continued to grow. A separate school for blacks was built shortly after Wagoner's first school for white children opened.

Wagoner ended the 20th century enjoying a reputation as a spirited community with a new water park, plans for a new library, a developing industrial park, a wonderful holiday lights program, and the one thing that has remained constant in the city's history—wonderful people.

One

Queen City of the Prairies

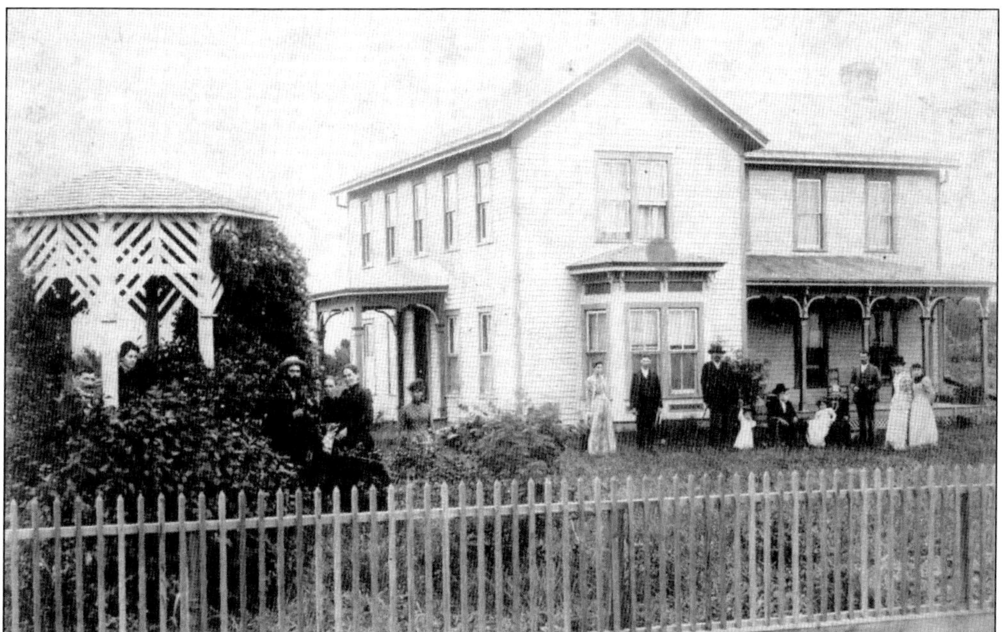

In 1883, shortly after settling two miles east of present-day Wagoner, the Joseph Benson Cobb family built what is today the oldest house in Wagoner County. This photograph from 1891 shows several members of the Cobb family. (Courtesy of the Cobb family.)

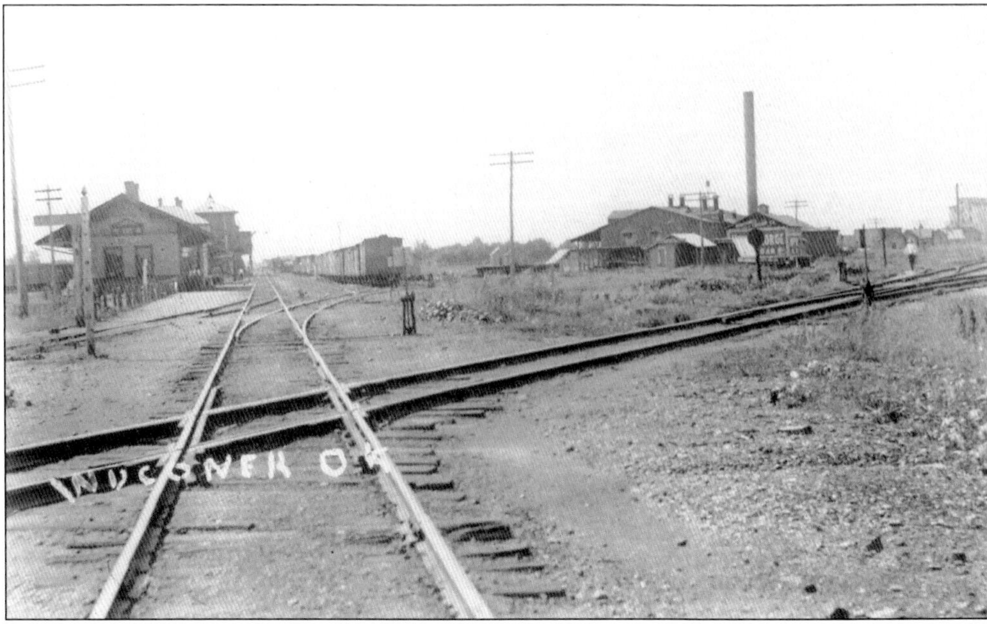

The Katy Railroad brought many visitors to Indian Territory. Learning that the Kansas and Arkansas Valley Railroad planned a line to intersect the Katy, William and Sallie McAnally decided to settle when they arrived at Wagoner Switch in 1887. This photograph shows the intersection of the Katy and the Missouri Pacific Railroads, with the Mo-Pac depot on the left and Merchants Cotton Co. at right. Wagoner is still a railroad crossroads city, with Union Pacific operating the two lines. Several dozen trains pass through the city each day. (Courtesy of Jerry Hickman.)

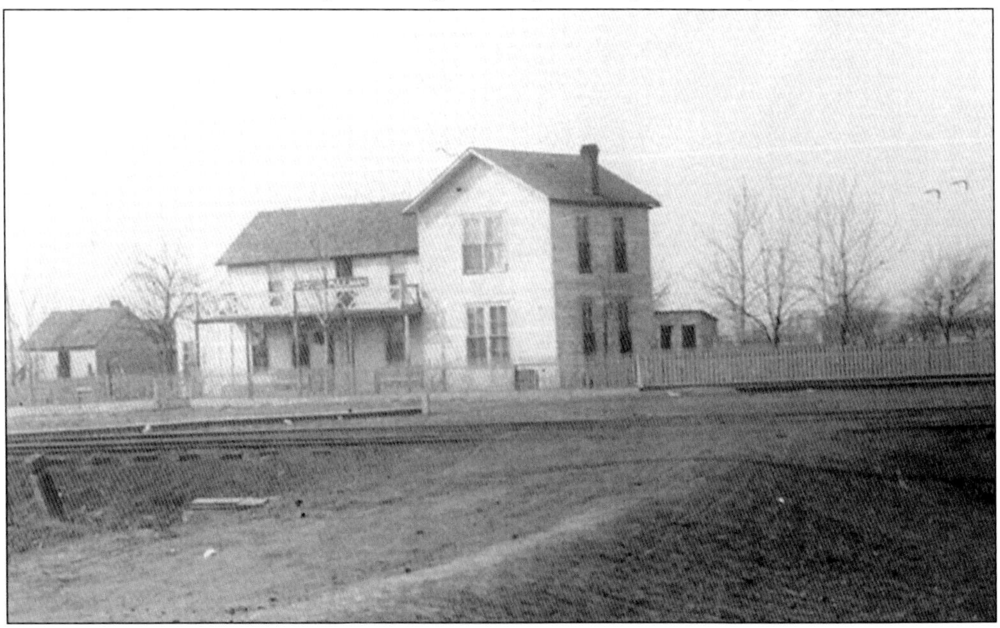

William McAnally built Wagoner's first business, the Cottonwood Hotel, near the intersection of Southeast Third and Main Streets in 1887. By the time this photograph was taken in 1895, it had become the Hotel Pullman. The building was destroyed by a fire sometime after 1901. (Courtesy of the Wagoner Public Library.)

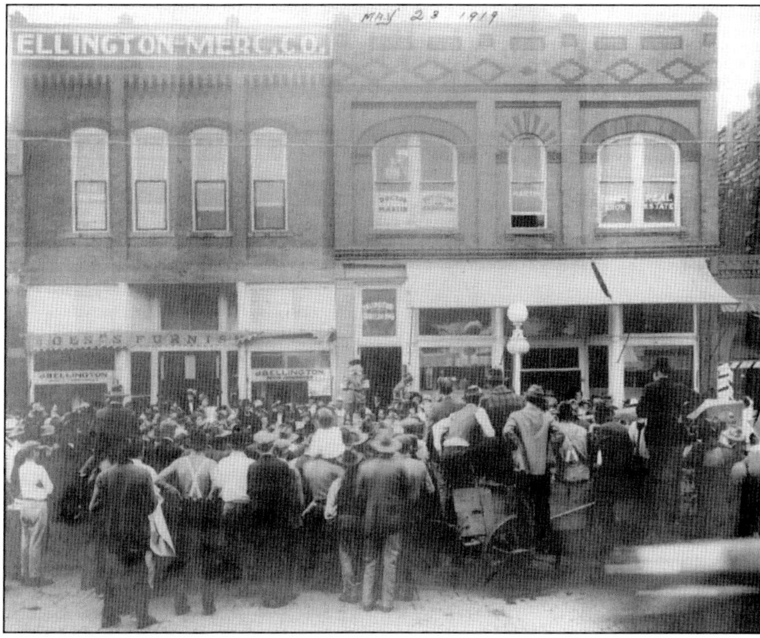

Buster Brown and his sidekick, Tige, are in full costume for this promotional event for Buster Brown Shoes on May 28, 1919, in front of Ellington Mercantile on the west side of Wagoner's South Main Street. (Courtesy of Don Daniel.)

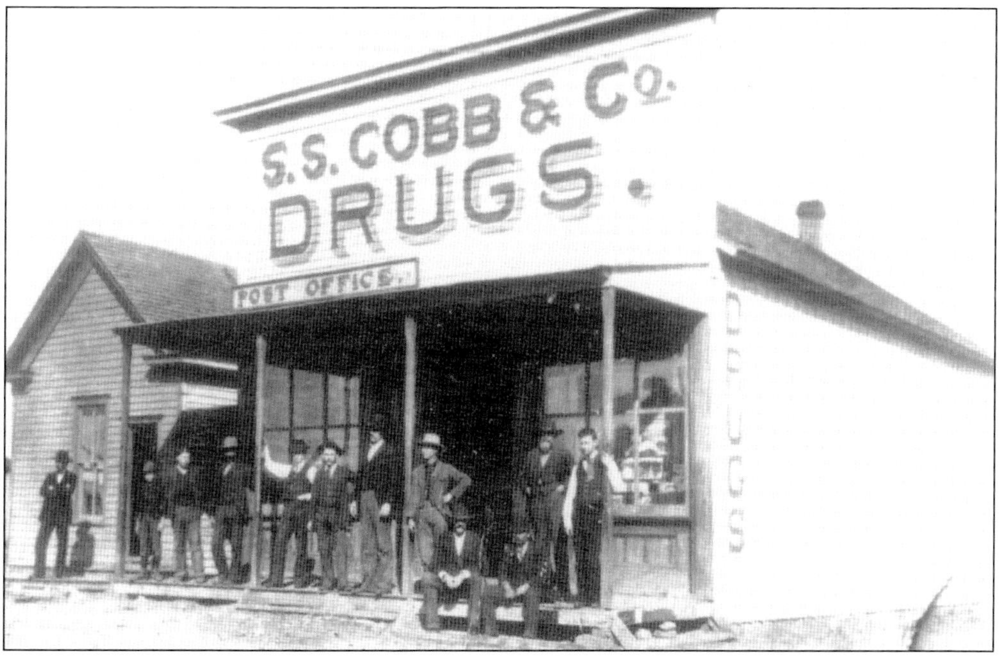

S.S. Cobb opened Wagoner's first drugstore in July 1890 just north of the intersection of Main and Cherokee Streets. The building was a small frame structure. He moved the business into his grand new brick building just to the south in 1895. This photograph shows several of the town's businesspeople on the wooden porch, such as Carl and Ira Dunlap, Kirk Turnbo, Harry Bettis, Ben Parkinson, Sam Cobb, Joe Hall, J.E. Newberry, G.D. Sleeper, ? Sears, and Jack Lisenbee. (Author's collection.)

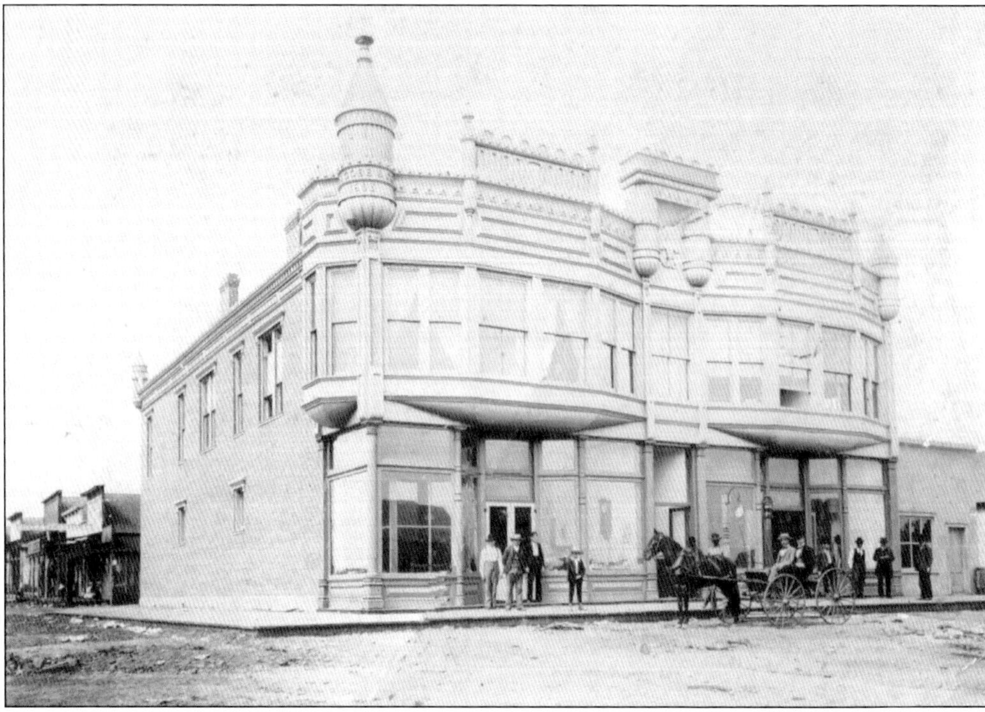

The S.S. Cobb Building, at the northeast corner of Main and Cherokee Streets, has been the centerpiece of downtown Wagoner since 1895. The structure is listed in the National Register of Historic Places and today is the home of American Bank. (Courtesy of Margie Semore.)

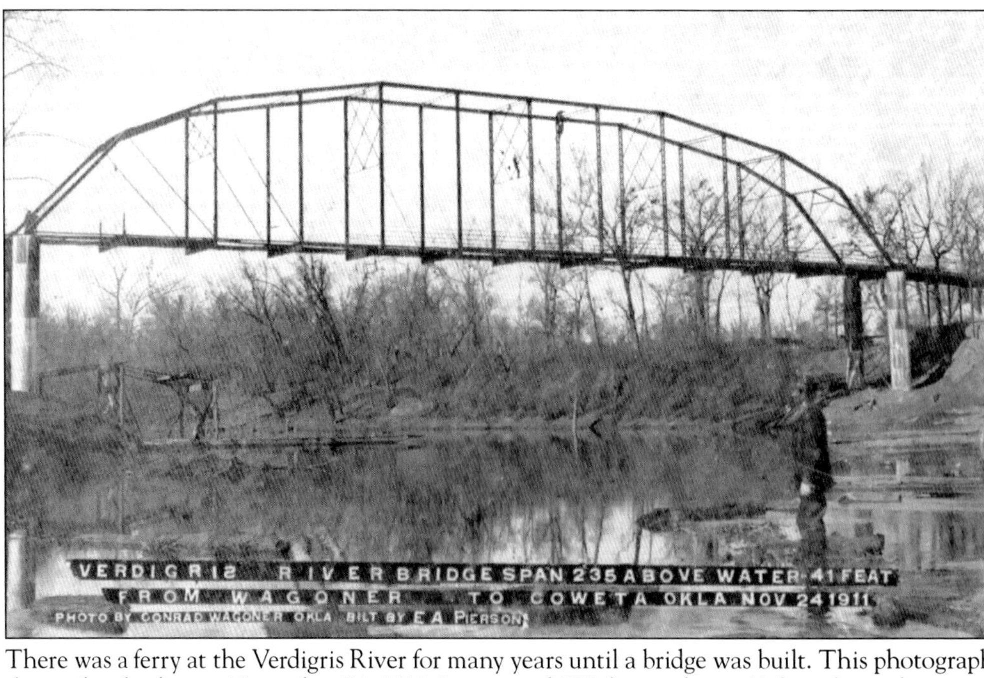

There was a ferry at the Verdigris River for many years until a bridge was built. This photograph shows that bridge on November 24, 1911. It spanned 235 feet and was 41 feet above the water, according to the photographer, Conrad. (Courtesy of Lindall Hughes.)

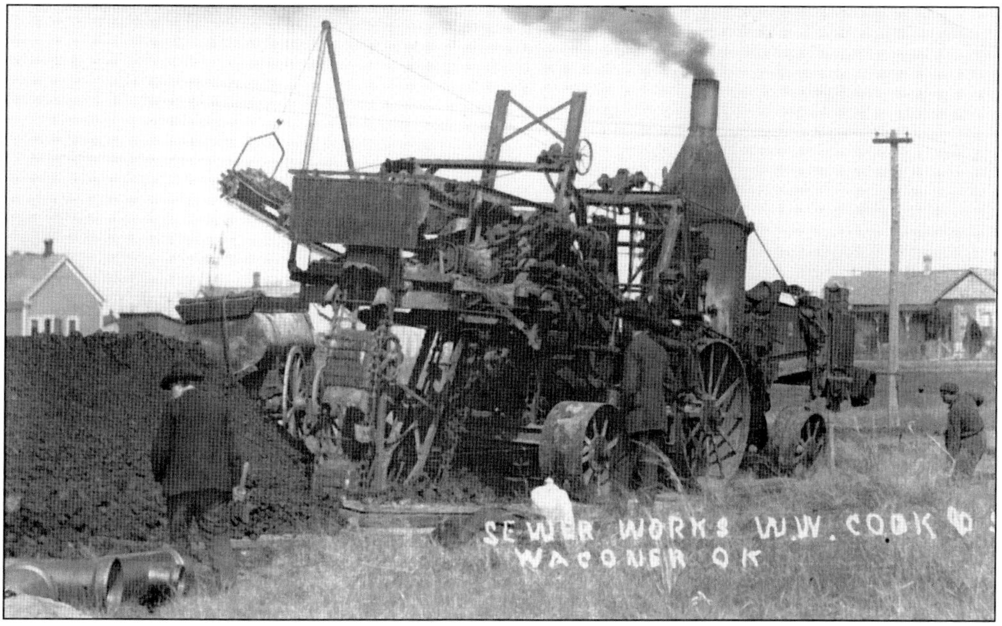

W.W. Cook was the contractor for installing sewer lines in Wagoner in 1909. (Courtesy of Shirle Lamb Williams.)

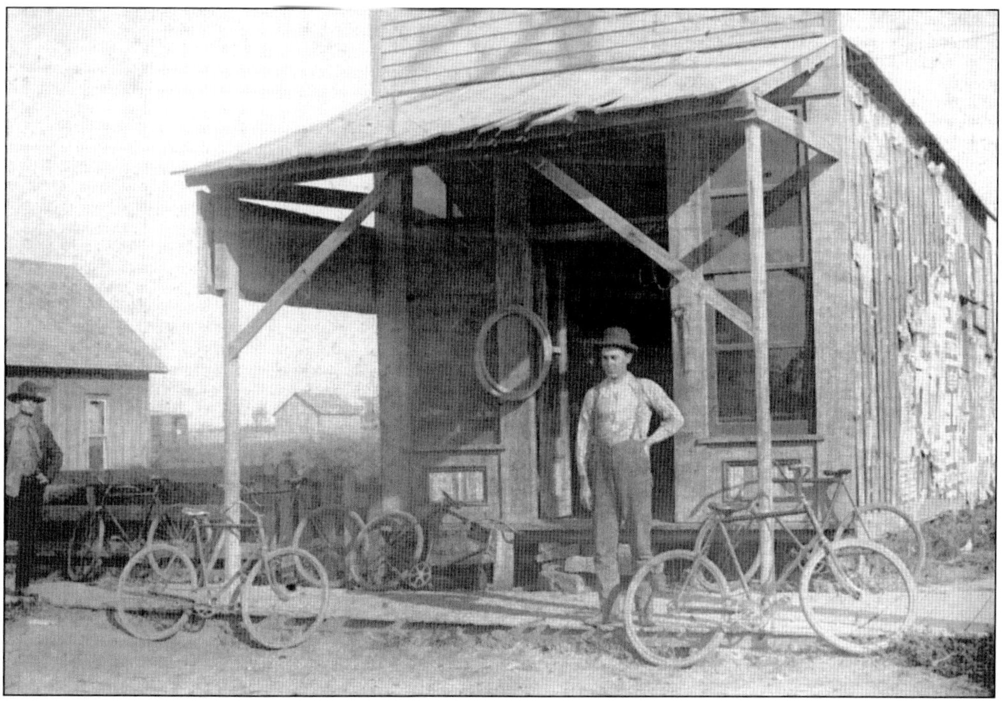

Mun Sprangel's bicycle shop was at the northwest corner of Cherokee Street and Casaver Avenue in the early 1900s. Sprangel came to Wagoner from Missouri on a bicycle, to which he had added a third wheel so that he could ride it on railroad tracks. (Author's collection.)

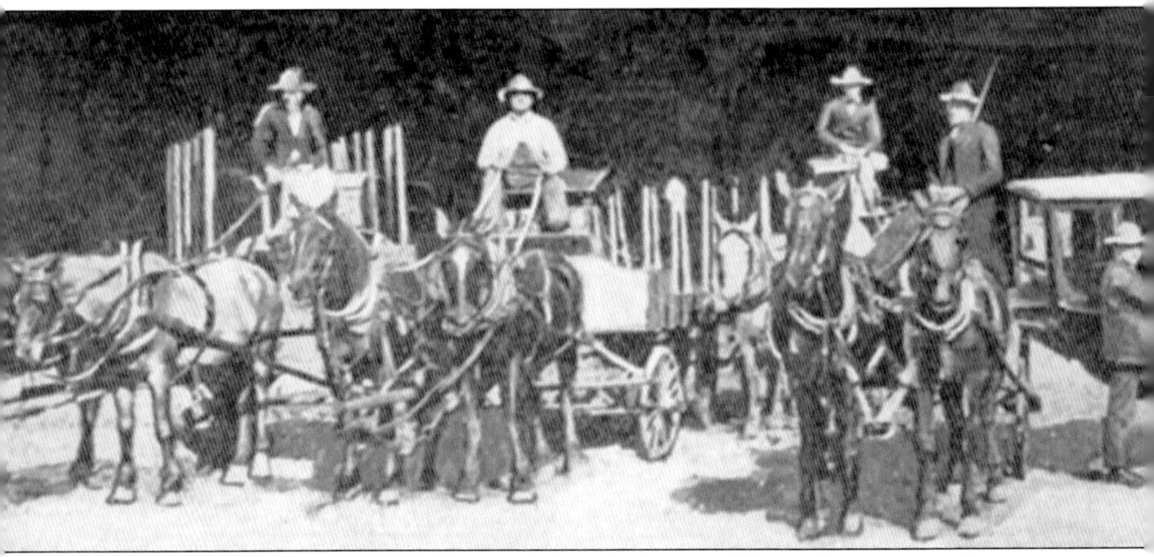

E.D. Lord bought out the City Dray and Transfer Line in 1900 and operated it from a stone building in the middle of the block on the east side of North Main until his death in 1936. This photograph is from an early-day advertisement for the building that boasts the business can

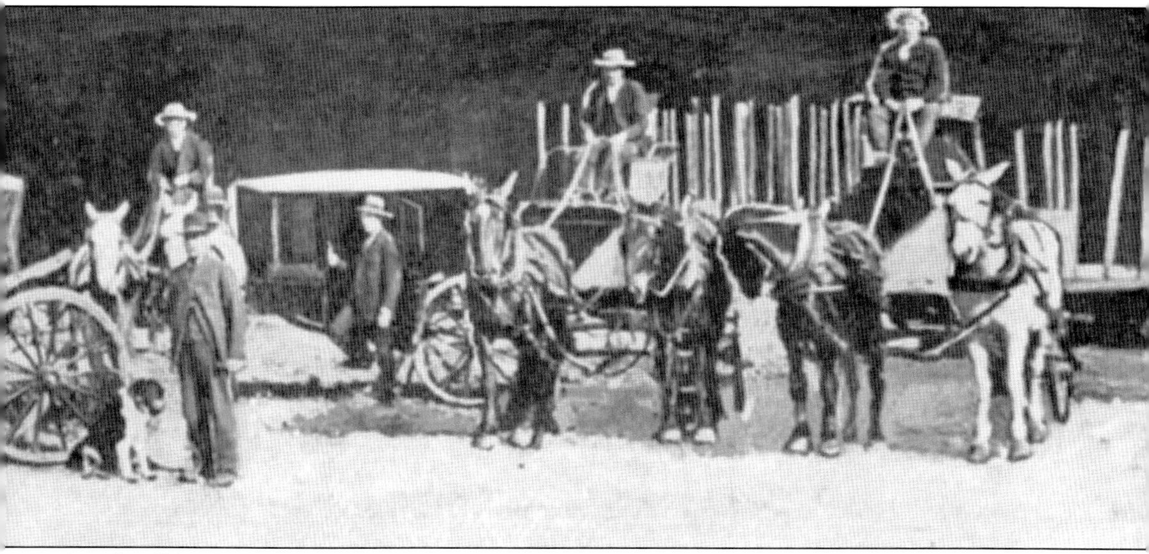

"handle all kinds of freight wagons. Cabs and baggage wagons are up-to-date. Ship your goods to us with instructions for delivery." (Courtesy of Shirle Lamb Williams.)

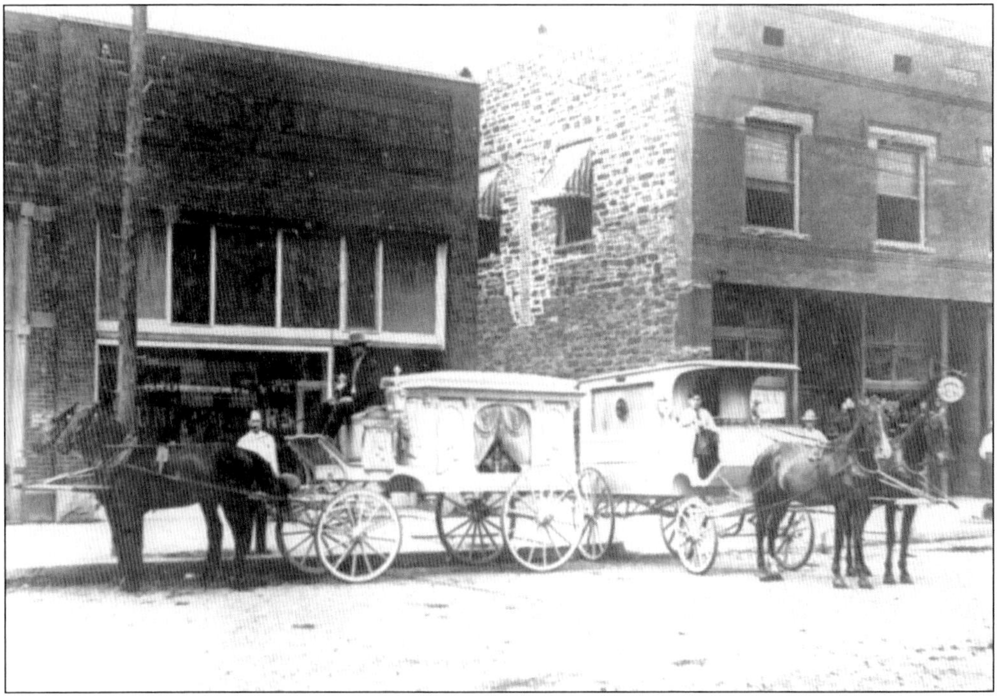

Brown, Cayo & Co., the forerunner to Hersman-Nichols Funeral Home, advertised in a 1913 Wagoner newspaper that it had two hearses, the silver gray one at left and the ambulance at right. The hearse cost $2,000. The company bought the ambulance for $950. (Author's collection.)

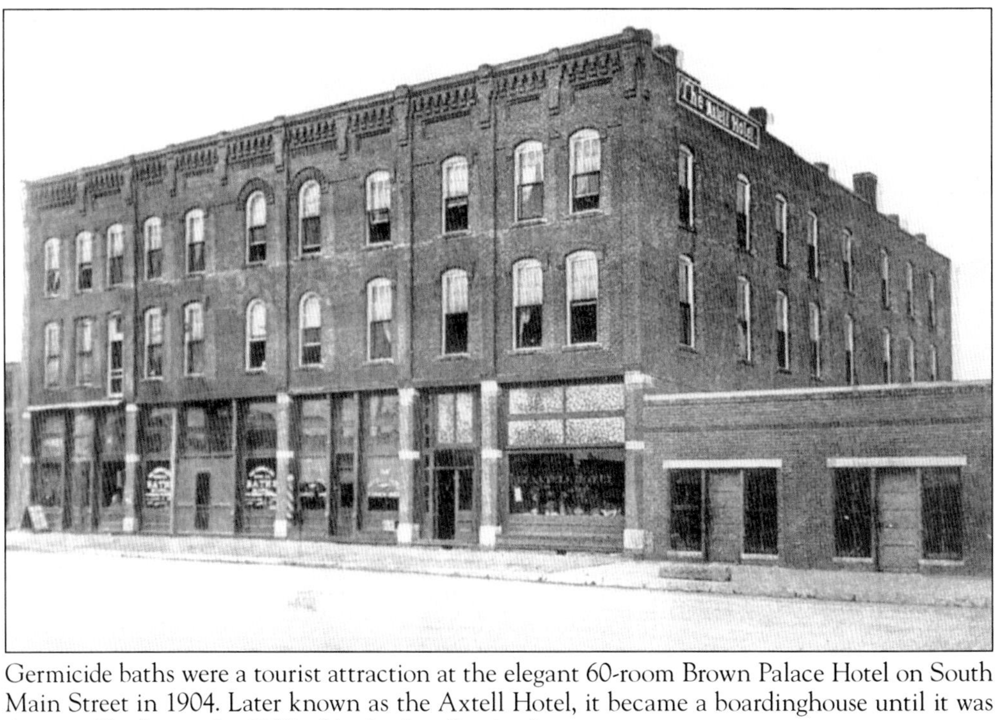

Germicide baths were a tourist attraction at the elegant 60-room Brown Palace Hotel on South Main Street in 1904. Later known as the Axtell Hotel, it became a boardinghouse until it was destroyed by fire in the 1950s. (Author's collection.)

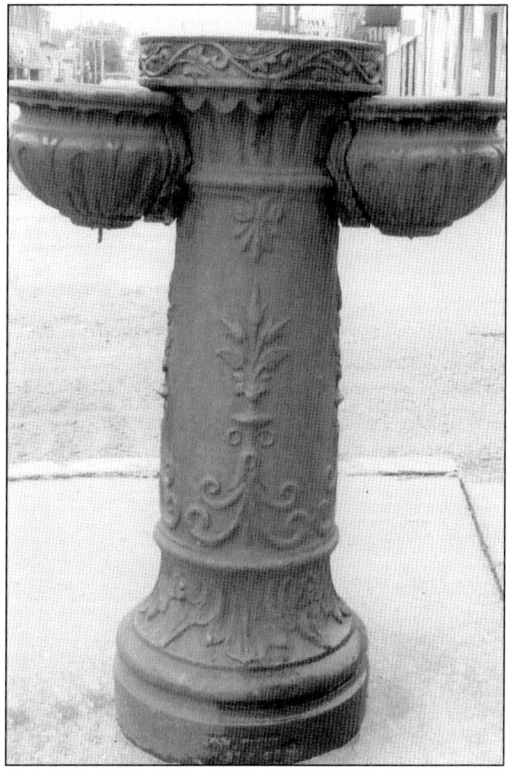

This two-sided fountain offered city visitors a choice between germicide water on one side and plain water on the other. The city bought the fountain in November 1906 for $53.65. It remains at the corner of Church and Main Streets. (Author's collection.)

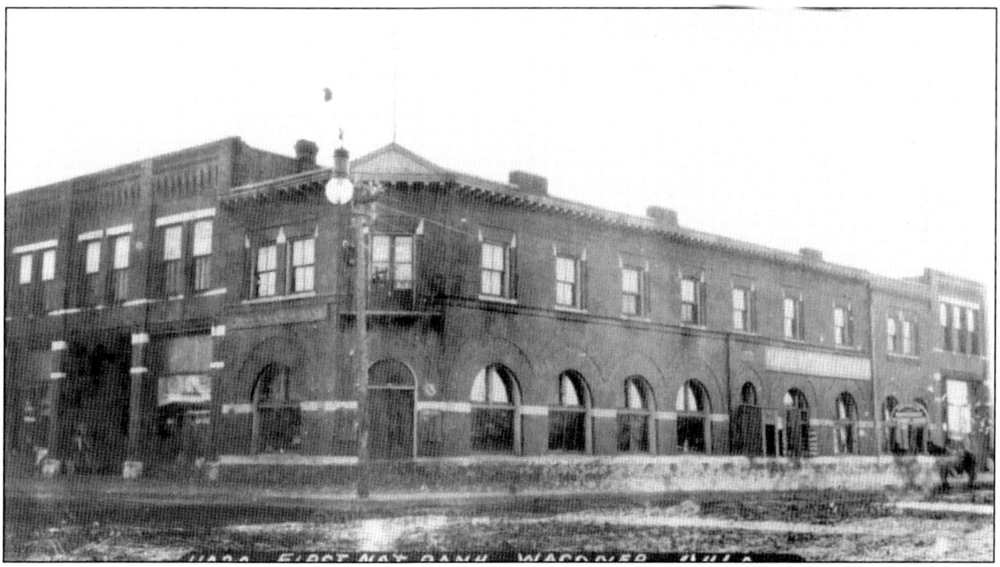

First National Bank was chartered on August 1, 1895, making it the sixth bank chartered in Indian Territory. The bank opened a couple of months after receiving the charter, moving into this building, which still stands at the southwest corner of Main and Cherokee Streets. The property where the bank was built had been purchased by James Parkinson for $1,600 and the structure was erected for $6,500. The blue bricks on the front of the building today were added before 1915. First Bank and Trust now operates from a building at Casaver Avenue and Church Street. (Author's collection.)

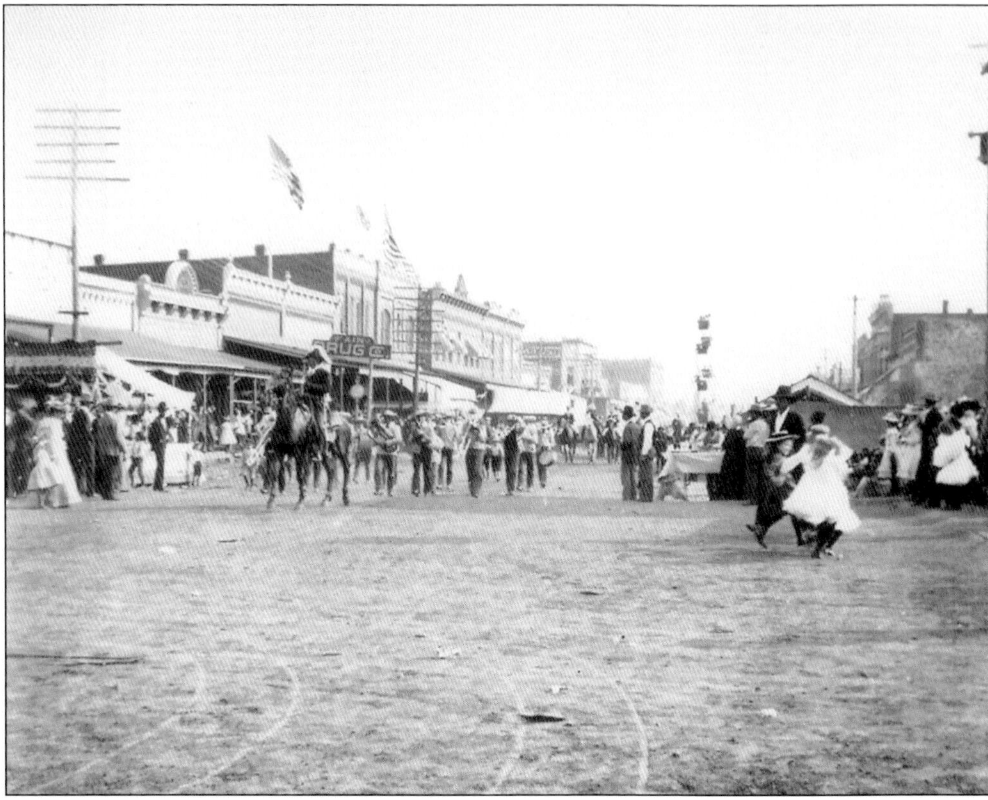

A carnival sets up on South Main Street in the early 1900s, erecting its Ferris wheel in the center of the street. (Courtesy of Shirle Lamb Williams.)

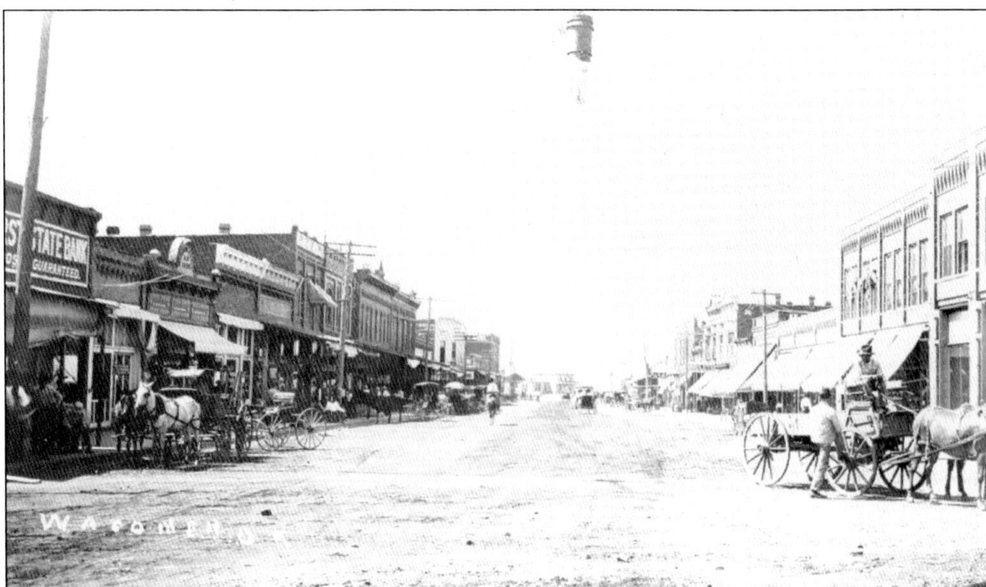

The view in this photograph looks south on Main Street on a busy trade day. (Courtesy of Jerry Hickman.)

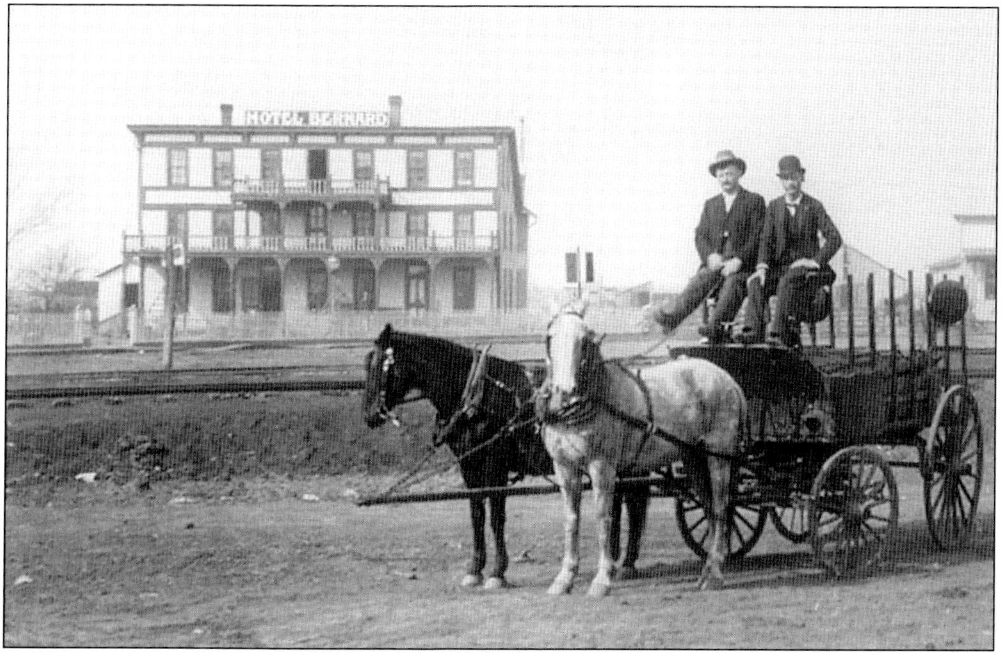

With Wagoner being located at the crossroads of several railroads, a number of hotels sprang up in town, even before the city was incorporated. Among the first was the Hotel Bernard. The hotels were on the west side of the tracks just before they cross Third Street. (Courtesy of Shirle Lamb Williams.)

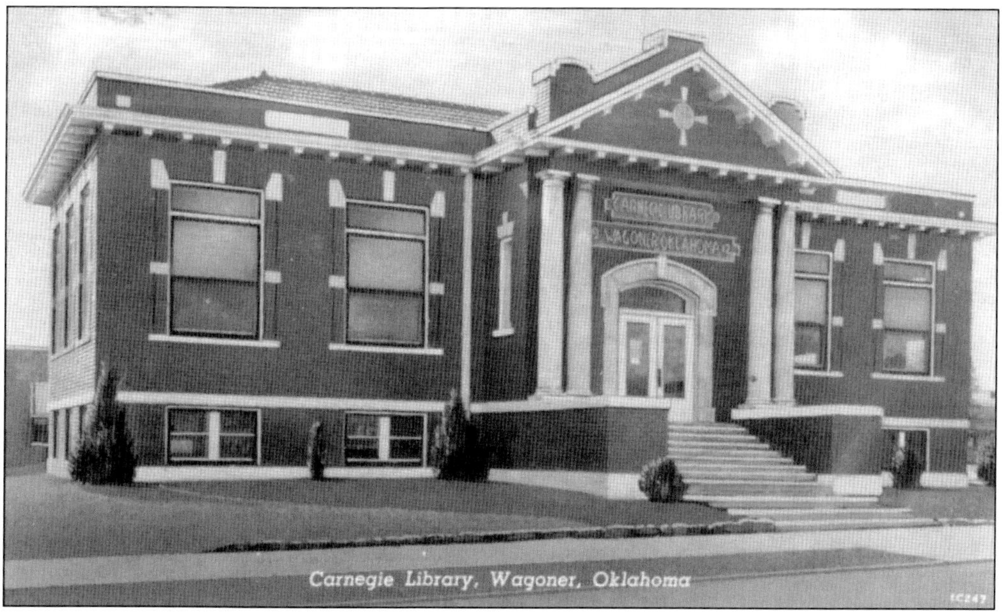

Wagoner's Carnegie library, which serves today as a genealogy library, was built with a $10,000 grant from the Carnegie Corporation in 1913. (Courtesy of Shirle Lamb Williams.)

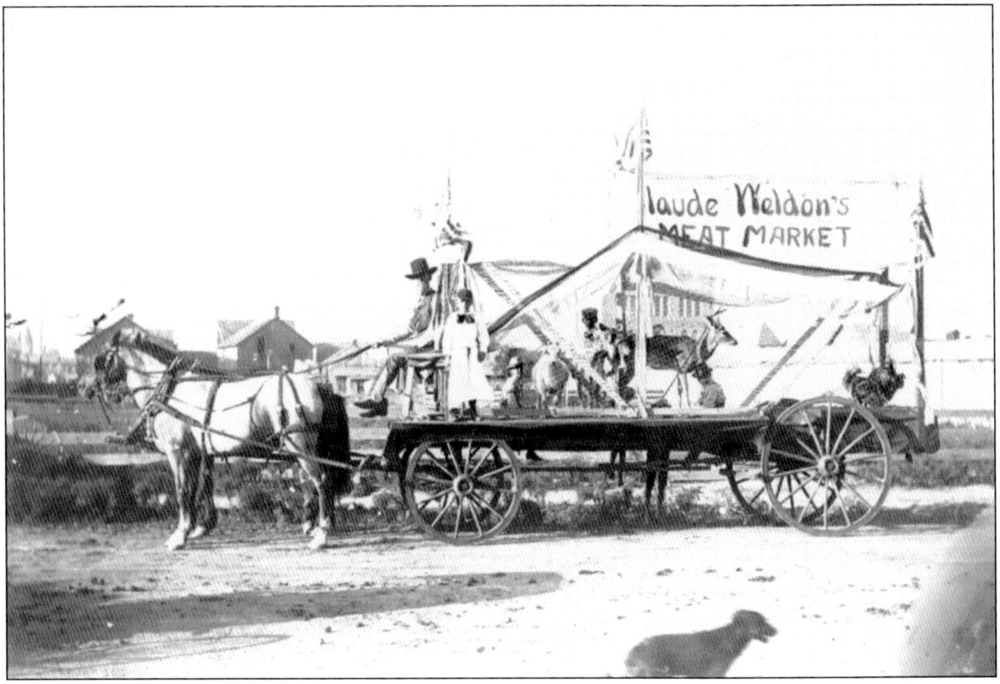

Claude Weldon advertised his meat market with this entry in an early-day parade. Species on the float include a sheep, a doe and a buck deer, and a pair of turkeys. (Courtesy of the Wagoner City Historical Museum.)

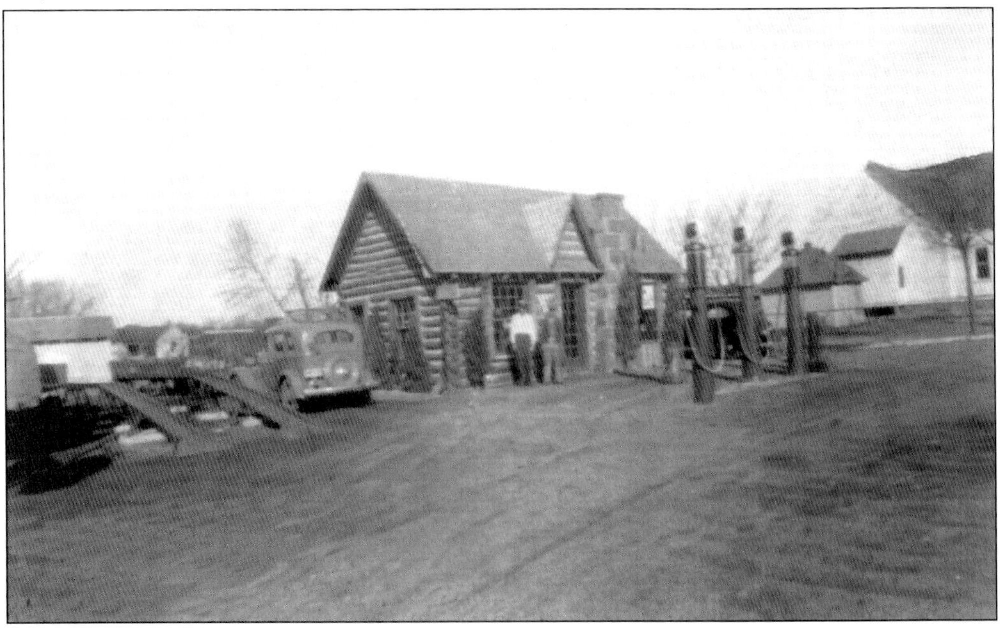

Located on State Street—the Jefferson Highway as it ran through Wagoner—the Log Cabin was the second service station in Wagoner. The Presbyterian church shown to the north of the station in this photograph was later moved. Wagoner historian Nellie Harris said Sinclair Oil Company did not like the primitive look of the log siding and had the station cover it up. (Author's collection.)

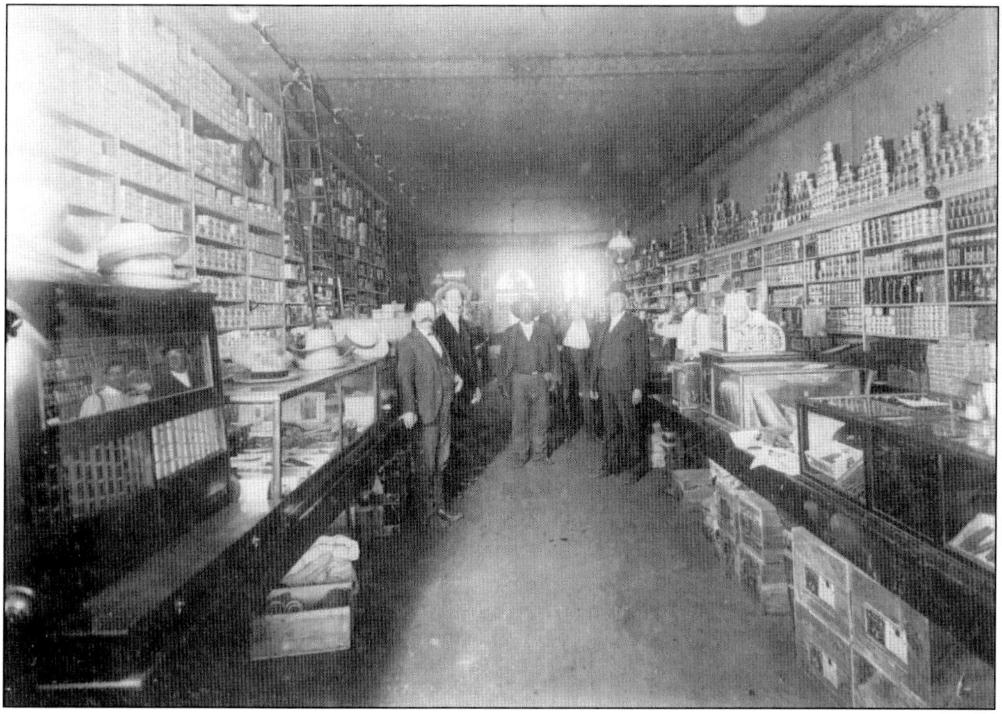

Quality clothes were among the offerings of Ellington Mercantile on South Main Street when this photograph was taken in 1905. J.B. Ellington is the first man on the left; O.H. Ellington is at far right. (Courtesy of Don Daniel.)

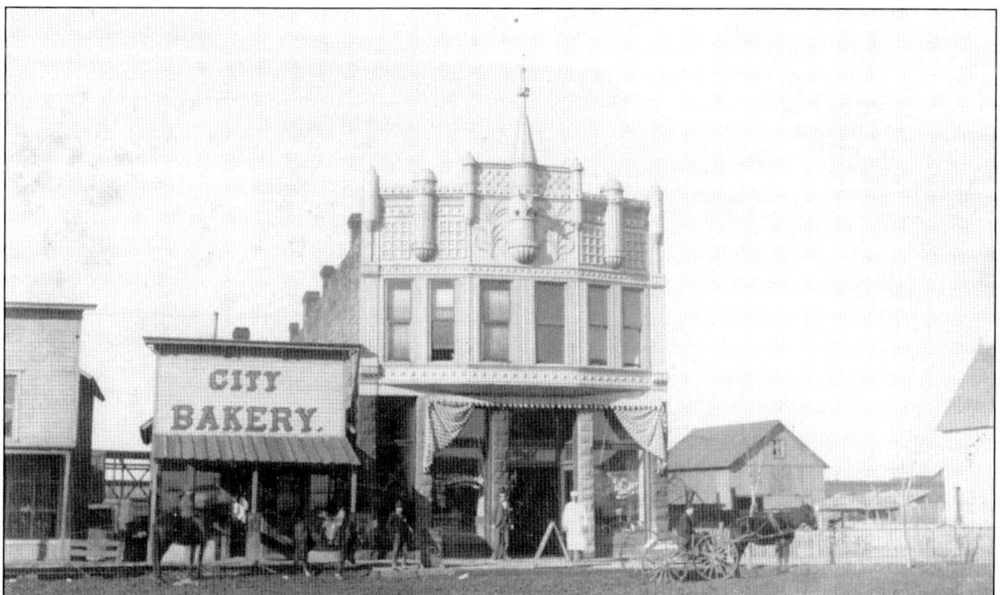

The metalwork on the front of H.A. Hills Meat Market on South Main Street looks very similar to that on the front of the Cobb Building, which was about one block north. They were among five storefronts in early Wagoner designed by Ed Lee. However, an ornate steer head set this building apart from the rest. (Courtesy of Shirle Lamb Williams.)

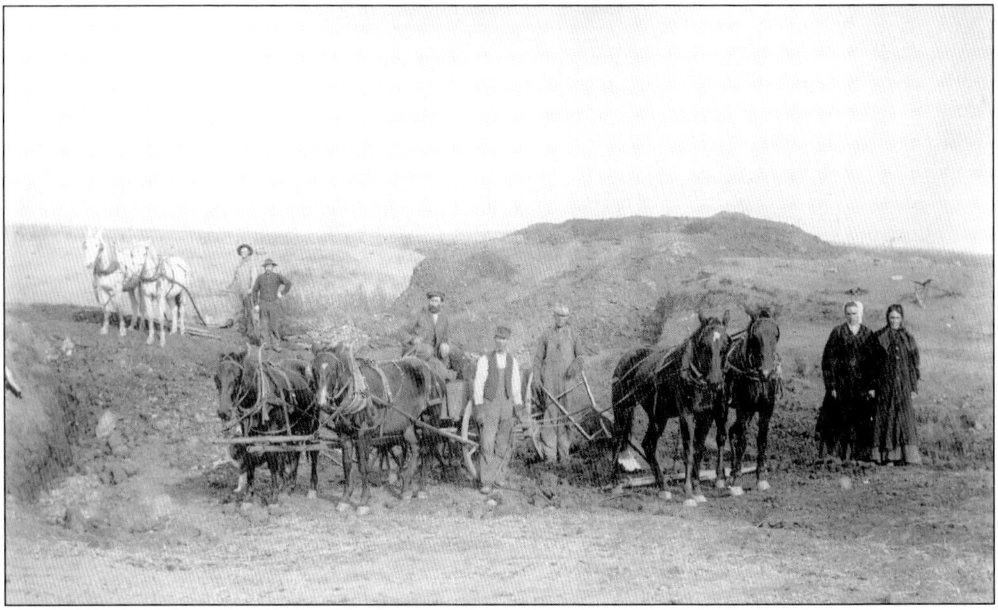

A coal mining operation along Bull Creek, west of Wagoner, diversified Wagoner's economy in its earlier days. (Author's collection.)

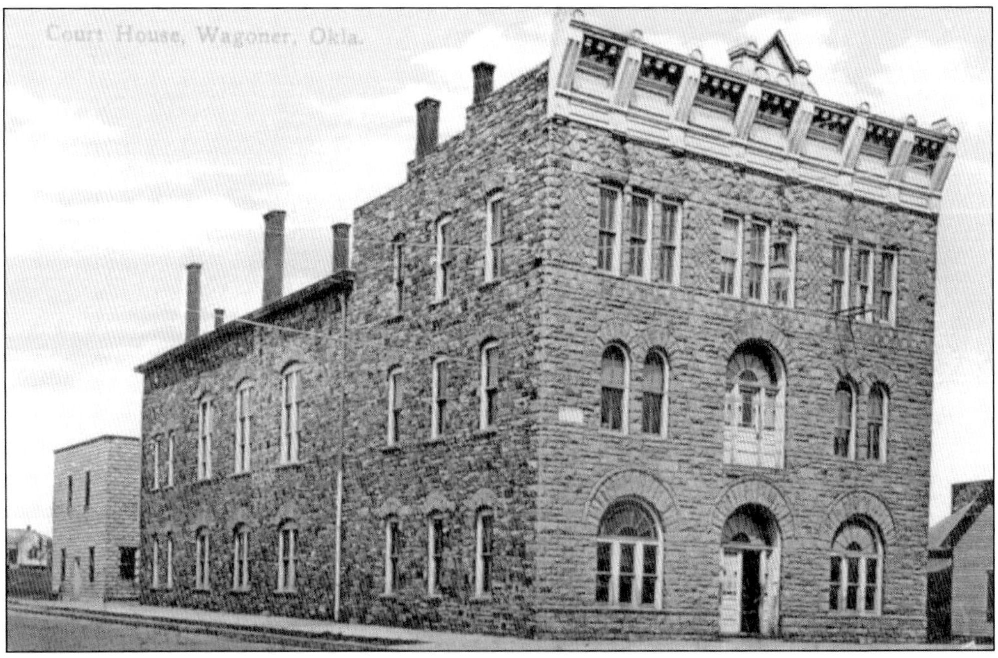

By the time statehood was granted in 1907, Wagoner already had a three-story federal courthouse at the northeast corner of Cherokee Street and Casaver Avenue. County commissioners rented it for $200 per month to serve as the county courthouse. The county purchased the building in 1932 for $8,000. It was razed in 1940, when it was replaced with a $90,000 Work Projects Administration structure that still serves as the center part of the current courthouse. (Author's collection.)

Pres. Theodore Roosevelt's train made a surprise stop in Wagoner in 1905. Hoping to get a look at the president's train as it passed through, local residents had gathered at the Katy depot and were delighted to get to see him in person. In this rare photograph, Roosevelt gives a special wave to one of his former Rough Riders in the crowd. The Rough Riders is the name bestowed on the 1st United States Volunteer Cavalry, one of three such regiments raised in 1898 for the Spanish-American War and the only one of the three to see action. (Author's collection.)

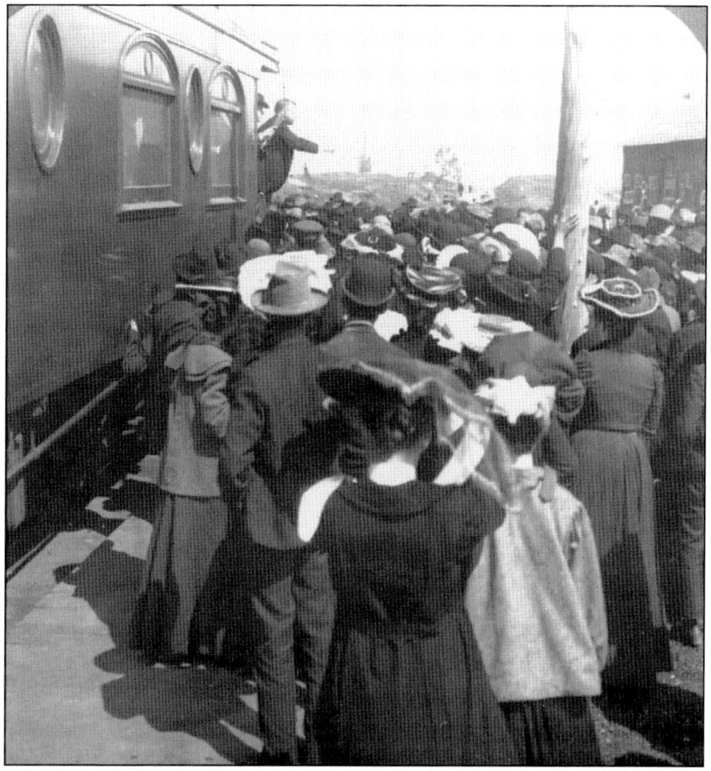

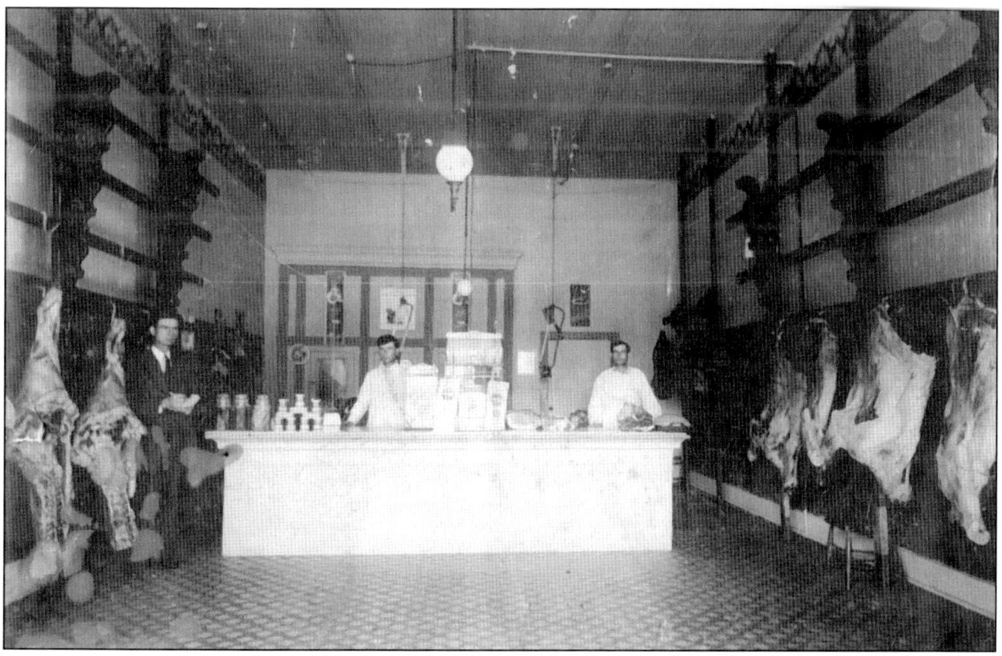

City Meat Market was operated by Leo Brumnett Sr. on the east side of South Main Street until 1929, when it moved to the west side of the street. He eventually relocated to Cherokee Street, where he operated Brumnett's Grocery and Meat Market until he retired in 1949. (Courtesy of the Brumnett family.)

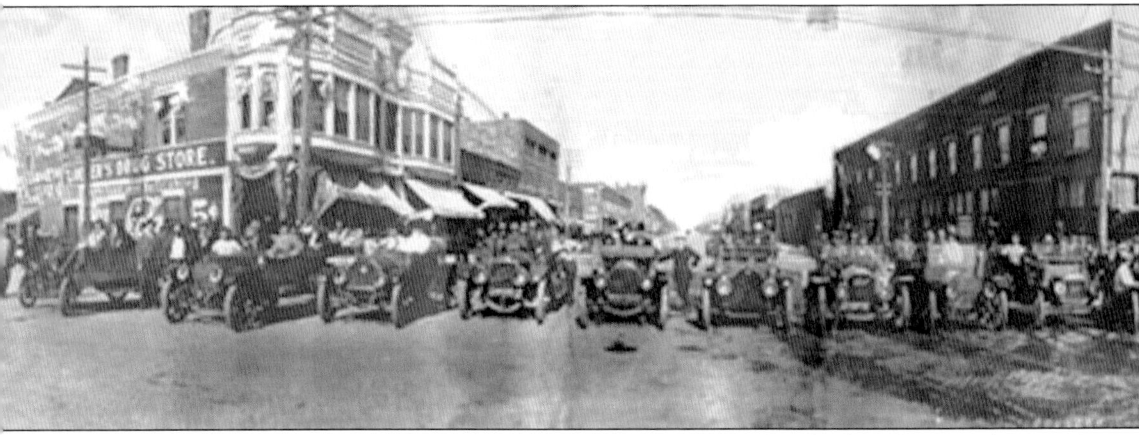

Pedestrians, a horse-drawn fire wagon, and automobiles are lined up for this photograph in 1913. At far left is the Cobb Building on the northeast Corner of Main and Cherokee Streets; in the

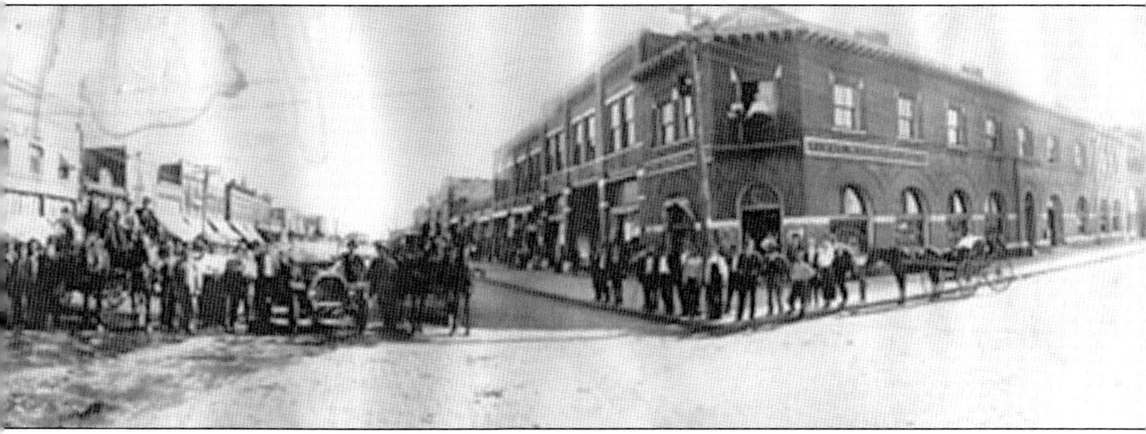

center is the Harris Building, on the southeast corner of that intersection; and First National Bank is on the right, the southwest corner of the intersection. (Author's collection.)

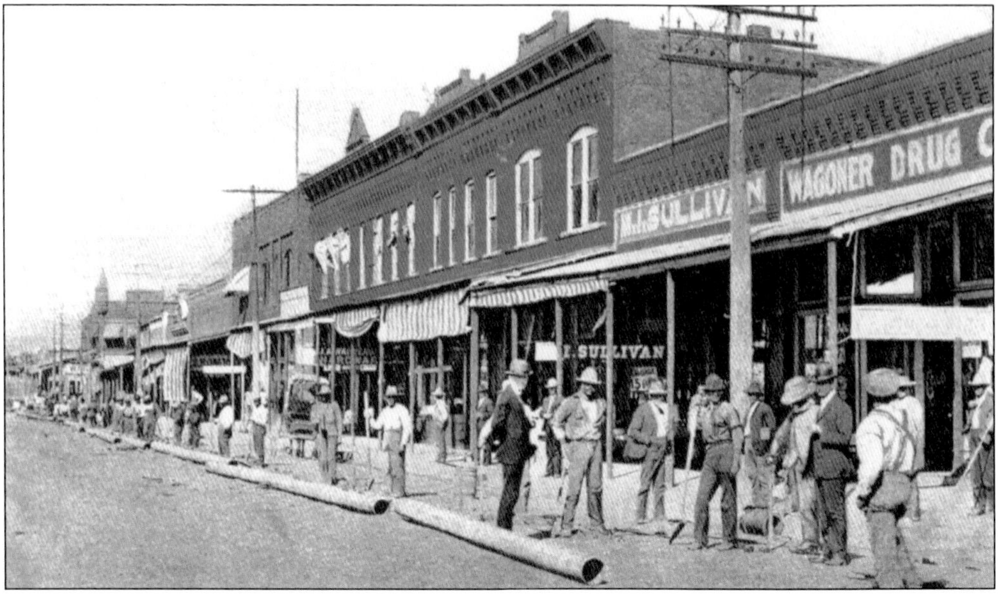

The Wagoner Gas Co. had nearly completed installation of natural gas lines on Wagoner's South Main Street when the photograph for this postcard was taken in 1906. (Author's collection.)

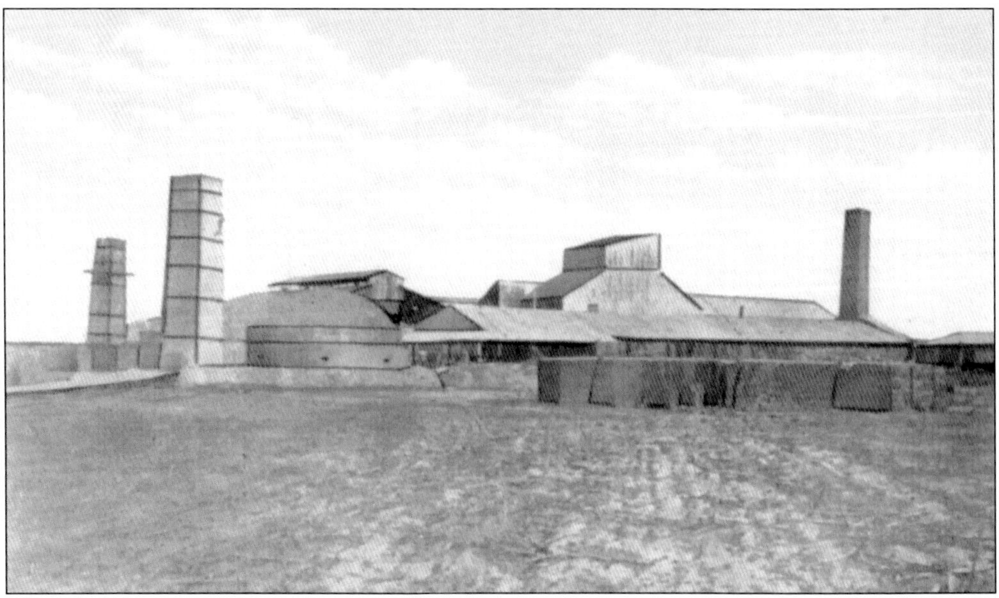

Wagoner's early years saw several brickmaking operations, including Reliance Clay Products Co., which was south of Wagoner, west of what is now Oklahoma 51 and east of Oklahoma 16. Other brick manufacturers included the Steam Brick Company, Wagoner Machine Brick Company, and Taylor and Raines. Brickmaking continued into the 1930s. (Author's collection.)

Two

Early Homes Were the City's Crown Jewels

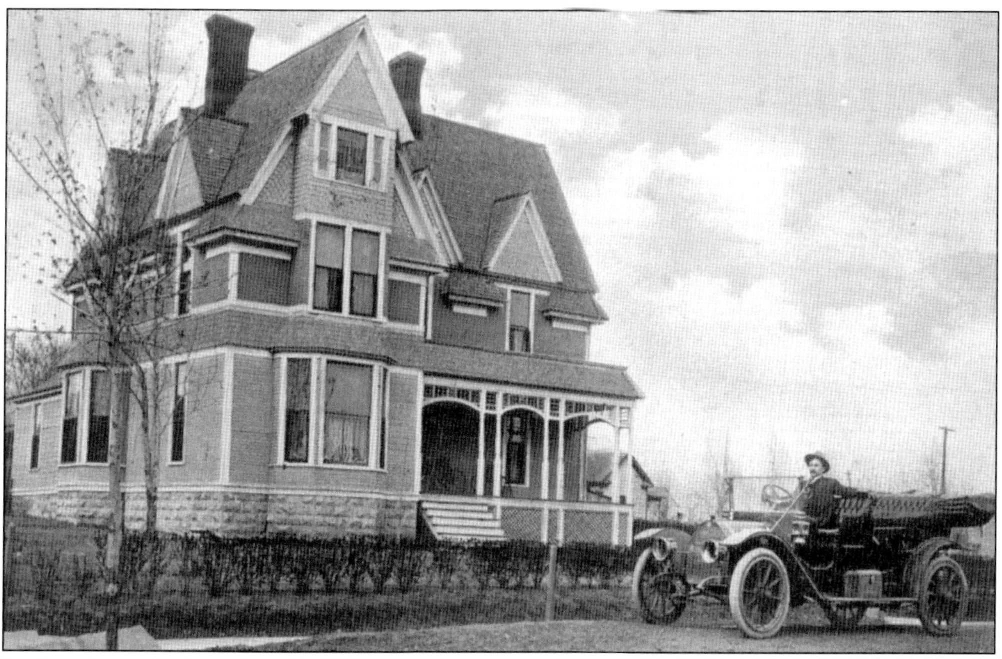

Luther Opry, the first sheriff of Wagoner County, is shown in his car in front of his house at 411 Northeast Second Street. After he left office, Opry was gunned down at Cherokee Street and Casaver Avenue by another law office in a dispute over bootleg whiskey. The house was built before 1901 by T.J. Way. It was destroyed by fire on April 19, 1992. (Author's collection.)

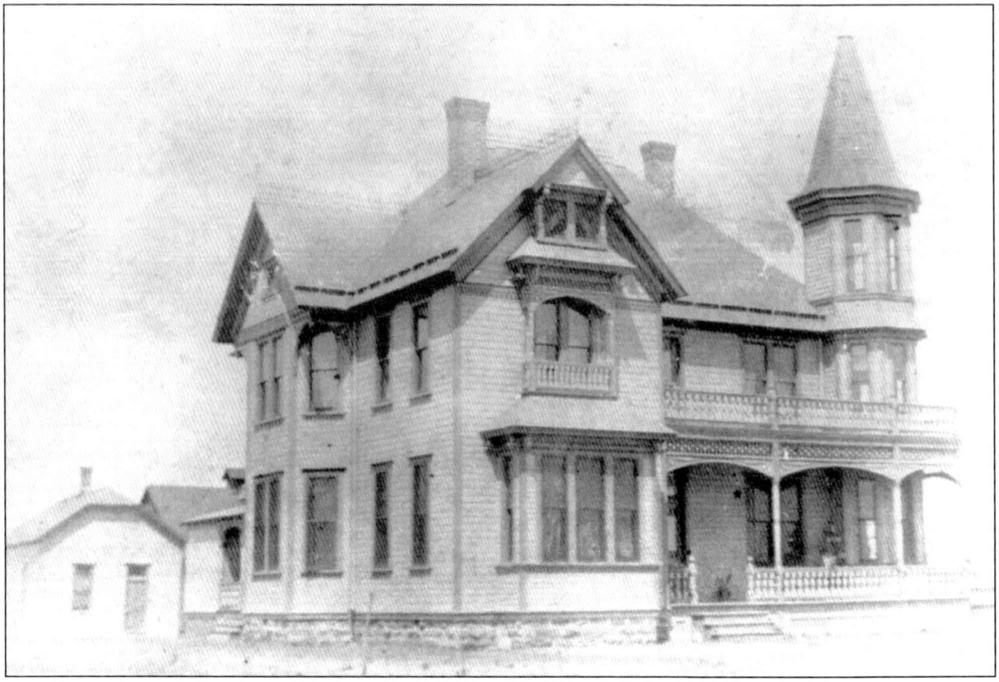

This photograph was taken shortly after James Parkinson built this elegant home at 207 Northeast Second Street in 1892. Parkinson owned a mercantile store at Main and Cherokee Streets and became president of First National Bank when it opened. (Author's collection.)

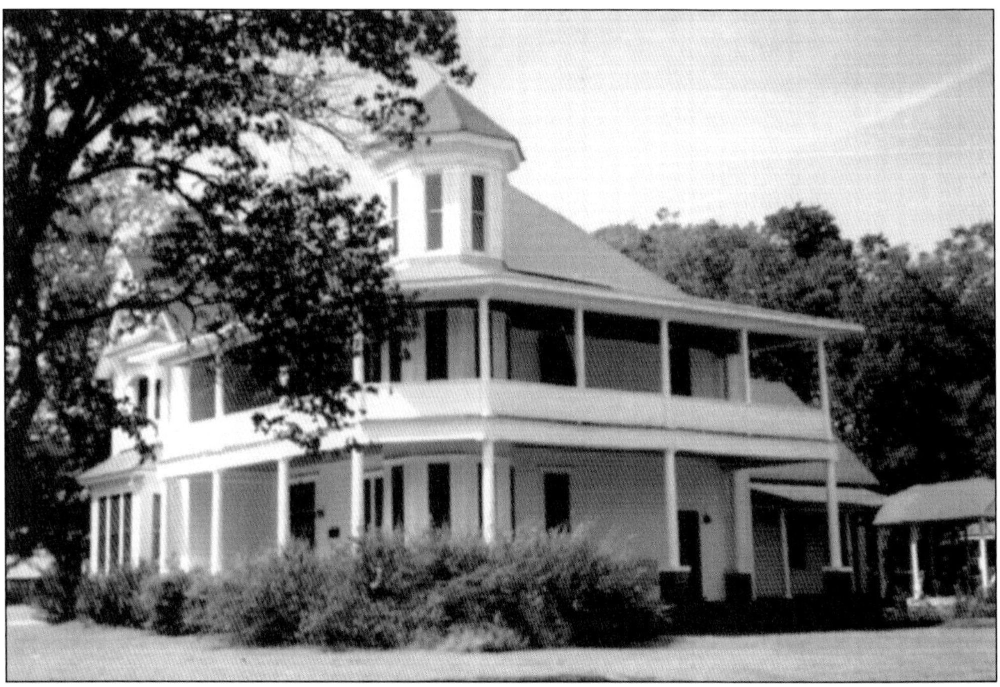

The James Parkinson house has been completely remodeled and upgraded by its present owners, Gary and Barbara Chappell. (Courtesy of Shirle Lamb Williams.)

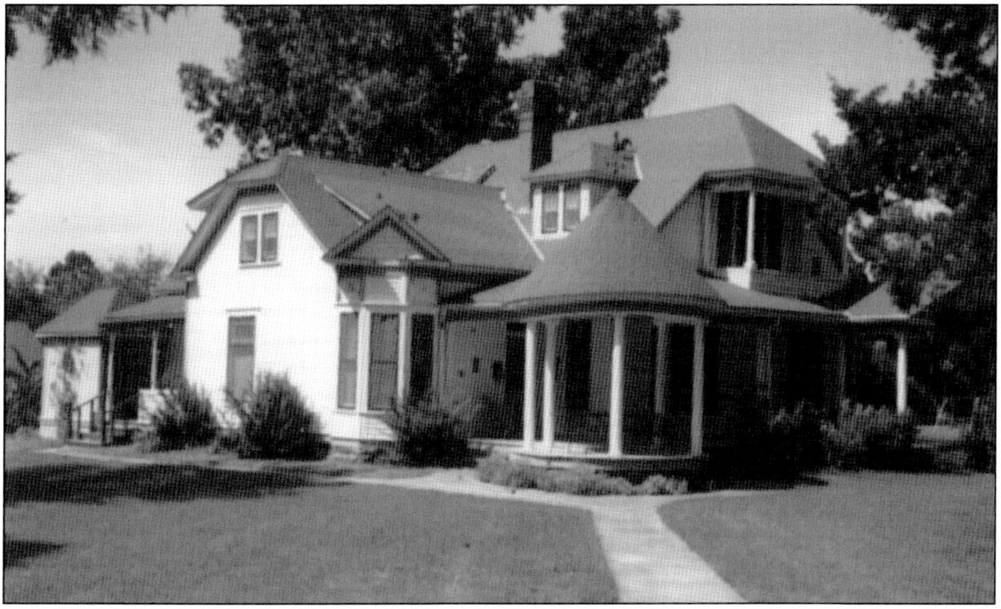

Amos Parkinson, owner of Wagoner Lumber Co., built this home at 603 Parkinson Avenue in 1893. It is listed in the National Register of Historic Places. (Author's collection.)

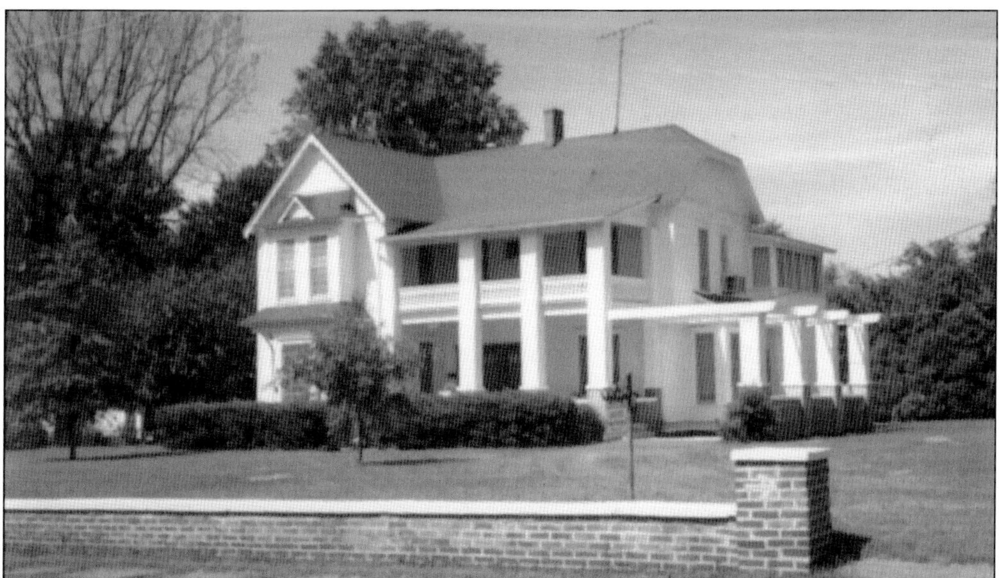

Another Parkinson family home was built at 407 Northeast Third Street about 1895. In 1903, it was assessed at $2,000. The home was purchased by J. Lee and Helen Stephens in 1946. Their granddaughter Pam Stephens-Karnes lives in the home today. (Author's collection.)

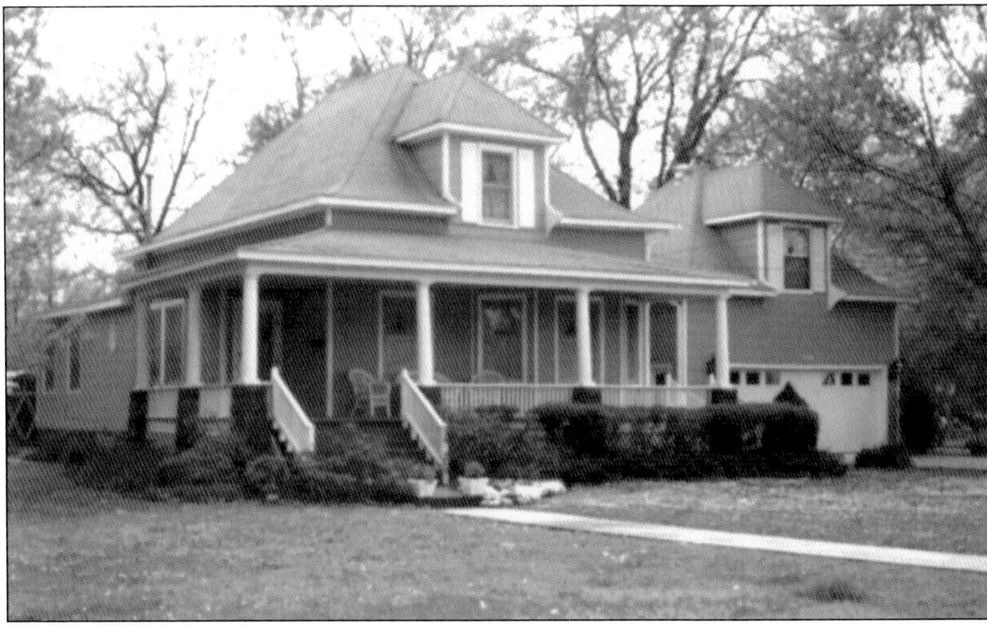

This home has been greatly enlarged since it was built by Walter G. Gibbon at 908 Southeast Third Street in 1894. Gibbons was a grocer. (Author's collection.)

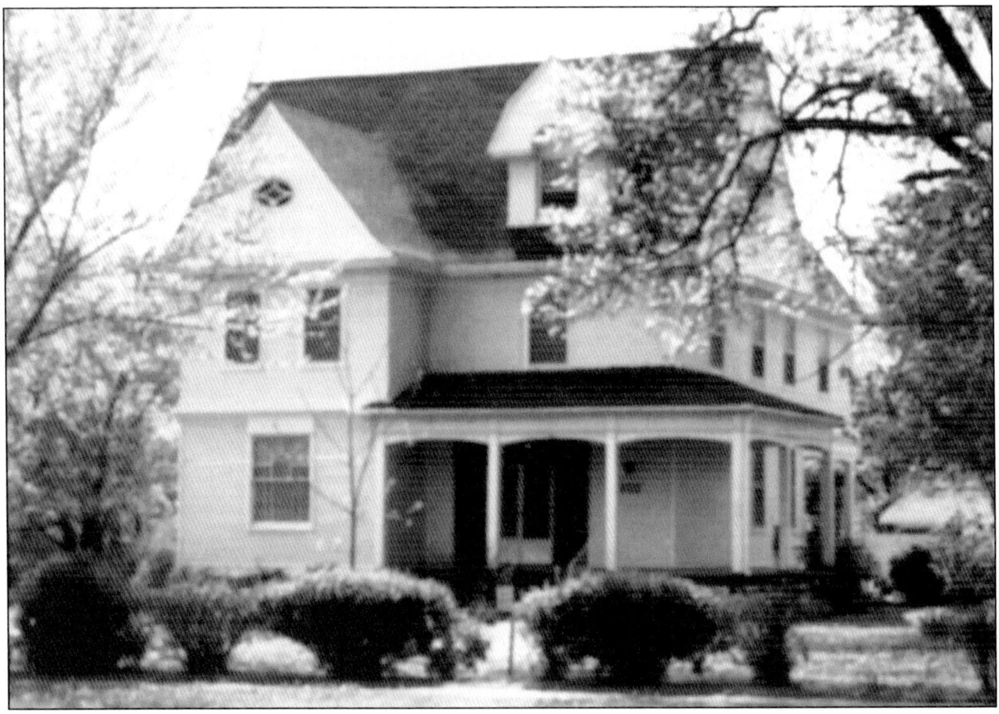

Painted a pastel yellow today, the John Gibson house was built in 1896 at 402 McQuarrie Avenue. He was a cattleman and president of First National Bank for many years. The home remains much as it was originally, with two handsome walnut and oak staircases and leaded stained-glass windows. One change that has been made is the installation of the brass fire pole from Wagoner's old city hall. It is between the second and third floors. (Author's collection.)

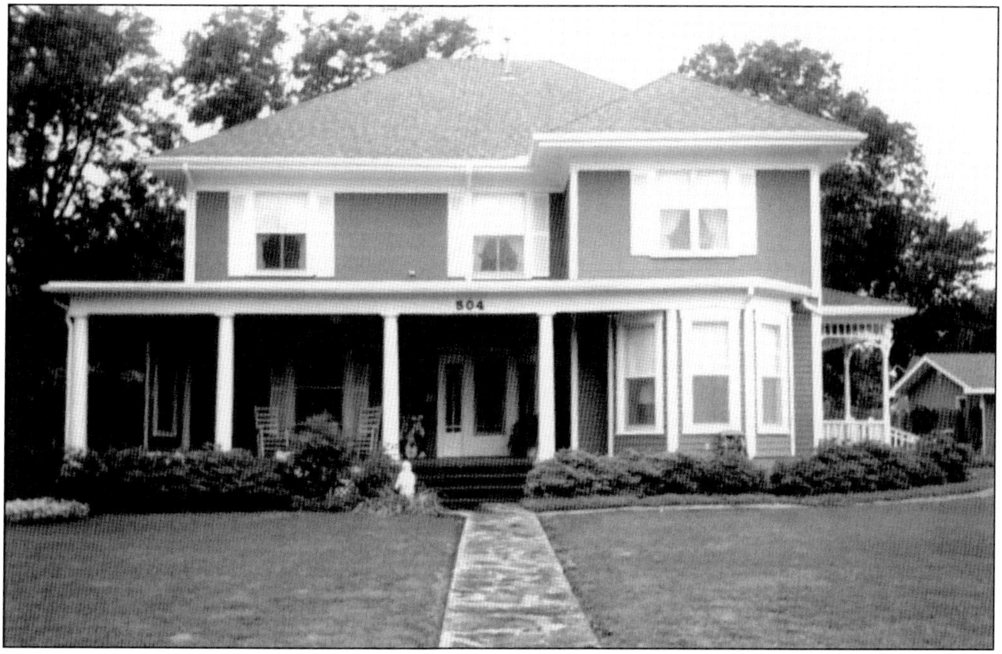

Located at 504 McQuarrie Avenue, this house that is painted green is one of the city's showpieces. It was built in 1901 by J. Morgan Livingston, a wealthy cattleman. The home was going to ruin when it was purchased by John and Agnes Sleeper in 1974. They restored and improved it to what it is today. This photograph was taken in the 1970s, after the restoration. (Author's collection.)

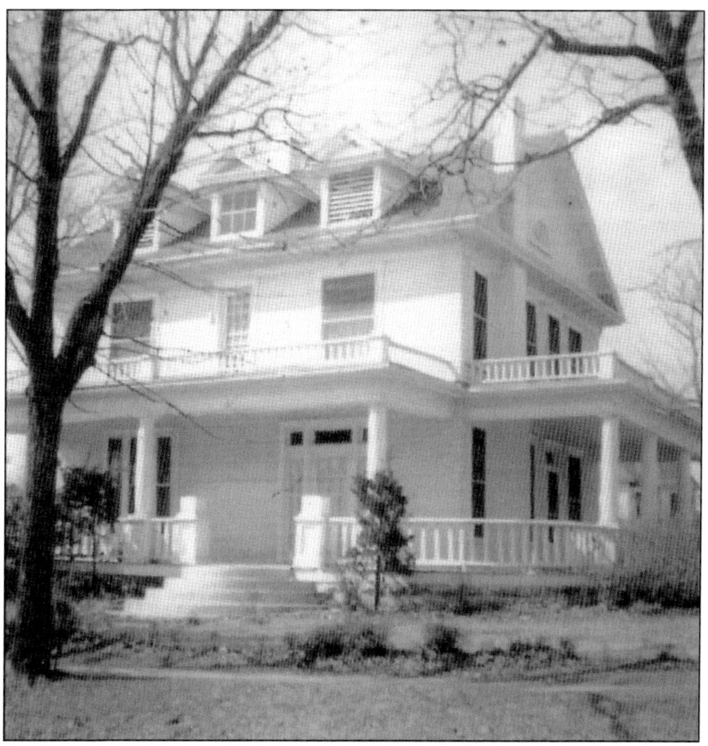

This beauty, which stood at the southwest corner of the intersection of Northeast Second and State Streets, was destroyed by fire several years ago. It was the A.C. Miller home. (Courtesy of Adam Miller.)

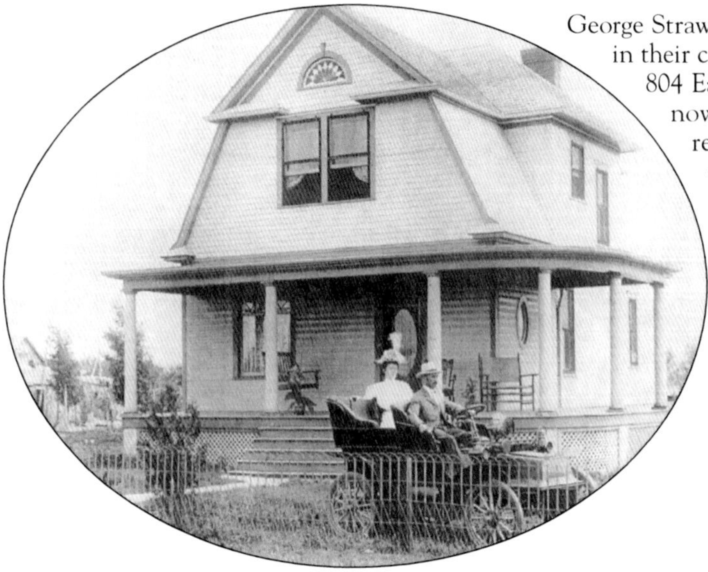

George Strawn is pictured with his wife in their car in front of their home at 804 East Cherokee Street, which now houses the Pink House restaurant. In 1910, Strawn owned a car dealership that operated from a building behind Walters Hardware on South Main Street. (Courtesy of the Wagoner City Historical Museum.)

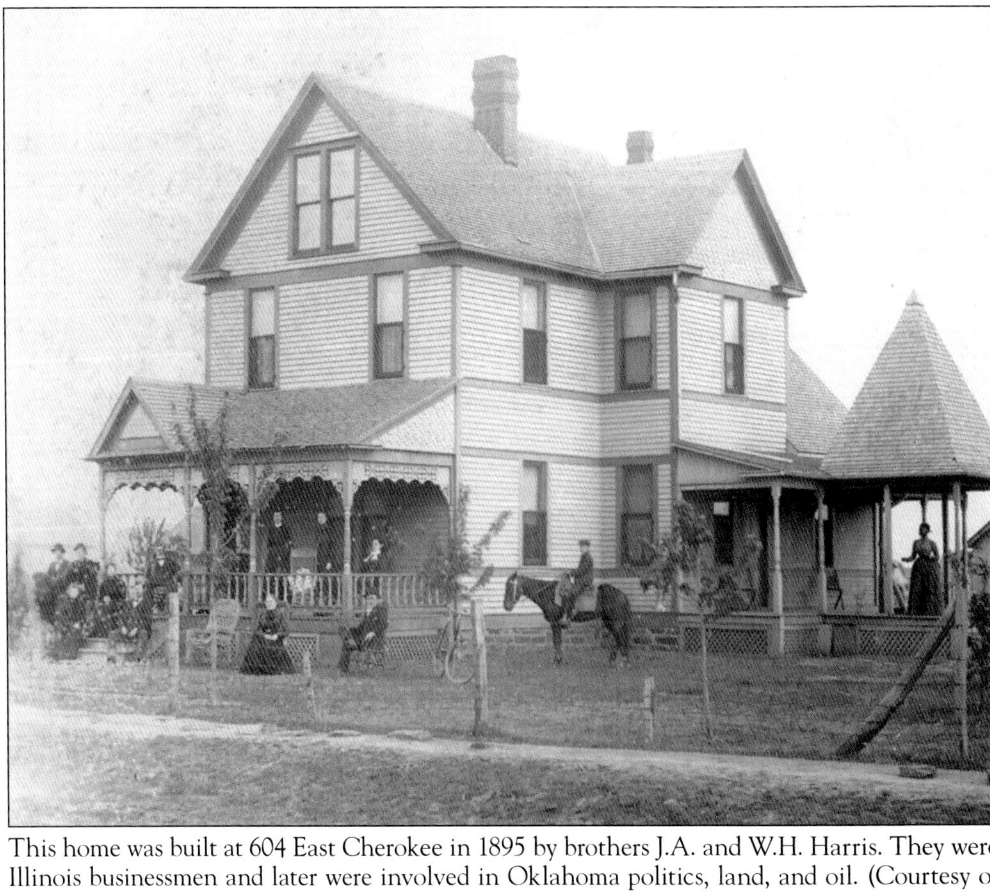

This home was built at 604 East Cherokee in 1895 by brothers J.A. and W.H. Harris. They were Illinois businessmen and later were involved in Oklahoma politics, land, and oil. (Courtesy of Jerry Hickman.)

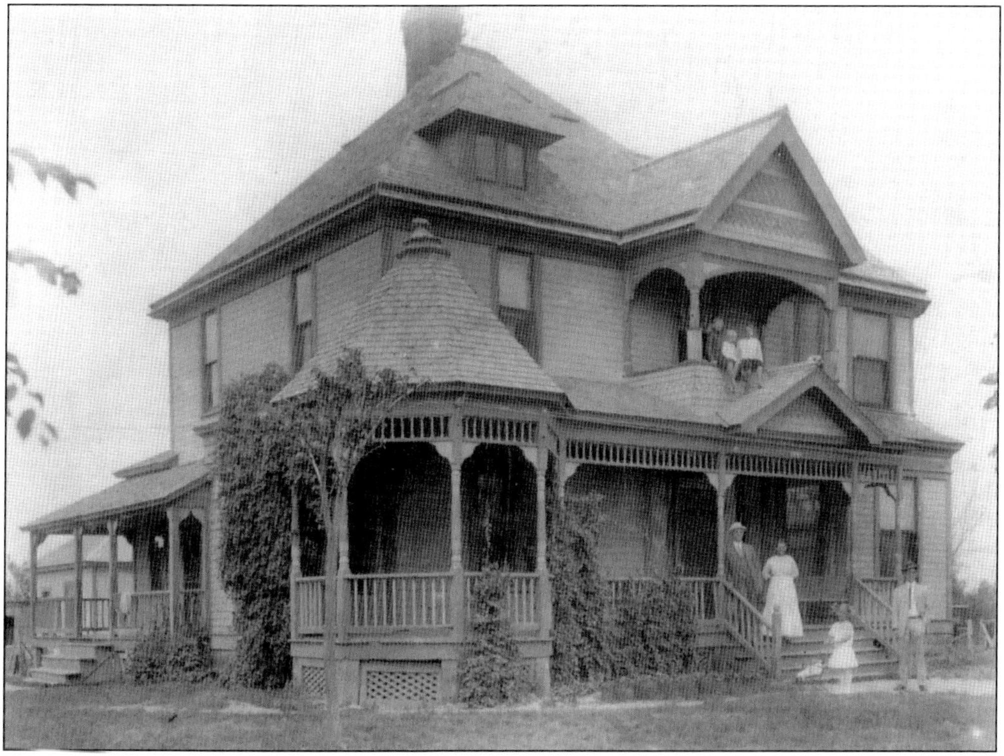

The home of Judge William T. and Mattie Hunt once stood at 1004 McQuarrie Avenue. The Hunts, who arrived in Wagoner from Arkansas in 1895, are standing on the front steps of the home. Judge Hunt served as mayor of Wagoner. The Hunts had 10 children, including son Russell, who was inducted into the Oklahoma Hall of Fame in 1981. He was a banker and was cited for his numerous civic activities. Another of the Hunt boys, Albert, was chief justice of the Oklahoma Supreme Court. The home was destroyed by fire. (Courtesy of Margie Semore.)

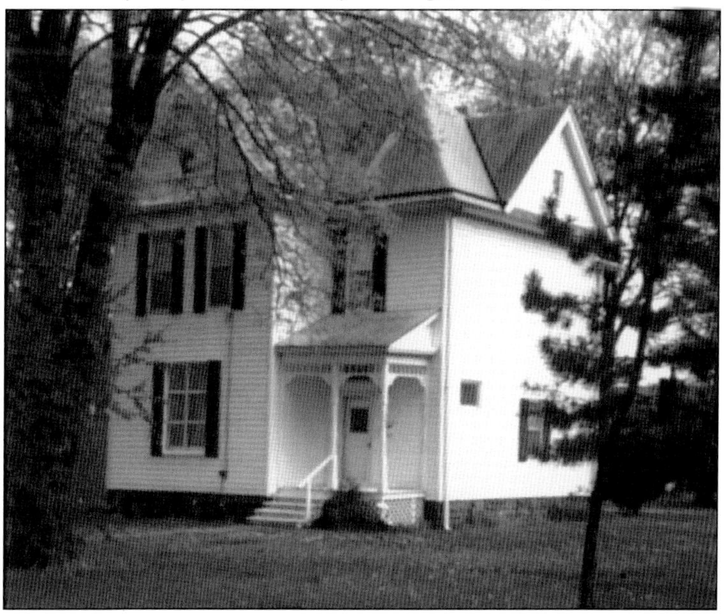

Built in 1896 by Hiram E. Dodge, this house is at 912 Southeast Third Street. Dodge came to Wagoner in 1895 as a stockholder in the First National Bank. He served as city treasurer in 1896. (Courtesy of Shirle Lamb Williams.)

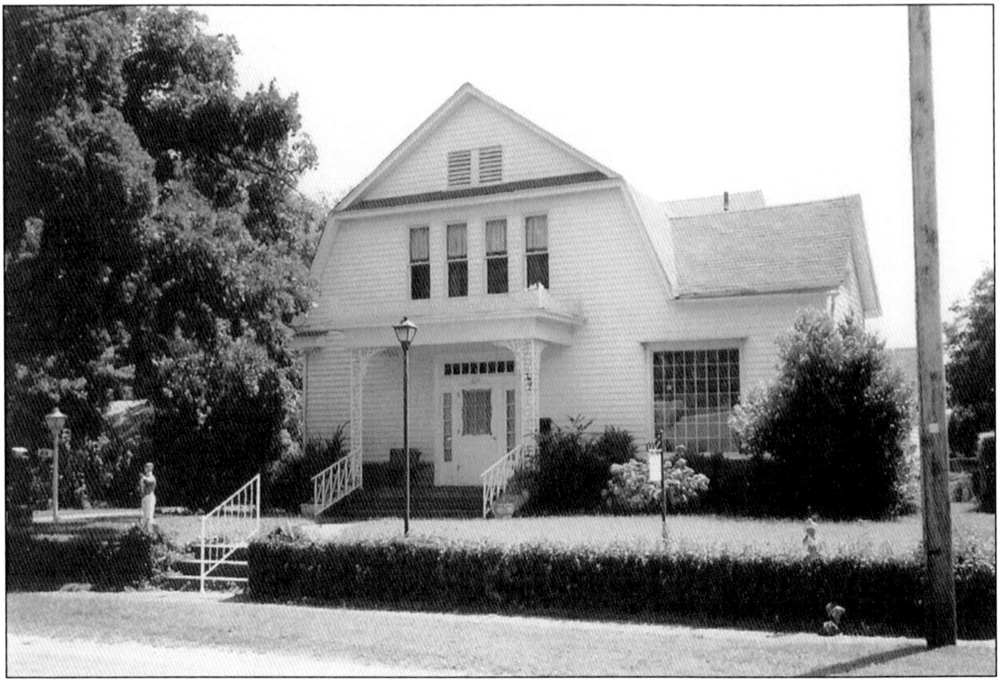

S.S. Cobb built this structure around a much smaller version that he had constructed for his bride in 1895. The home originally faced Second Street, and then was moved to State Street before finally being located on Northeast Third Street. (Author's collection.)

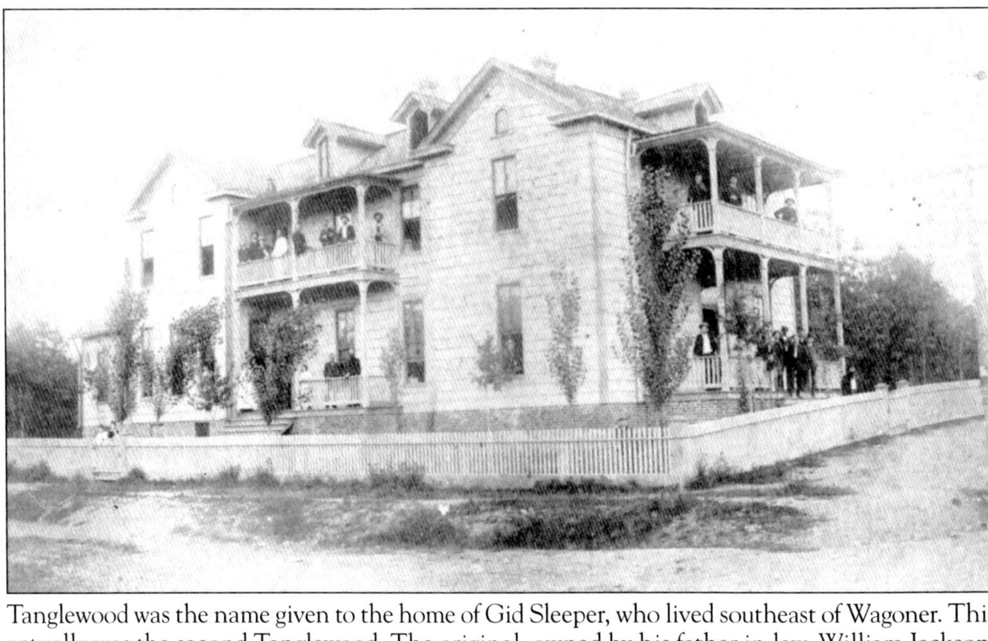

Tanglewood was the name given to the home of Gid Sleeper, who lived southeast of Wagoner. This actually was the second Tanglewood. The original, owned by his father-in-law, William Jackson, had been destroyed by fire, as was this one sometime after 1910. (Courtesy of John Sleeper.)

Three

New City Focused on Education and Religion

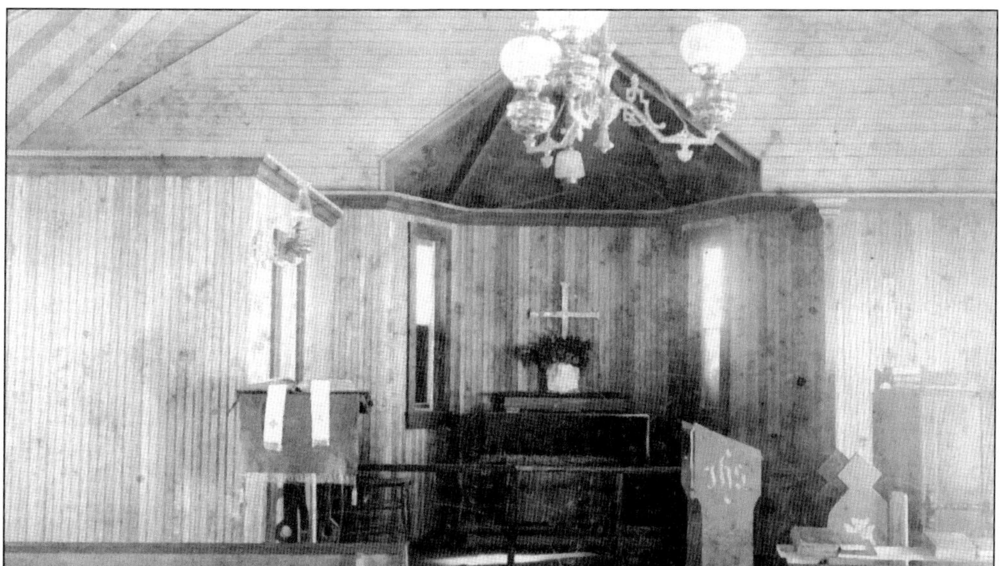

The first services were held in St. James Episcopal Church in April 1894. The church had been built at a total cost of $850. In 2015, the church still has its original, handcrafted furnishings and looks much the same as it when it was constructed. The building was moved three times after its construction and now sits at Lee and Church Streets. (Courtesy of Shirle Lamb Williams.)

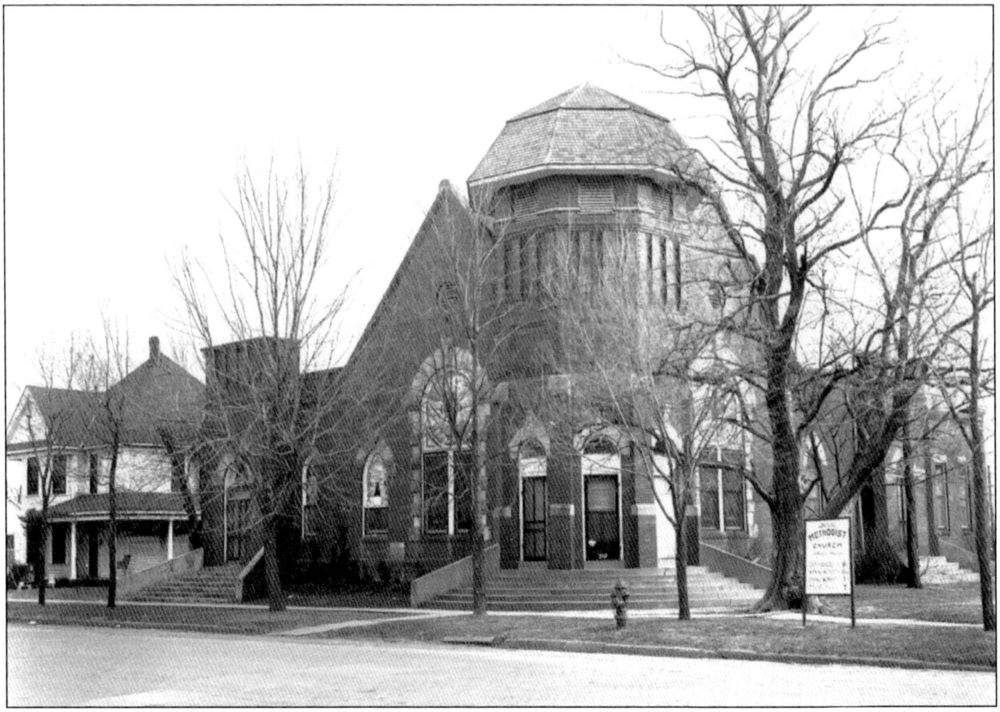

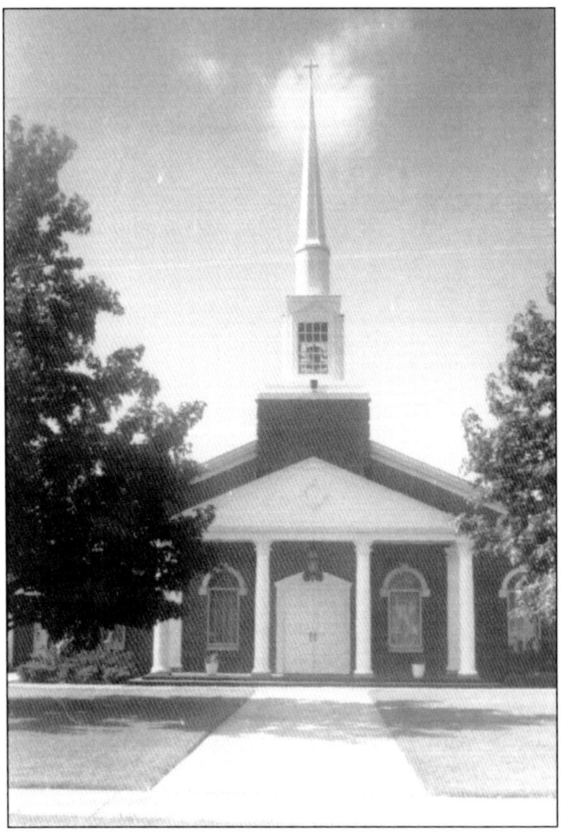

The Methodist Episcopal Church South's original 1893 wooden building was replaced with this magnificent structure in 1907. The two-story parsonage stands to the left. The church reunited with the M.E. Church North in the 1920s and today is known as the First United Methodist Church. (Courtesy of the Cradow Smith collection.)

In 2015, the First United Methodist Church stands at the south side of the intersection of Casaver Avenue and Church Street, just west of the former building. (Author's collection.)

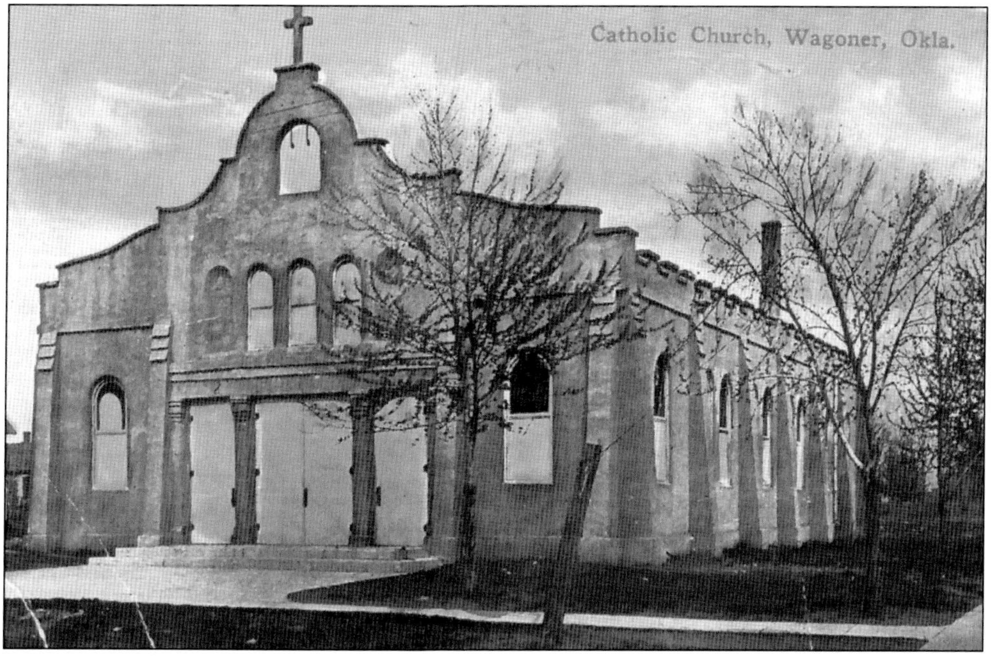

Wagoner's Catholic church was established in 1895 and erected this stucco building in 1910 at State and Cherokee Streets. The building still stands and houses Crossroads Community Church in 2015. (Author's collection.)

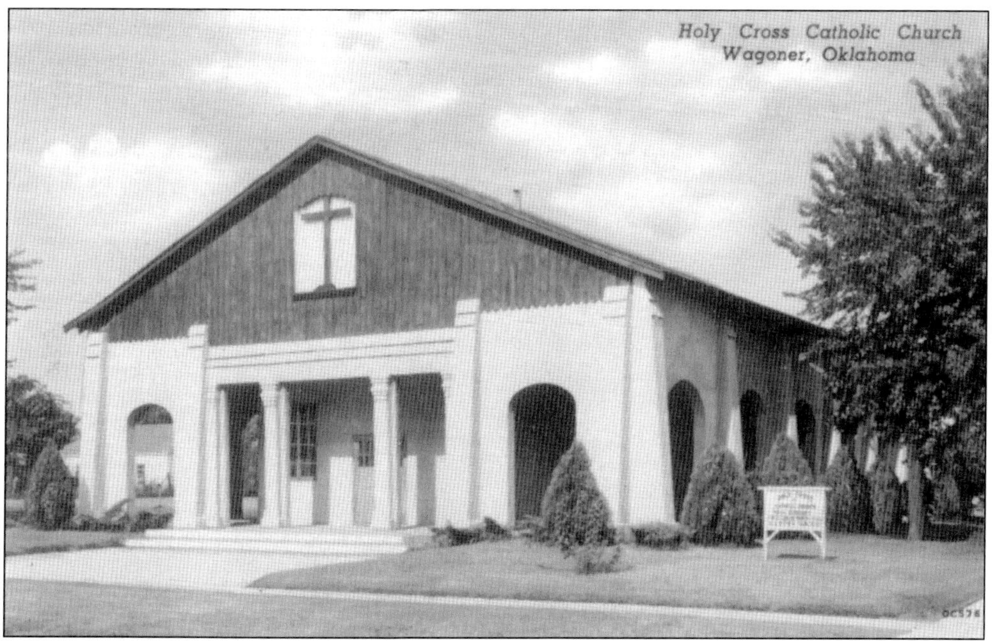

Holy Cross Catholic Church was remodeled several years after it was built. The Mission style was replaced to modernize the facility. Holy Cross later sold its building and erected a new church on Southwest Fifteenth Street. (Author's collection.)

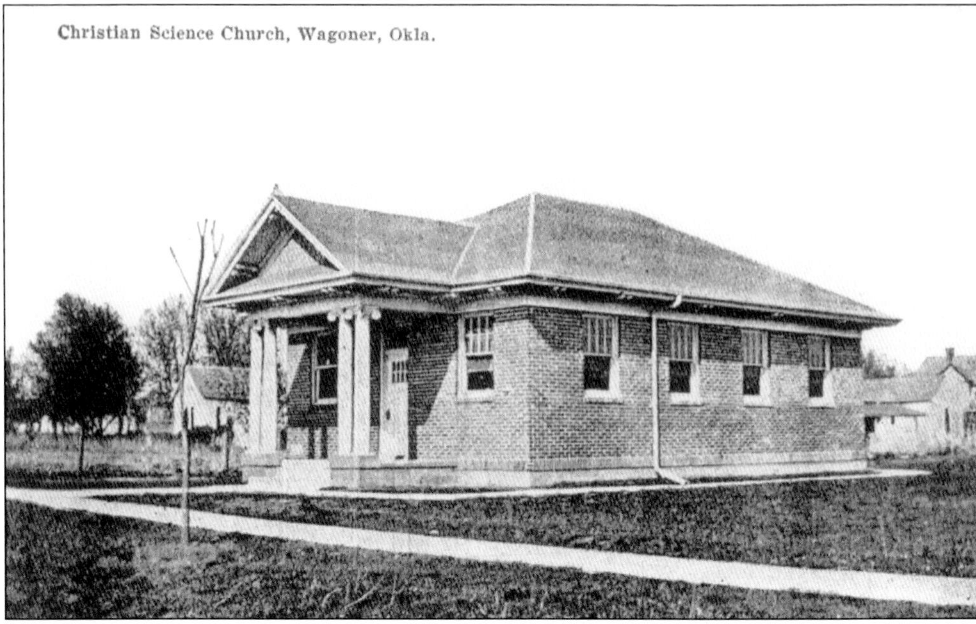

Organized in 1903, the Christian Science church built this brick church in 1917. It was across the street from the Carnegie library and was sold to the Church of Christ in 1936. It was later purchased by the county and, for many years, served as the office building for the county's welfare department. (Author's collection.)

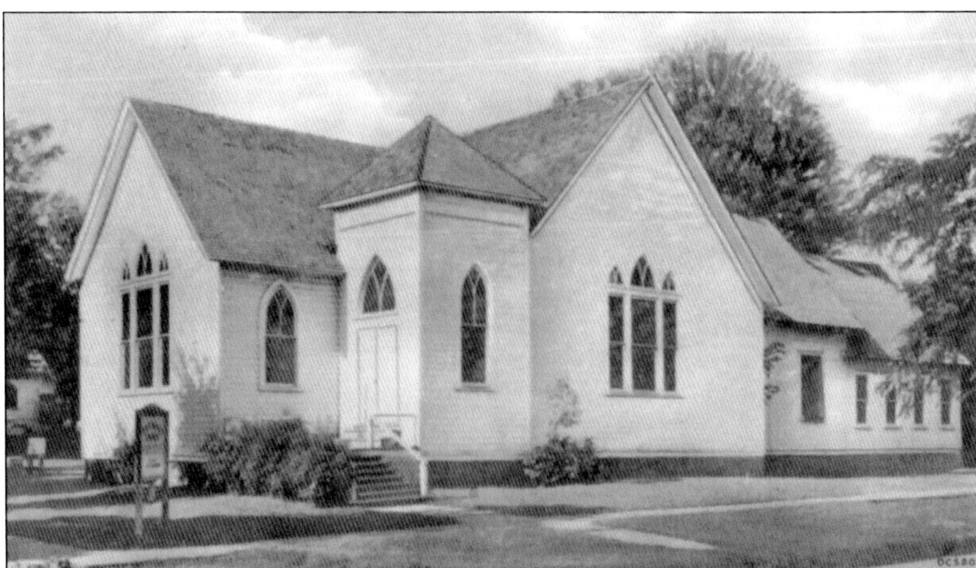

Wagoner's original First Baptist Church building was constructed in 1897 at Northeast Second and Parkinson Streets. It was replaced with a $100,000 brick building in 1956. (Author's collection.)

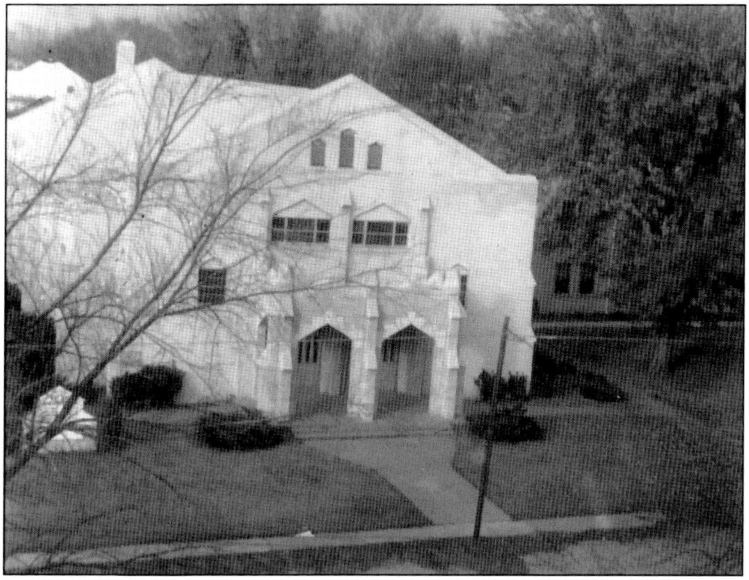

First Baptist Church is pictured as it appeared after the 1960s expansion. The courtyard area between the sanctuary and fellowship hall was enclosed in 2015 to provide a gathering place for the congregation. (Courtesy of the Cradow Smith collection.)

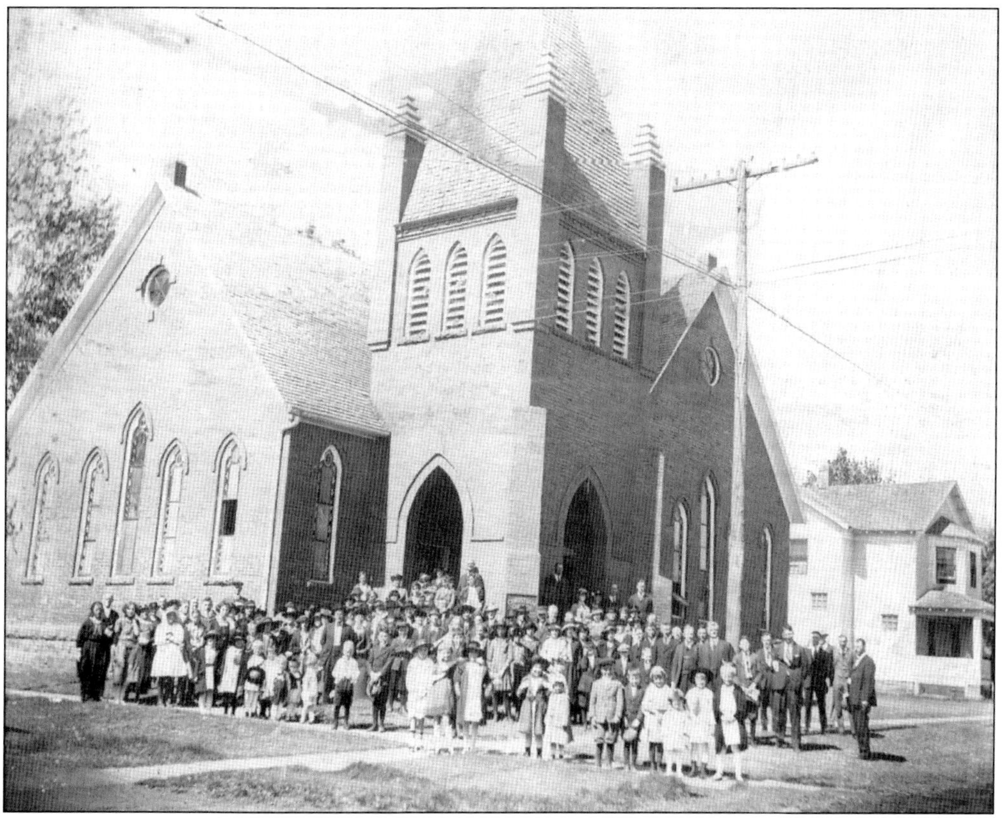

The First Christian Church bought the former North M.E. Church in 1920, when that congregation reunited with the South M.E. Church after a rift that dated to the Civil War. The church later razed this structure and built a new sanctuary that opened in June 2015. (Courtesy of Shirle Lamb Williams.)

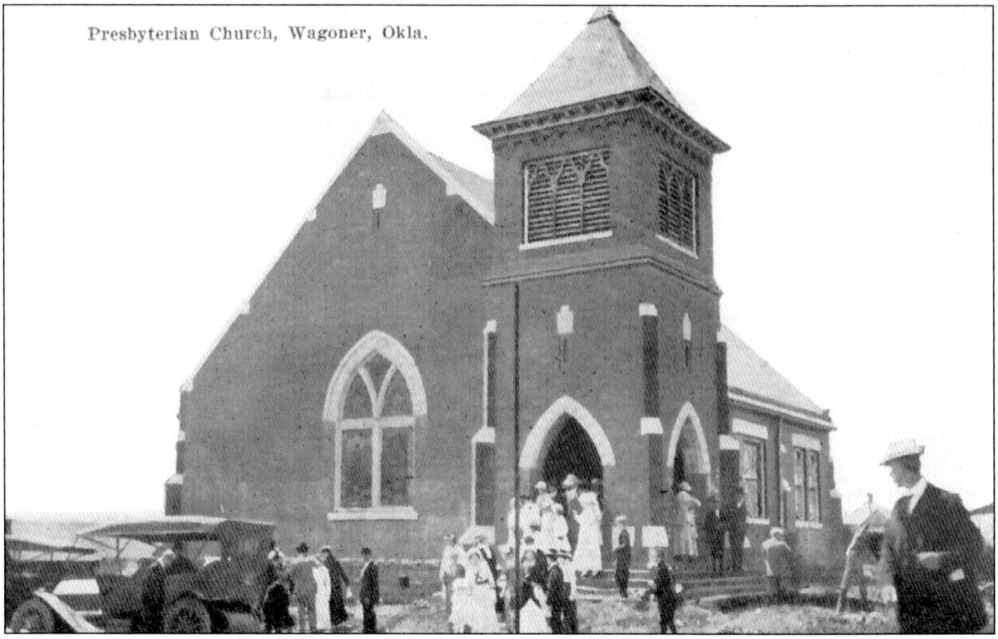

Sunday worshippers leave the First Presbyterian Church at Main and Northeast Second Streets in this postcard photograph. This building was erected in 1904 and has since been replaced. (Author's collection.)

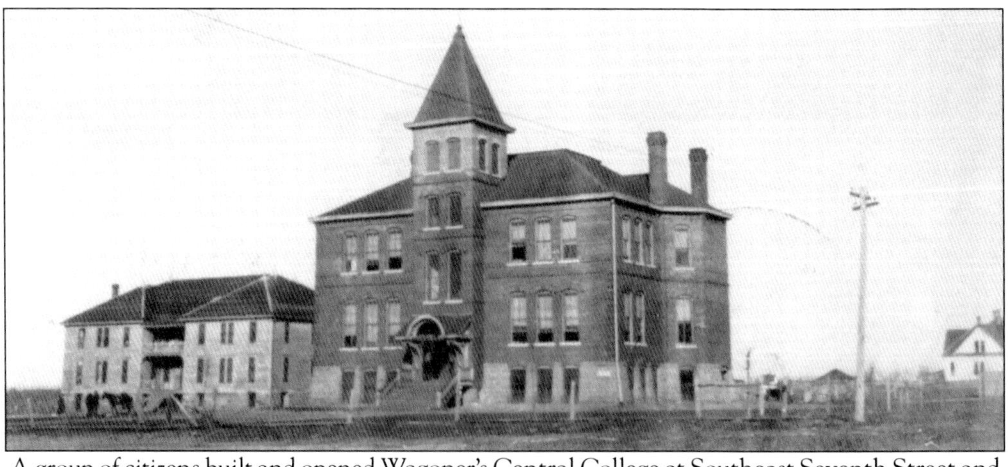

A group of citizens built and opened Wagoner's Central College at Southeast Seventh Street and Arthur Avenue for about $20,000 in 1898. A smallpox epidemic in 1900 permanently closed the school. Wagoner citizens passed the first bond issue in Indian Territory in 1902 and subsequently opened the territory's first public school. The old Central College building at right became Wagoner High School and the dormitory building, at left, became South School, for elementary grades. (Author's collection.)

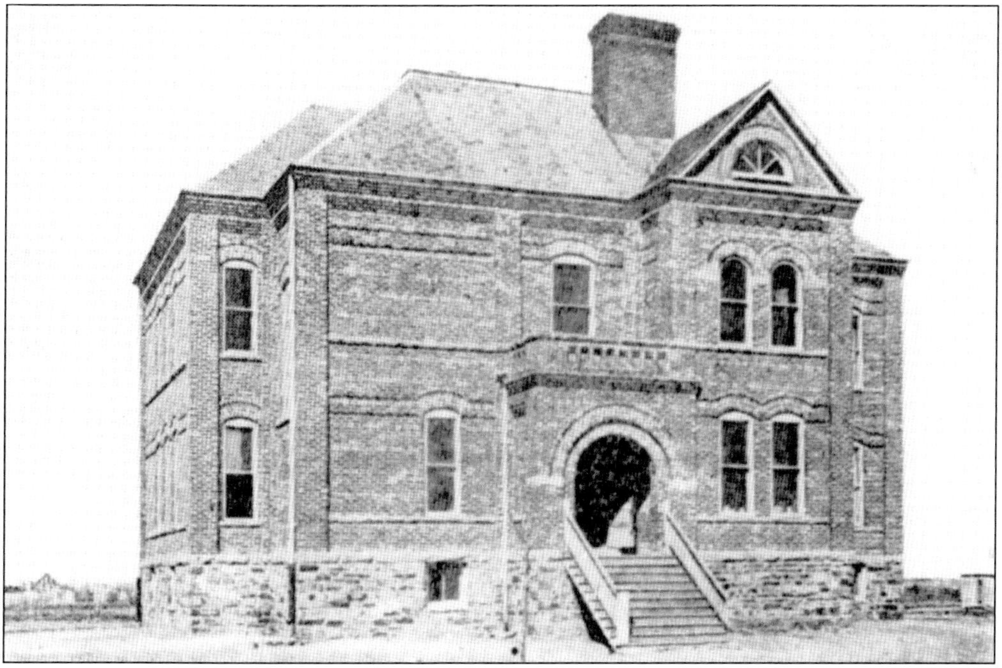

Originally called Franklin School, the West School served elementary students from 1905 to 1938; it was located at Northeast Third and Taylor Streets. When the school closed, the building was razed and materials used in the construction of the new Central Elementary on Northeast Second and Lee Streets. (Author's collection.)

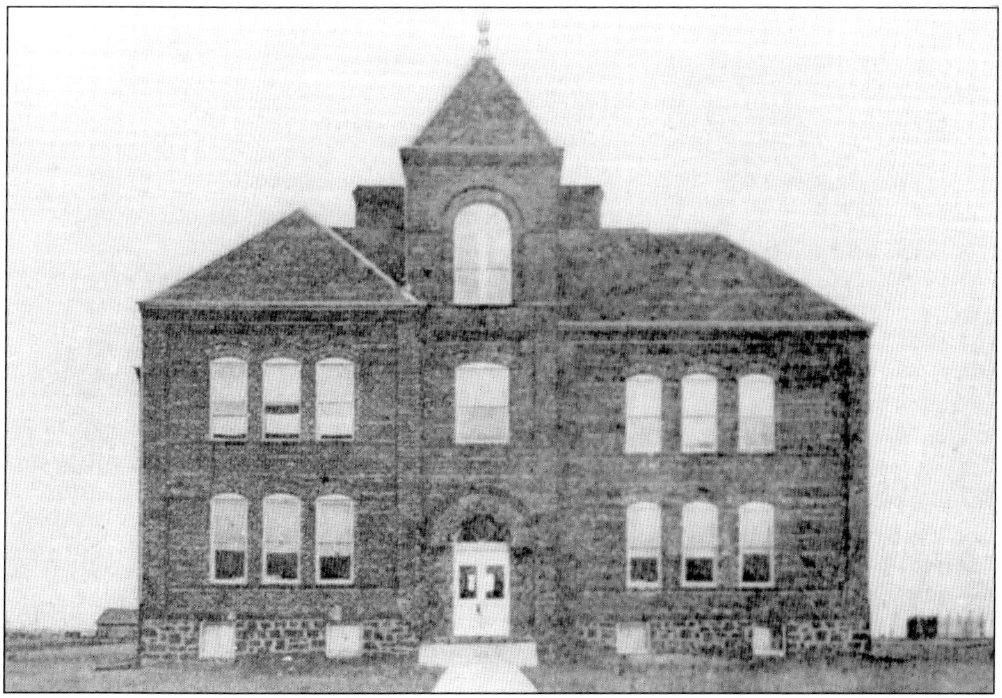

North School, located at North State and Northeast Sixth Streets, originally was called Crown Hill School. It operated from 1905 to 1938. (Author's collection.)

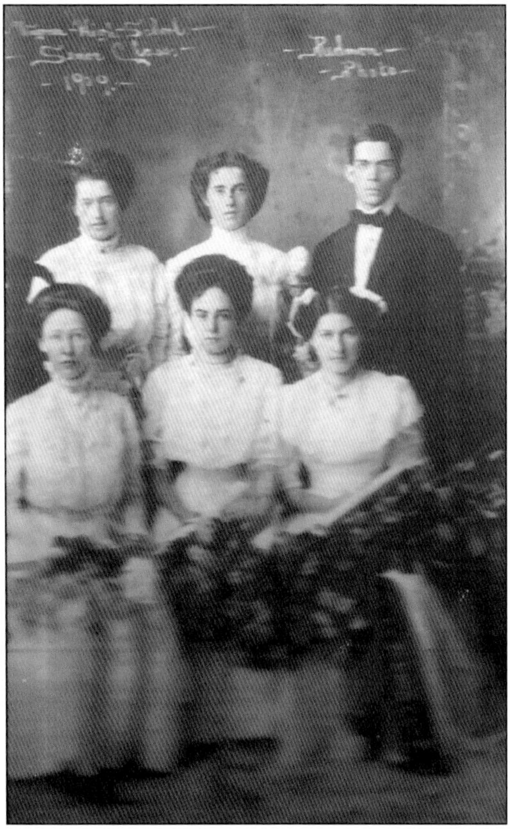

The second class to graduate from Wagoner High School was this group in 1909. Ora Ellington, who taught many years in Wagoner schools, is seated in the front row on the left. (Courtesy of Wanda Lee Hicks.)

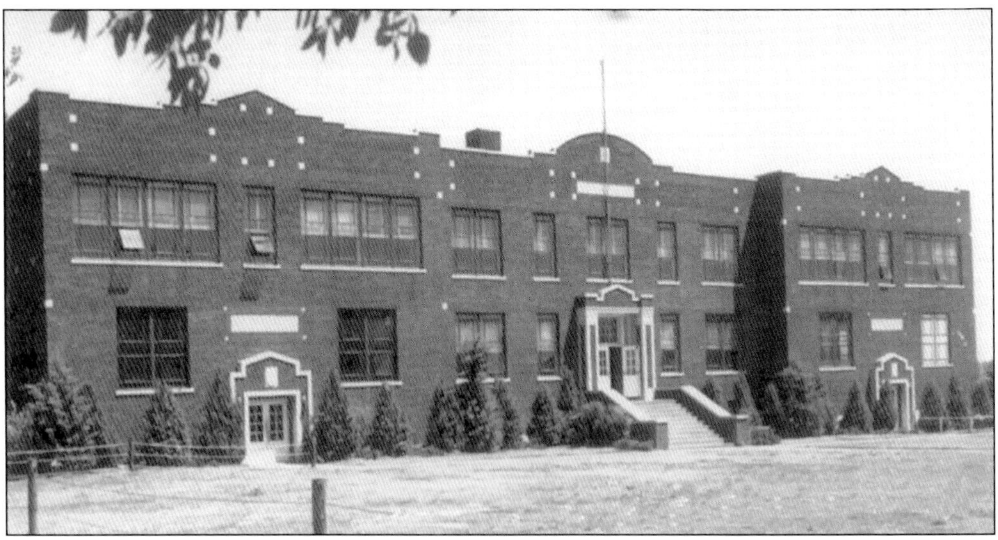

Wagoner High School moved into this building at Northeast Second Street and Casaver Avenue in 1926. It had been built at a cost of $78,000 and was located on North Casaver Avenue, south of Northeast Second Street. The building was used as a high school through 1965, and then used for several years as a junior high. It was demolished in 2004. Only white students were allowed to attend Central Elementary and the high school. Black students first attended Pitt School, which became Lincoln School. The school system was integrated in 1966. (Author's collection.)

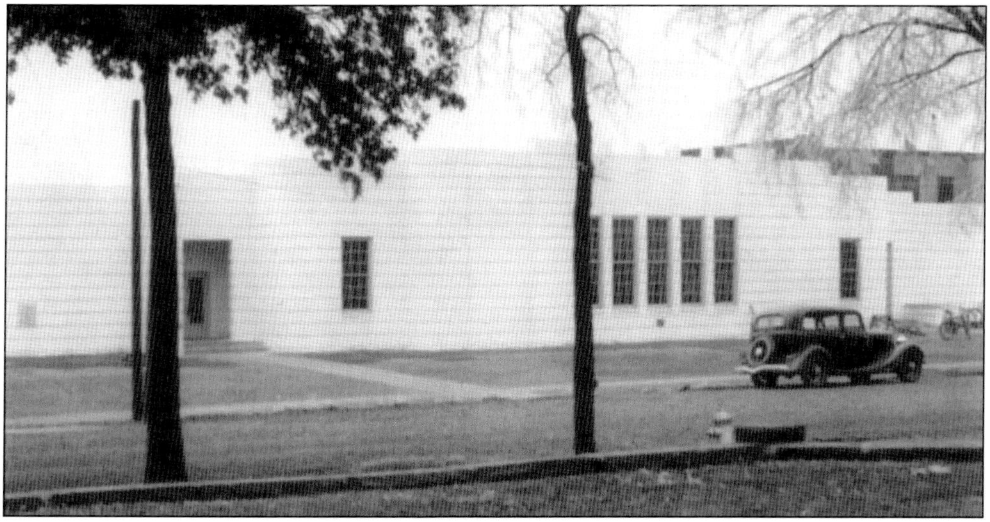

Bricks from North School, West School, and the old Central College were used to build Wagoner's Central Elementary in 1938. It was a project of the Works Progress Administration and cost $66,000. The building now houses the school district's administrative offices. (Courtesy of the Elmer Thomas Collection, Carl Albert Center, University of Oklahoma.)

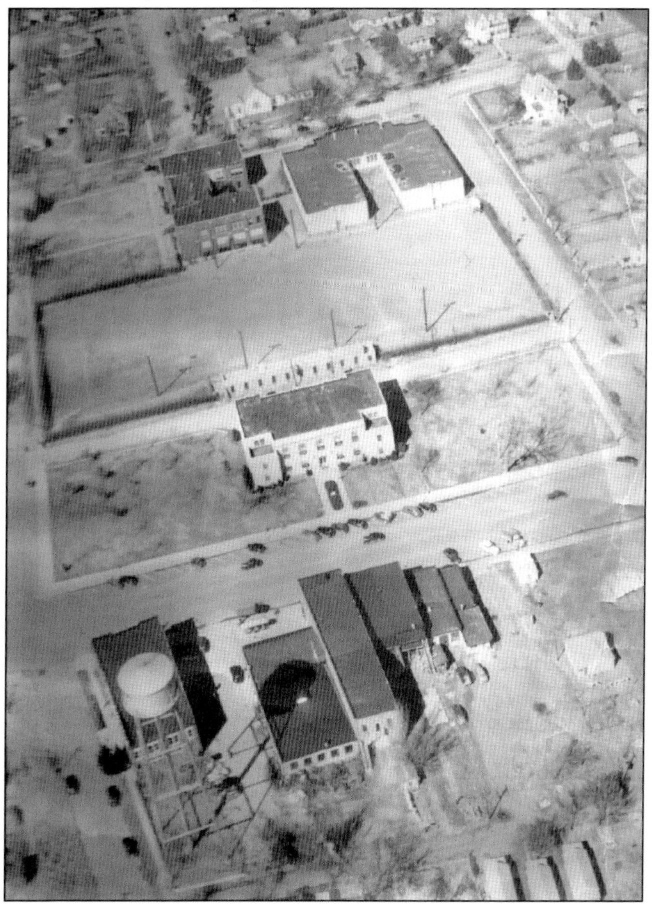

At the center of this aerial photograph is the playground behind Wagoner High School and Central Elementary. The Wagoner County Courthouse is the light-colored building toward the bottom center. The playground served as a football field until the school moved its football program to the east of Maple Park in 1954. (Courtesy of the Cradow Smith collection.)

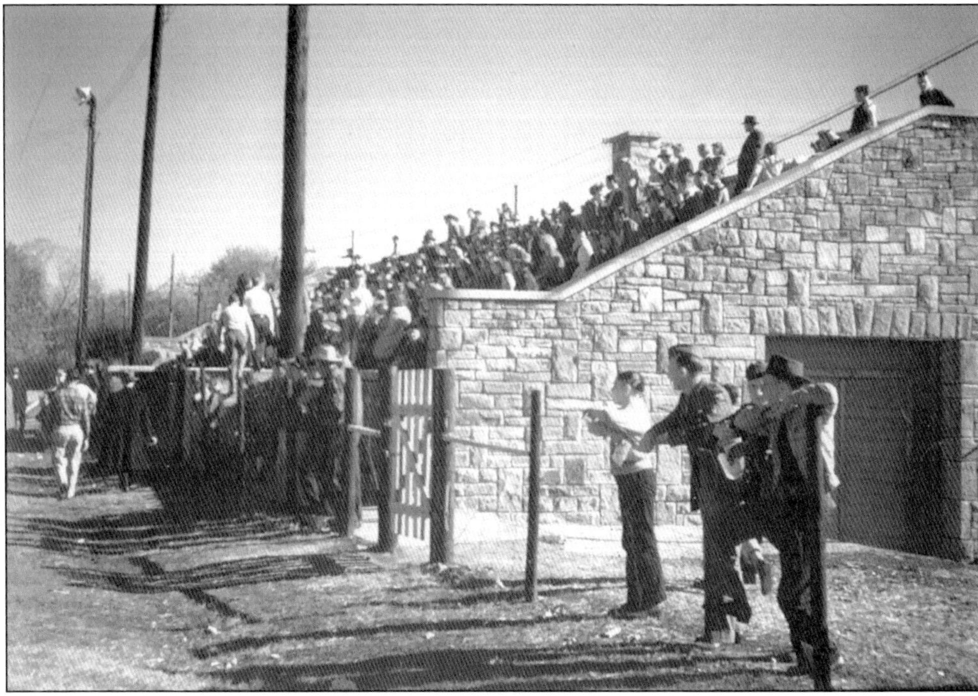

Wagoner High School's football stadium was this WPA-built rock structure behind the courthouse. (Courtesy of the Bob Jeffrey collection.)

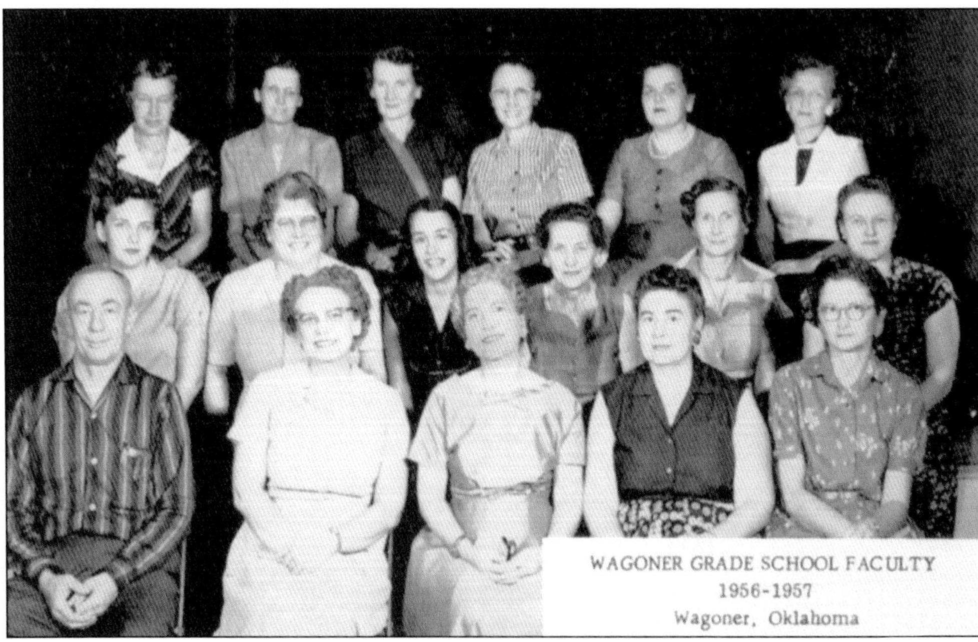

This group of Central Elementary teachers helped create many fond memories for students. Pictured, from left to right, are (first row) A.M. Callaway, principal; Virginia Banks; Ruth Lorenz; Helen Grissom; and ? Garrett; (second row) unidentified; Louise Langston; Mary Deal; Ruth Timmons; Kate Cochran; and Lois Mills; (third row) Ora Ellington; Helen Stephens; Betty Breedlove; Grace Bethell; Lillian Bryant; and Waleah Hornsby. (Author's collection.)

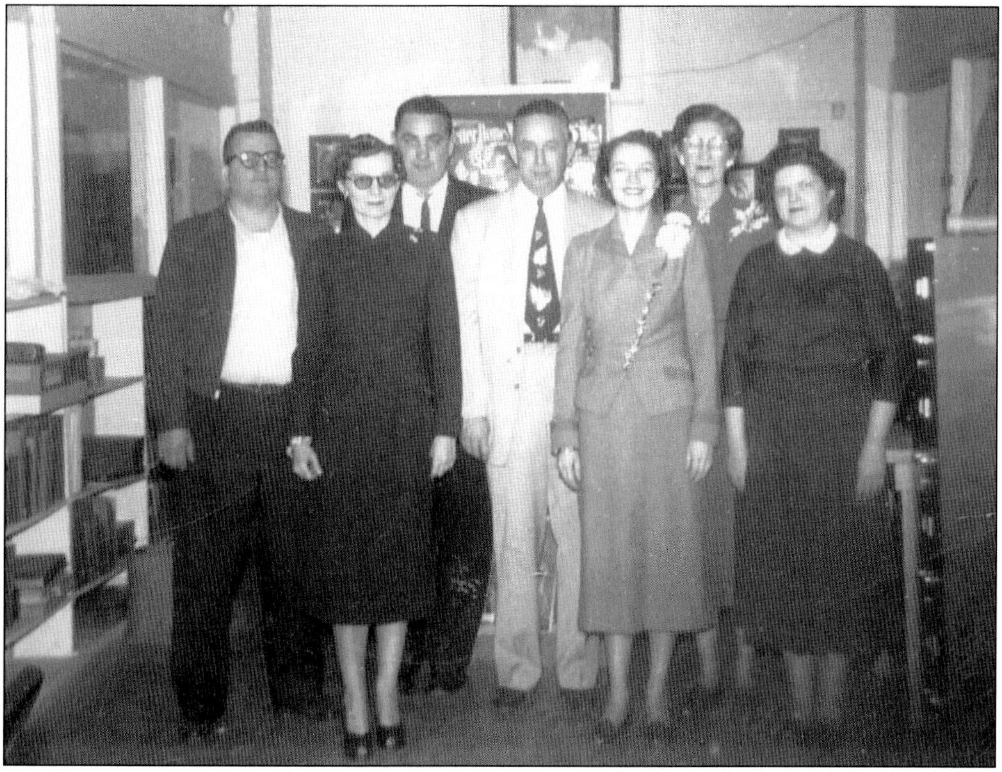

Wagoner Junior High faculty members in 1956 are, from left to right, unidentified, Ila Hicks, Don Riederer, J.C. Atchley, Betty Ritch-Lombardi, Grace Cherry, and ? Lees. (Courtesy of Betty Ritch-Lombardi.)

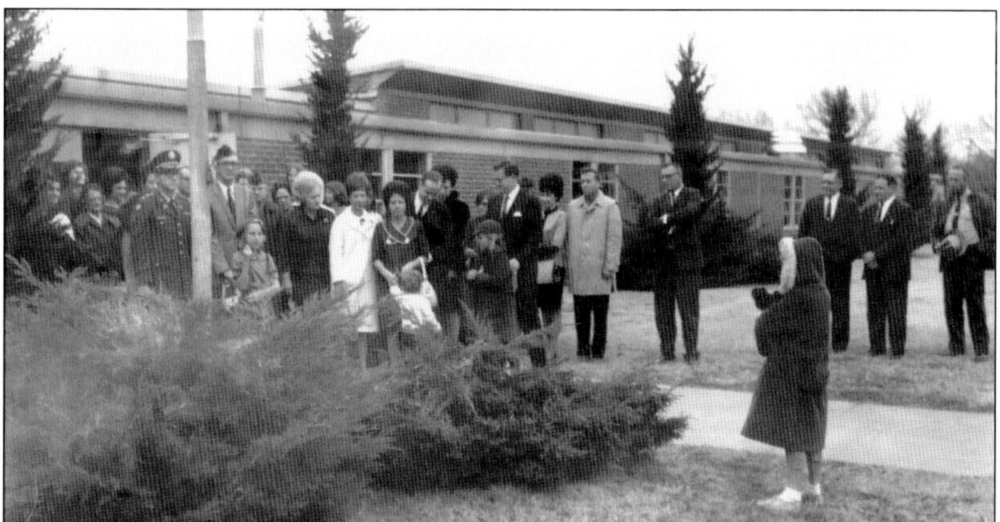

US congressman Ed Edmondson was guest speaker at the dedication of Ellington Elementary, the first new building Wagoner Public Schools had added in 20 years. Among those attending are Sally Russell (in the white coat) and Mattie Faye Carroll (directly behind Russell). Edmondson is two people to the right of her, looking down at the little girl. Bob Hill is in the light-colored overcoat to his right. (Courtesy of the Cradow Smith collection.)

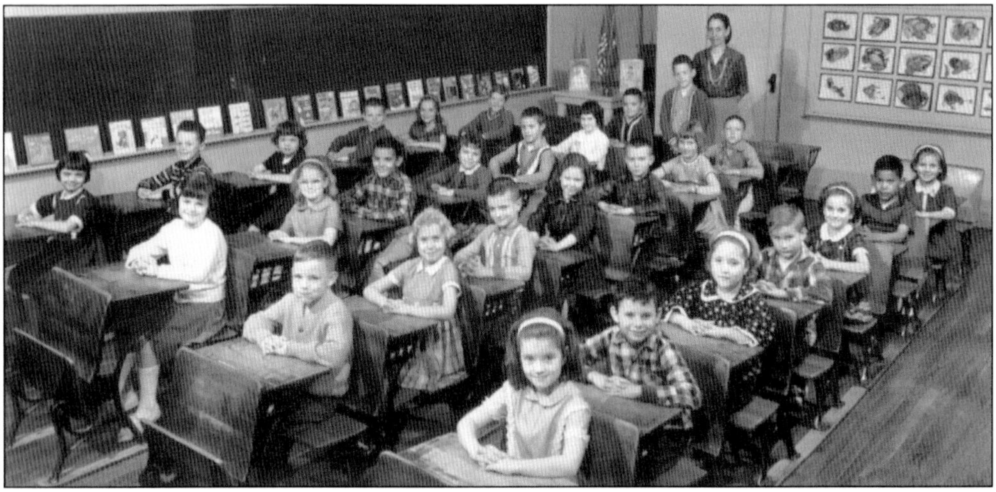

This photograph from Mary Deal's class at Central Elementary in 1965 shows how classrooms used to look. Pictured are, from left to right, (first row) Lori Frost, Tommy Hill, Janet Beck, Jeff Shipman, unidentified, Ronald Carey, and Susan Gilbert (second row) Greg Smith, Regina Thieleke, Ronald Ross, Betty Young, Wayne Harding, Jerri Olson, and unidentified; (third row) Janis Lancaster, Glenda Pratt, Homer Johnson, unidentified, Gary Allison, Diana Palone, Paul Adams, unidentified, and Deal; (fourth row) Janet Baker, Mike Gilbert, Pam Teeters, unidentified, Sharon Greathouse, and unidentified. (Author's collection.)

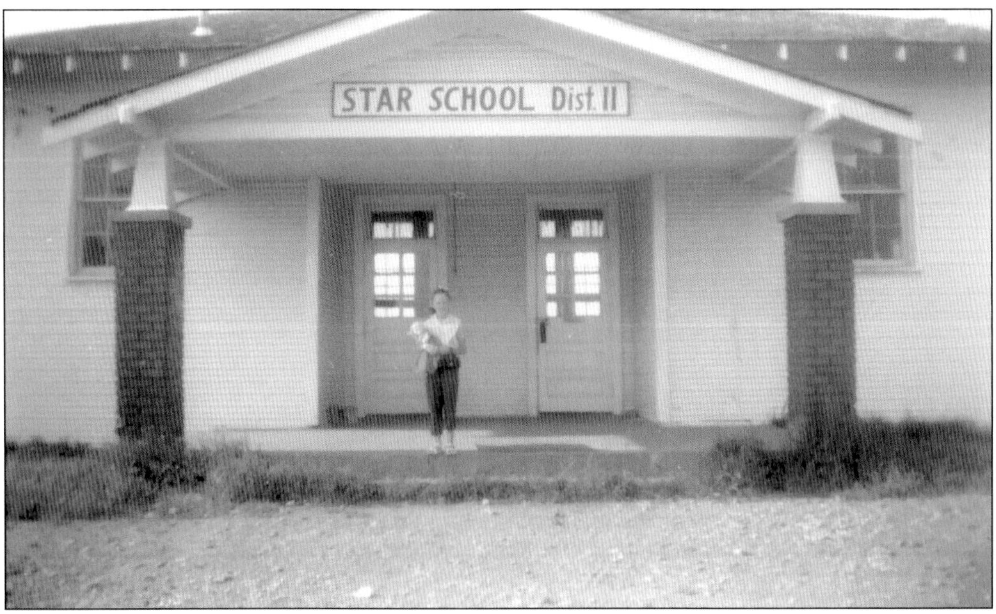

Wagoner was surrounded by small, rural schools; there were more than 60 in Wagoner County in 1918. One of those was Star School, which operated west of Wagoner until the early 1960s. In 2015, there are four districts in Wagoner County—Wagoner, Coweta, Porter, and Okay. (Courtesy of Doreen McMahan.)

Four

Agriculture Was King

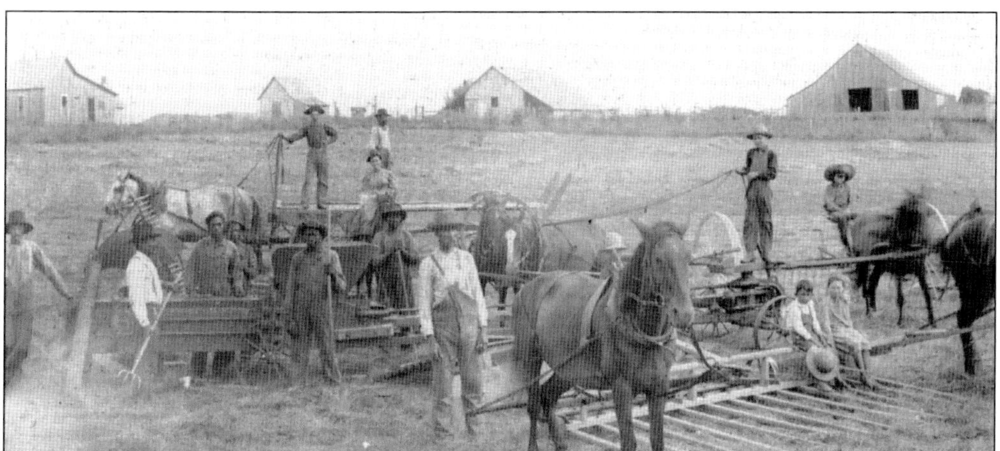

Farming was a mainstay in Wagoner's economy for most of its first 100 years. This farm scene, from about 1900, is on the A.J. Ahrens farm, just east of the present-day Wagoner High School. The little boy sitting on the rake is Henry Ahrens. The little girl is his sister Julianna. (Courtesy of Jerry Hickman.)

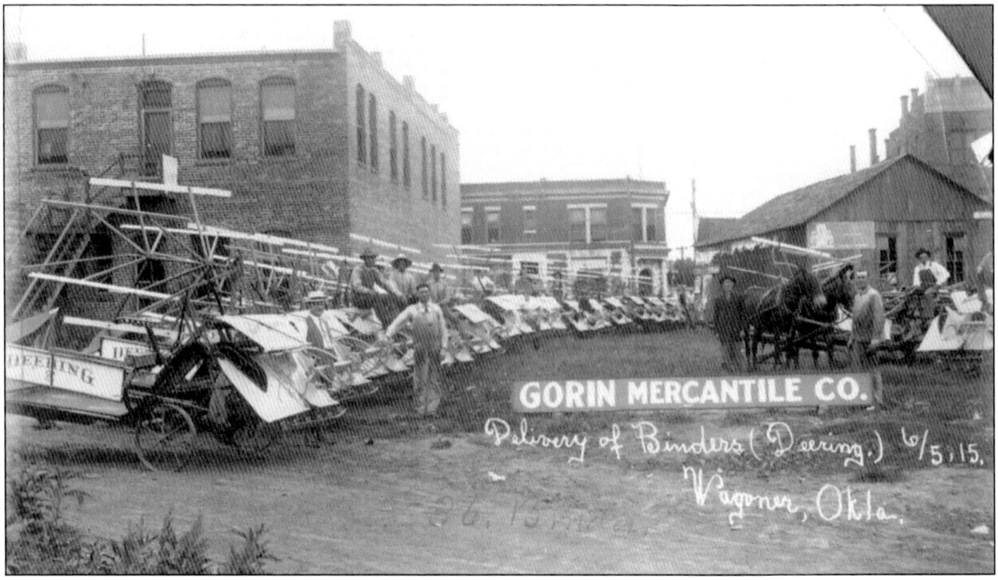

The delivery of Deering binders to Wagoner was the occasion for this photograph on June 5, 1915. Those pictured include H.J. Kennedy, on the left in the white shirt. A mechanic named Grimes is seen standing. Seated individuals include Renfro B. Brady, Peck Noe, Henry Mannon, and others. On the far right are Grant Johnston, John Redfern, and Elijah Johnston. Grant Johnston purchased three binders that day. The building on the left is the Majestic Hotel. On the right is Bill Thome's blacksmith shop. In 2015, the back center building housed Wagoner County Abstract Co.'s closing office. (Author's collection.)

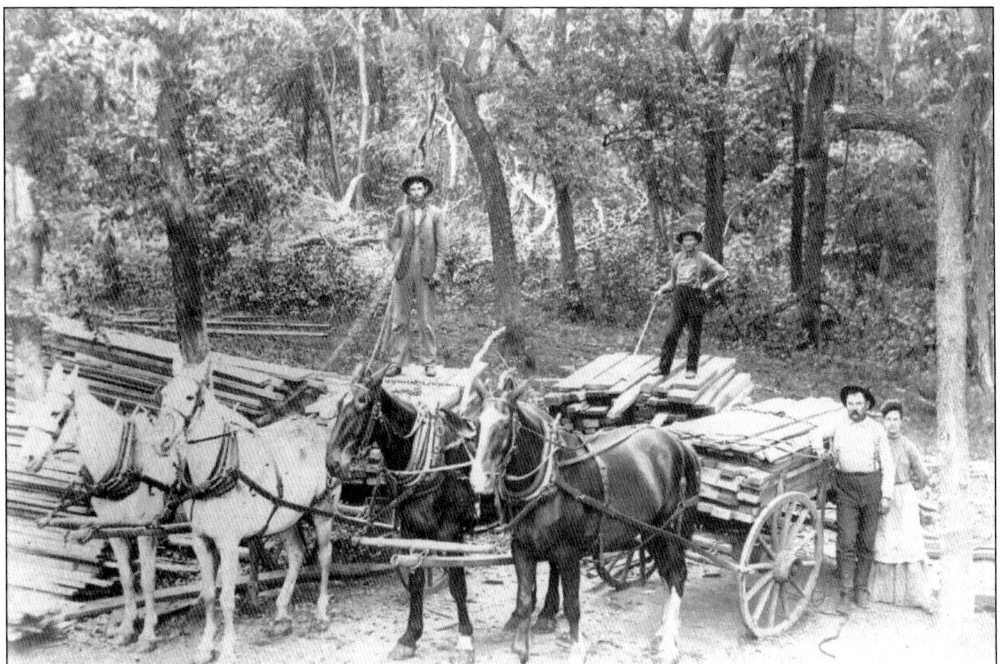

A load of lumber is headed to Lawson's Saw Mill on Grand River in 1907. (Courtesy of Jerry Hickman.)

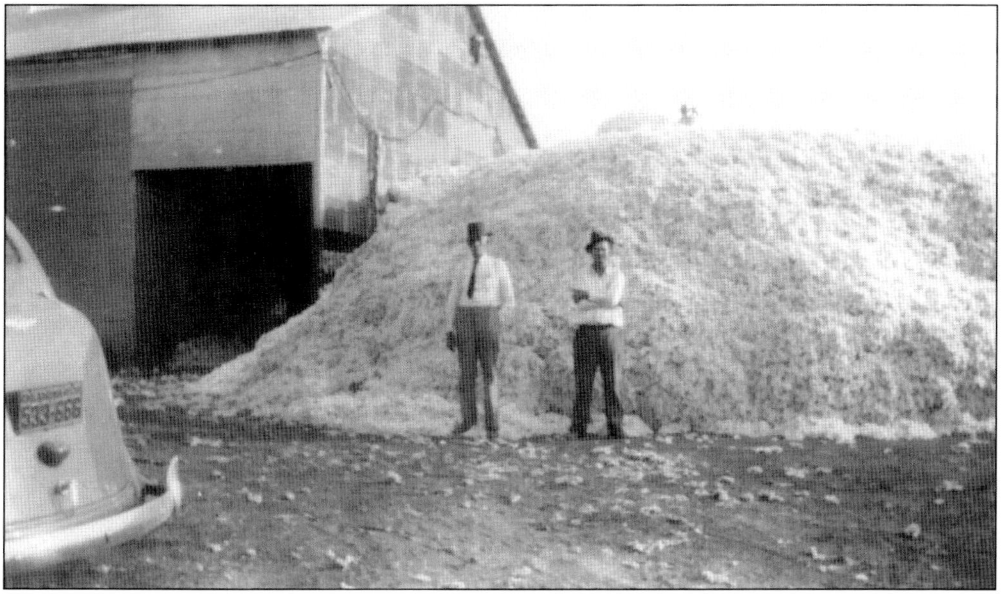

Wagoner had several cotton gins in the early 1900s, including the Farmers and Merchants Gin, owned by W.A. "Cap" Lamon Sr. (left). To his right is his son, W.A. Lamon Jr. Lamon Sr. built his gin in 1895 and it operated until 1954. (Courtesy of the Lamon family.)

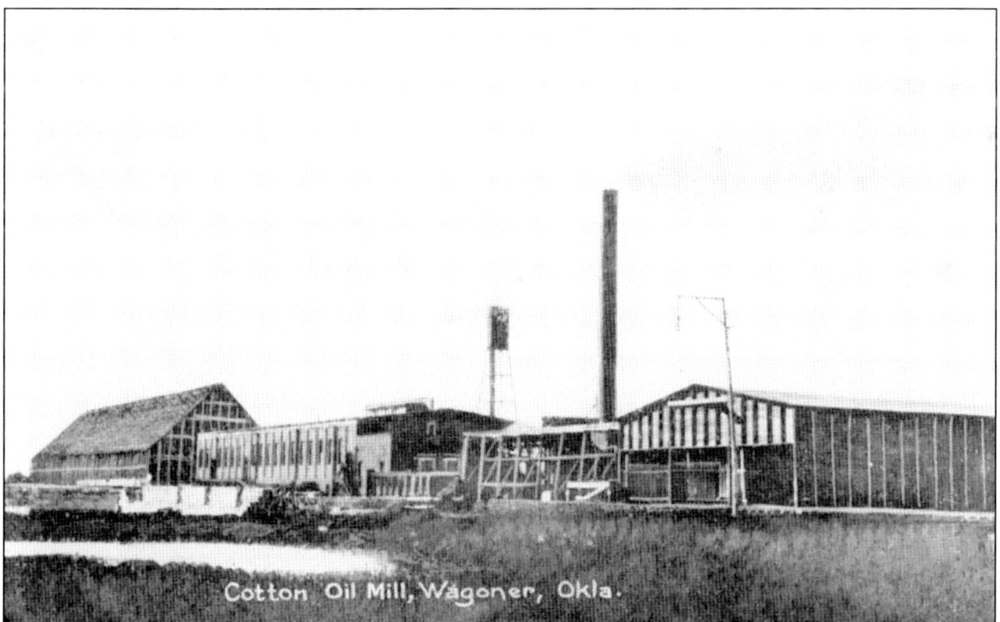

Located at West Fourth and Rice Streets, the National Cotton Oil and Mfg. Co. was a large presence in Wagoner. The company removed cotton hulls from the ginned cottonseed and steamed and pressed them, producing edible oil. The defatted seeds and hulls were used for livestock feed. The plant burned in 1926. (Author's collection.)

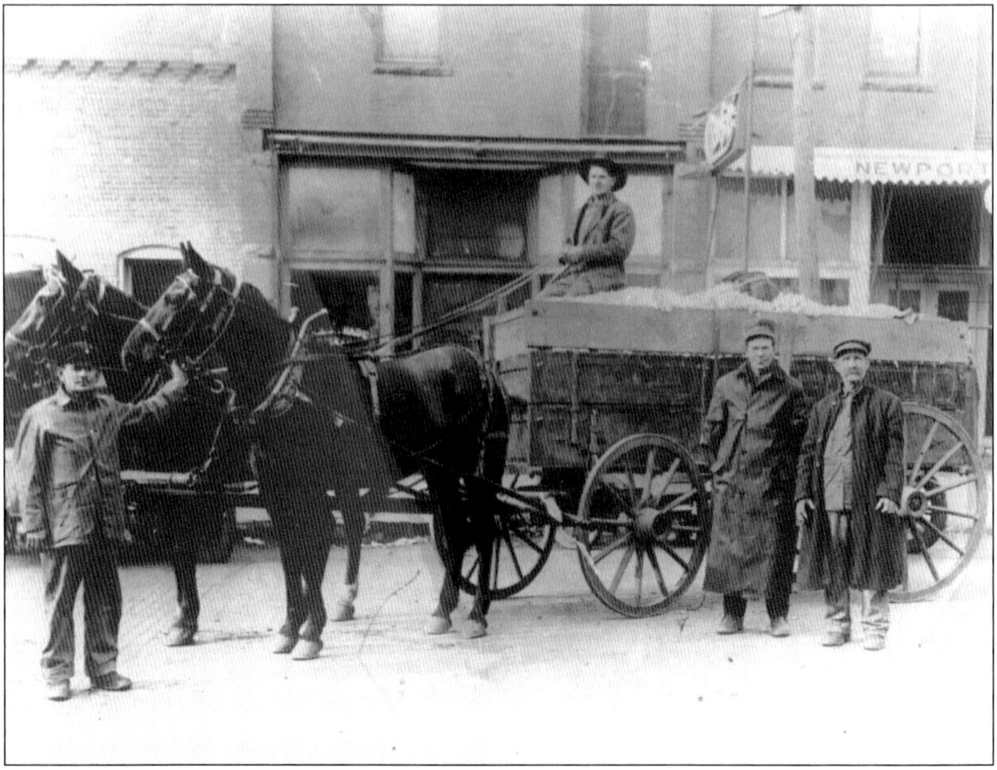

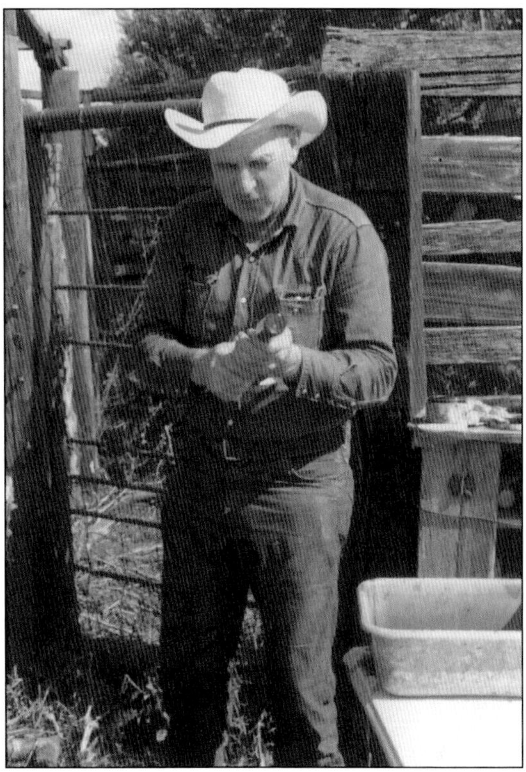

Isaac Newton Rhodes, sitting in the wagon seat, brings a load of cotton to Wagoner to be ginned. He is posing for this photograph on South Main Street. At the front of the wagon is his uncle Bob Brewer. (Courtesy of Jim Rhodes.)

Getting ready to vaccinate a calf is rancher Tom Gilbert, who had a large cattle operation north of Wagoner from the 1950s to the 1980s. (Author's collection.)

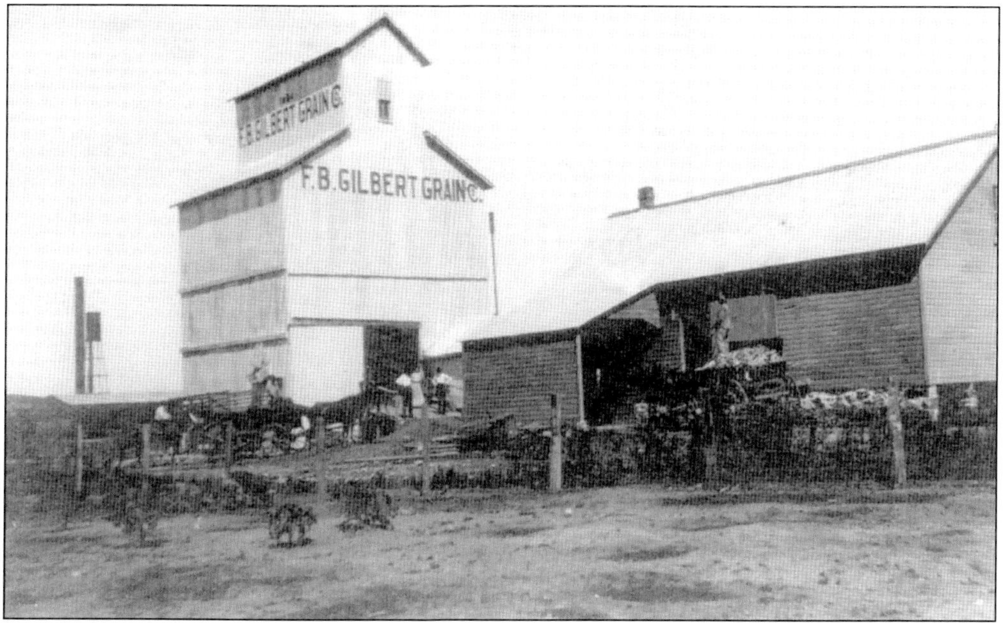

F.B. Gilbert established a grain elevator at Northwest Fourth Street and Prairie Avenue in 1905. The elevator was rebuilt after a 1907 fire. (Courtesy of Shirle Lamb Williams.)

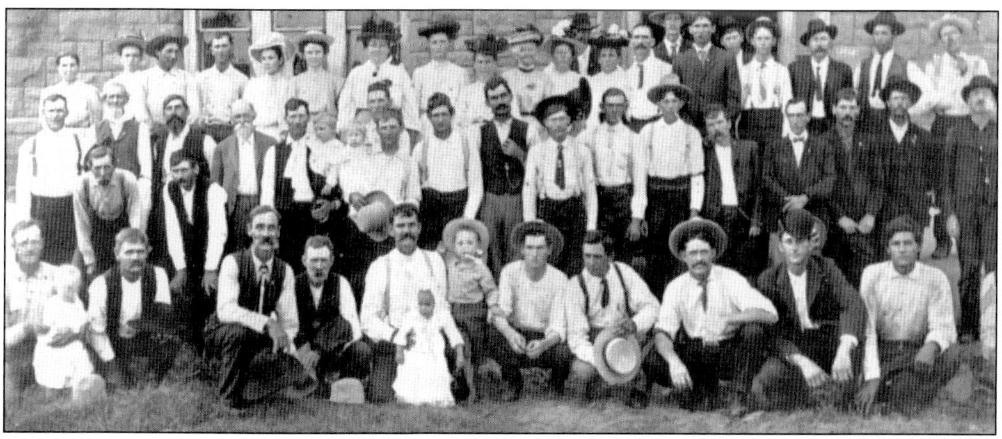

This photograph of members of the Anti-Horse Thief Association of Wagoner County was taken in front of the old rock building in the Pipeline School District that was used as a store that was run by a Mr. Piers. Those who have been identified in the photograph are Bill Eaton and baby, Frank Nickle, Ross Nickle, Frank Higgins, ? Piersall, Bill Turnham, ? McCormick, ? Dorr, John Burris, Sherman Lane, Alvin Stoehand, Henry Ferrill, Jim Dyer, ? Friman, George Williams, Sam Brady, Liza Brady Damet, Zora Stadalman Stoehand, Doll Nickle, ? Burris, Pearl Eaton, ? McCormick, Ollie Buckley Sowers, ? Stadalman, Fred Stadalman, John A. Bellah, ? Stoehand, and Herschel Jones. (Courtesy of Margie Semore.)

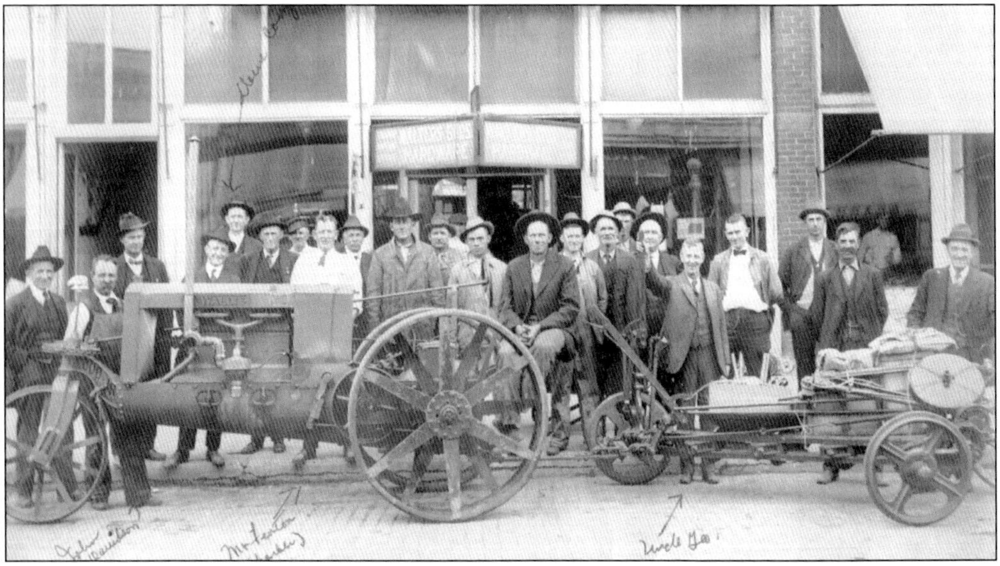

This Wallis tractor is believed to have been the first tractor sold in Wagoner. This photograph is from about 1914 and was taken in front of Walters Hardware, 120 South Main Street, around 1914. Those in the photograph are, from left to right, unidentified; John W. Davidson, tinner for G.H. Walters; J.A. "Jess" Goddard; J. Francis "Frank" LeMaster; Dave T. Campbell, manager for Chesnutt-Gibbons Wholesale Group; unidentified; Robert E. Doggett, magistrate and attorney in Gibson Building, Wagoner mayor in 1910; Littrell B. Fenton, barber; William B. Moss, lawyer in Citizen's Trust Building; John White, farmer; Arthur P. Thomas, livery; unidentified Walters employee who assembled the tractor; unidentified farmer who bought the tractor; Edward N. McAllister, clerk for Chesnutt-Gibbons Group Co.; Charles H. Bennett, carpenter, father of George Bennett; two unidentified; George H. Walters, owner of hardware store; Harold Sleeper; two unidentified; Rufus Leach, laborer; and unidentified. (Courtesy of Adam Miller.)

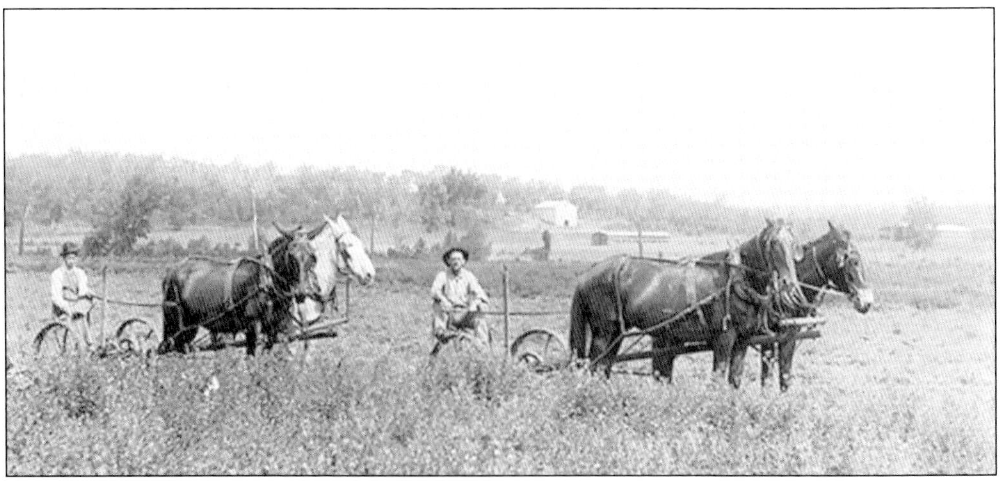

This photograph, from about 1913, shows Wagoner County sheriff J.E. Long (right) in a field of 90 acres of alfalfa on his Grandview Farm northeast of Wagoner. The farm was in the area of what is now Grandview Addition. In the background is a bunk barn. It was about 40-by-60 feet with a cement floor and tin roof. Remnants of the barn still stand. Long was removed from office for a number of offenses and convicted of embezzling $37.80 from the county. He declared bankruptcy in 1915. (Author's collection.)

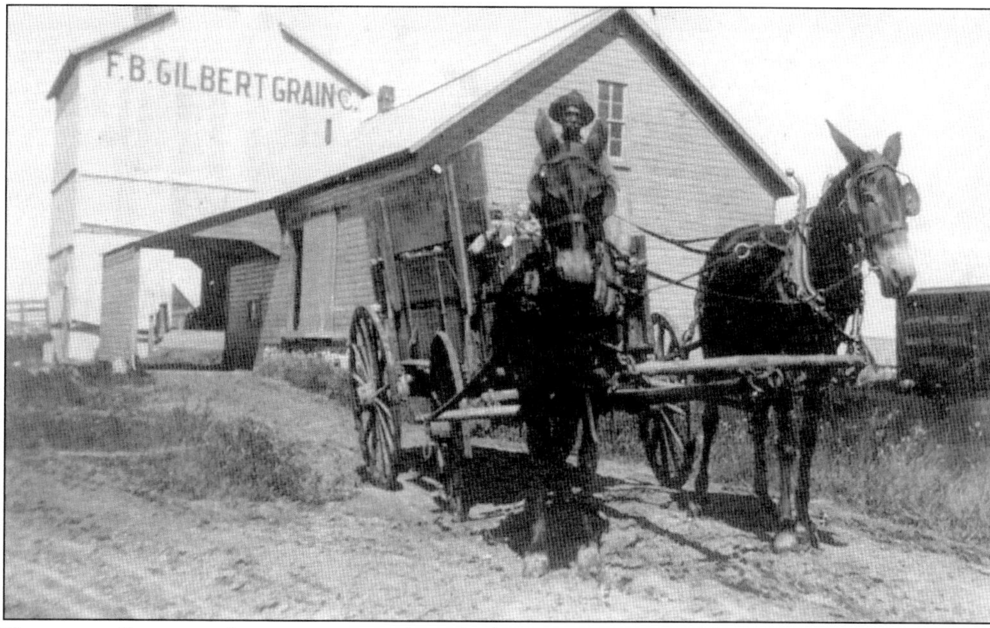

Known as Bumpus, the man pictured worked many years as a deliveryman for F.B. Gilbert Grain Co. There is no actual name listed on the photograph. (Courtesy of the Wagoner City Historical Museum.)

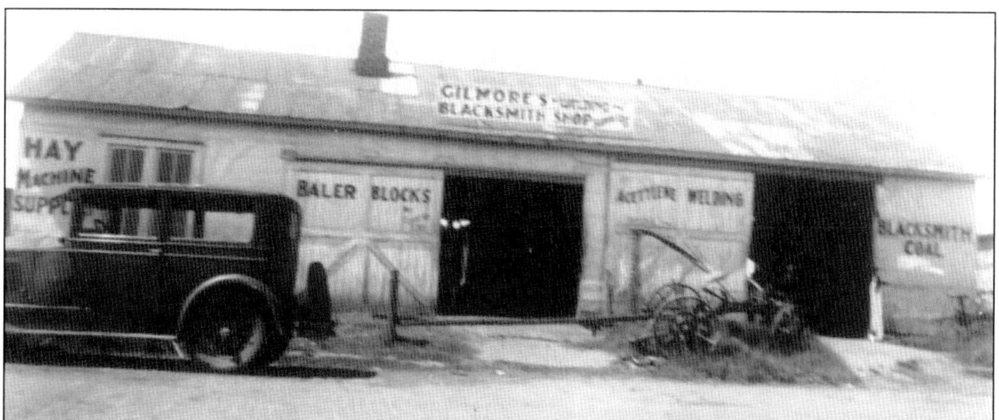

The village blacksmith played an important role in the community when its economic base was agriculture. The Gilmore Blacksmith Shop, formerly the Benny Harris Blacksmith Shop, went from shoeing horses to making hay baler repairs as farming shifted from horses to depending on machines. (Courtesy of Barbara Harris Chappell.)

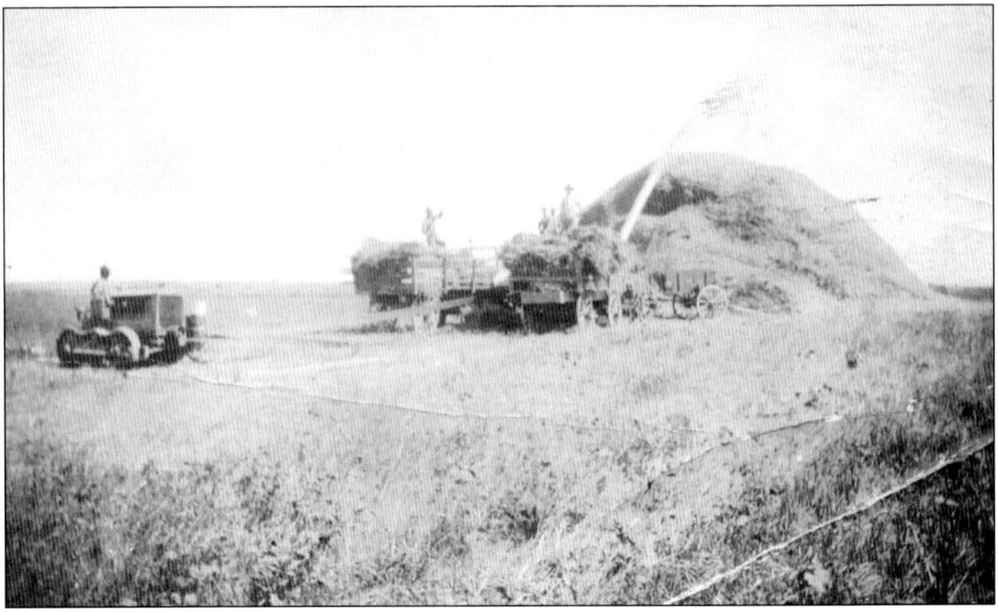

Workers stack hay after cutting the field at the Ahrens farm, just east of Wagoner, around 1900. (Courtesy of Jerry Hickman.)

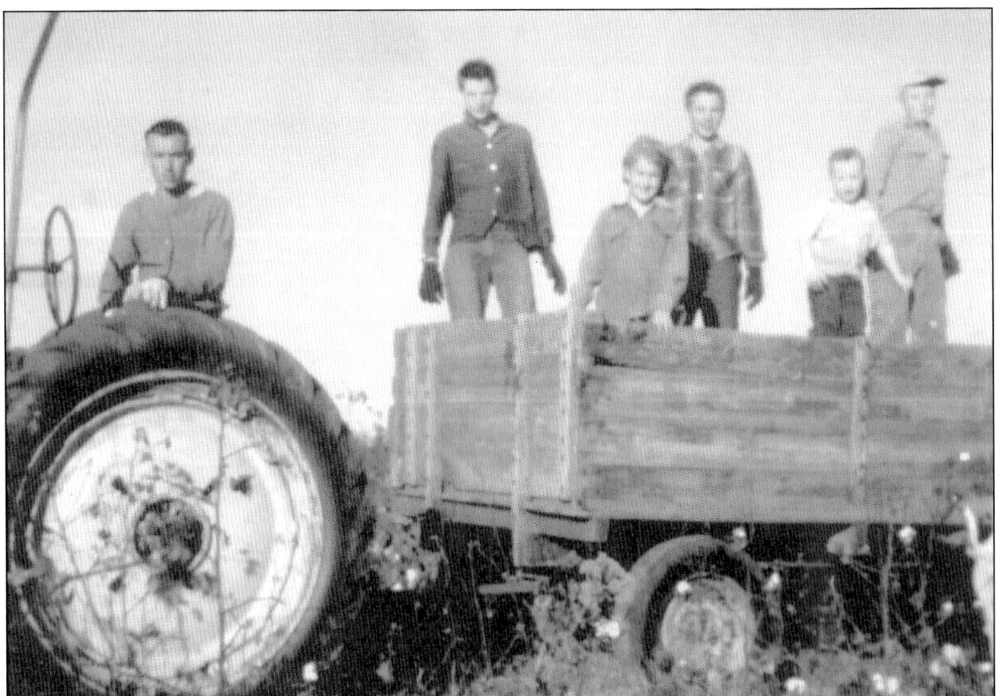

Growing up on a farm meant chores, including picking cotton, for the children of John and Maggie Rice. They are, from left to right, Joe, Johnny, Margaret, Jerry, Ronnie, and Charles. (Courtesy of Billie Rice.)

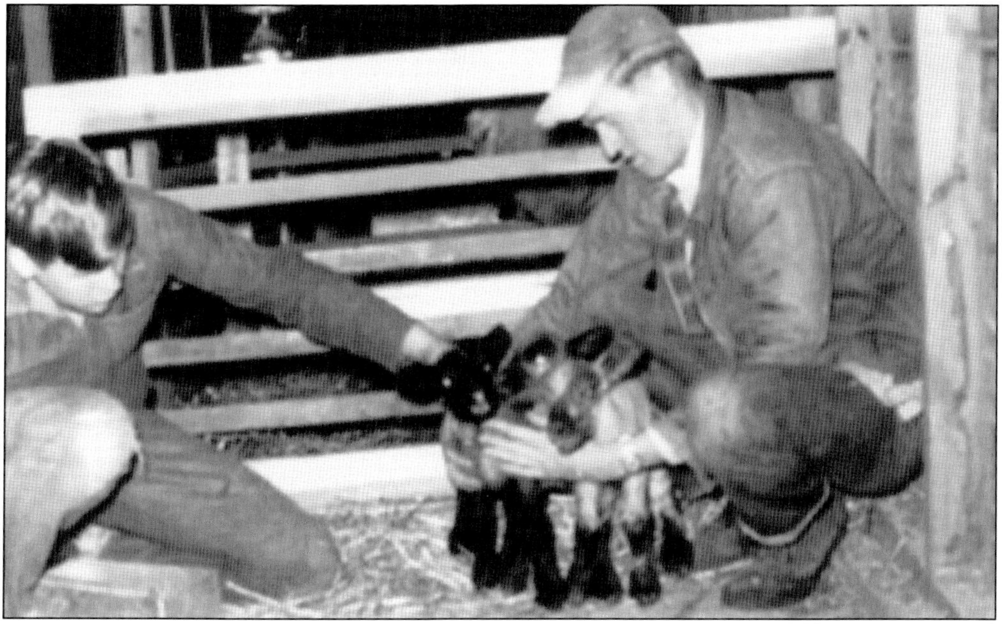

Carl (left) and Robert Brady admire new baby lambs at the family farm near Wagoner. (Courtesy of Beth Brady Edwards.)

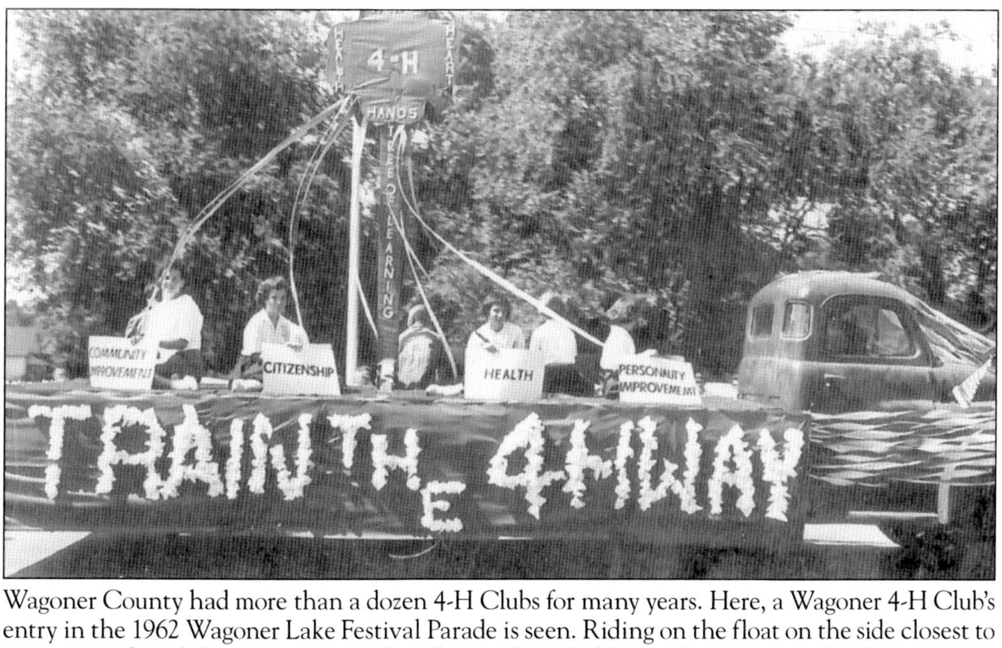

Wagoner County had more than a dozen 4-H Clubs for many years. Here, a Wagoner 4-H Club's entry in the 1962 Wagoner Lake Festival Parade is seen. Riding on the float on the side closest to camera are, from left to right, Elizabeth Gilbert, Alene Webb, Carolyn Peters, and Judy Satterfield. (Courtesy of the Cradow Smith collection.)

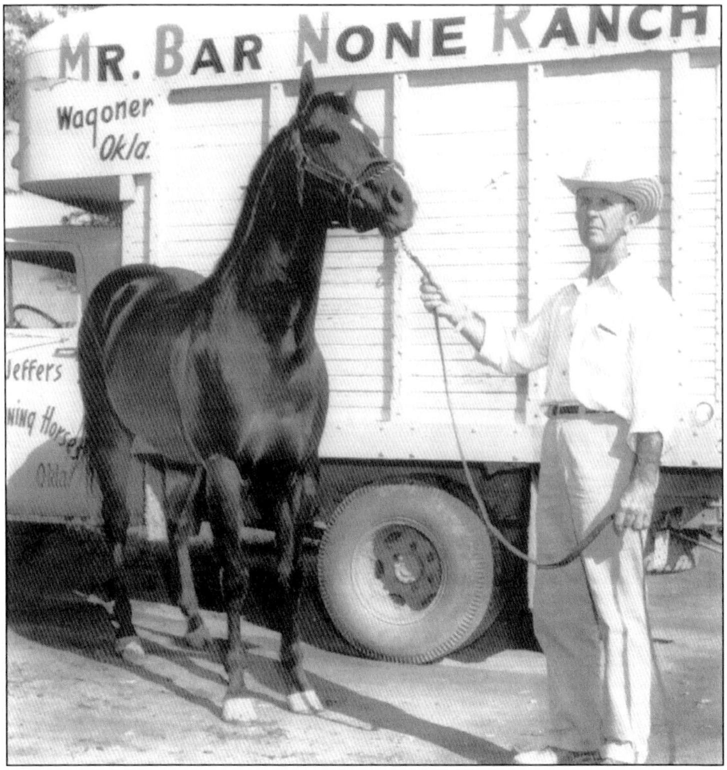

The legendary racehorse Mr. Bar None was the pride of Wagoner as he set national quarter horse speed records. Here, he is pictured with Oscar "June" Jeffers, who owned the horse with his wife, Zelma. Mr. Bar None was the Champion Running Horse and World Champion Stallion quarter horse in 1957 and 1958. (Author's collection.)

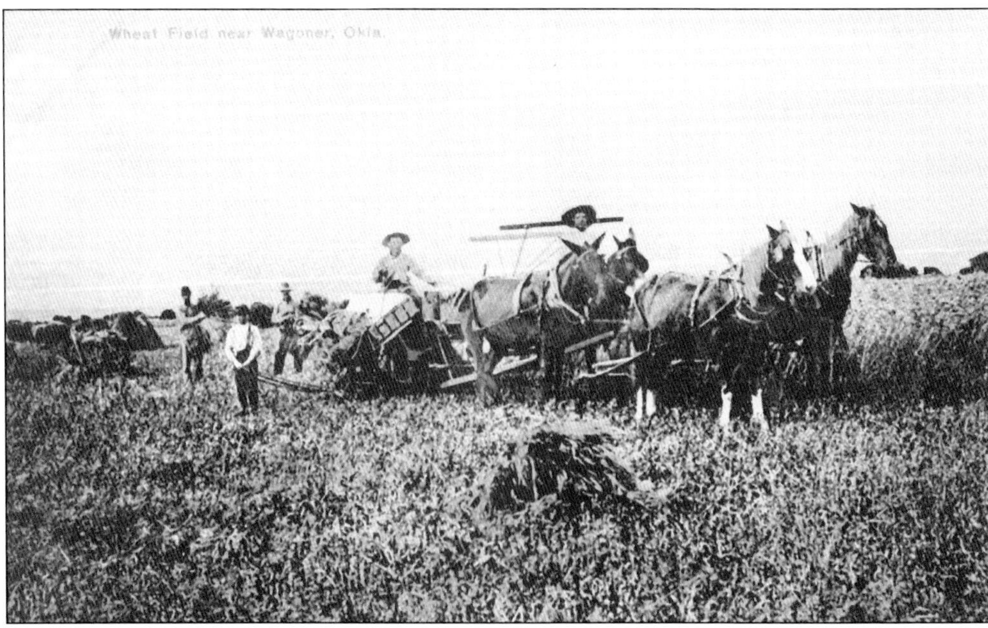

Area farmers planted thousands of acres of wheat when the photograph for this postcard was taken in about 1906. In 2015, soybeans are the area's main farm crop. (Author's collection.)

Being involved in agriculture has not always involved farming. Charles Lamb owned Lamb Seed Store on North Main Street. Delivering a load of feed here is Cletus Geurin, who hauled not only feed but also cattle over the years. Pictured are, from left to right, Jim Owen, Tony Rizzo, two unidentified, Geurin, unidentified, and Lamb. (Courtesy of Shirle Lamb Williams.)

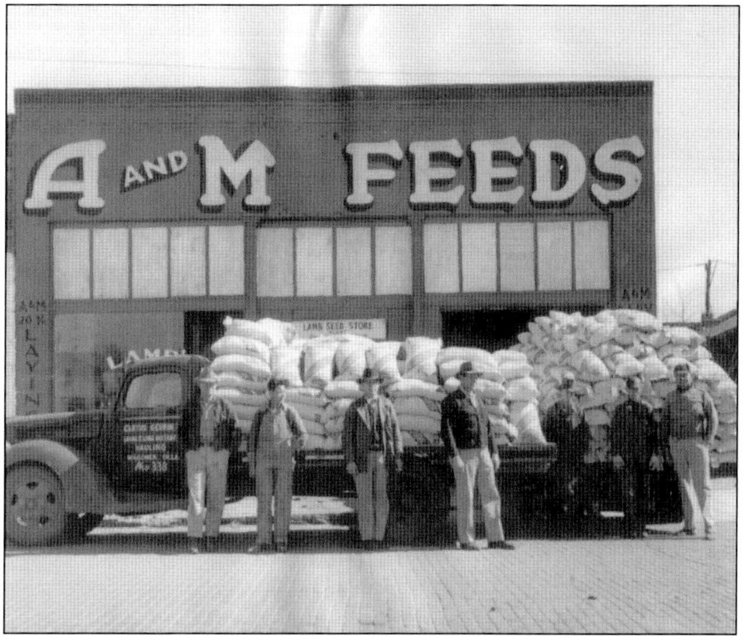

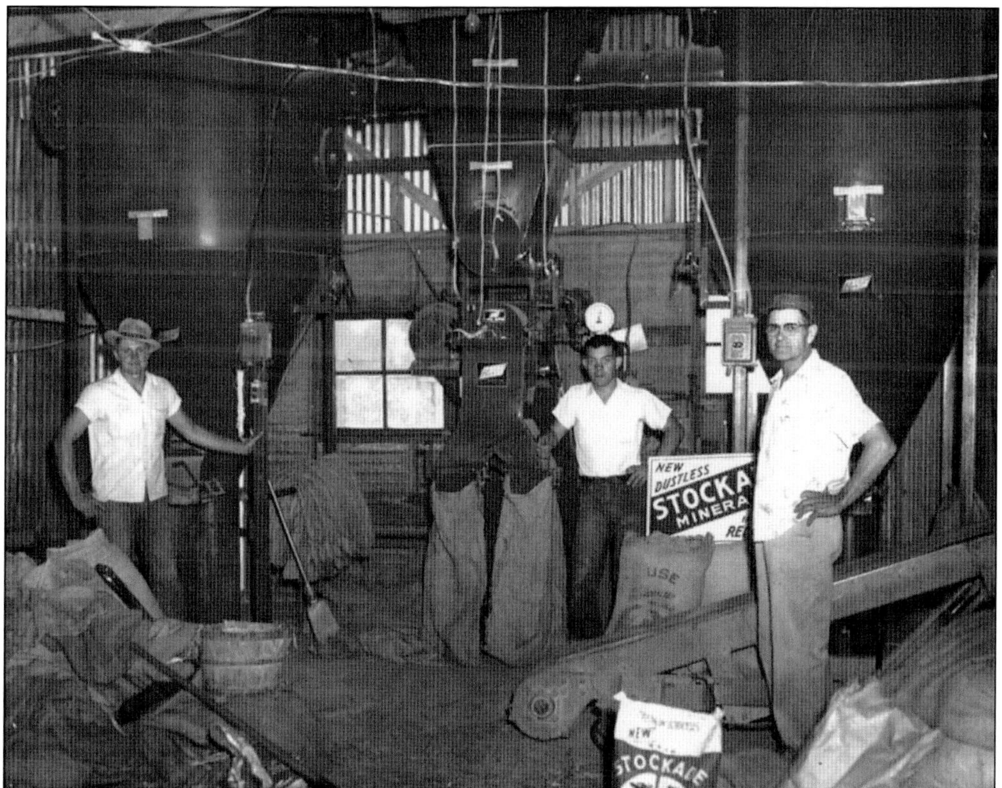

Showing off the Wright's Mill operation on West Cherokee Street in the late 1950s or early 1960s are, from left to right, Leroy Champlain, Spuddy Wright, and John Wright. (Courtesy of Spuddy and Ginger Wright.)

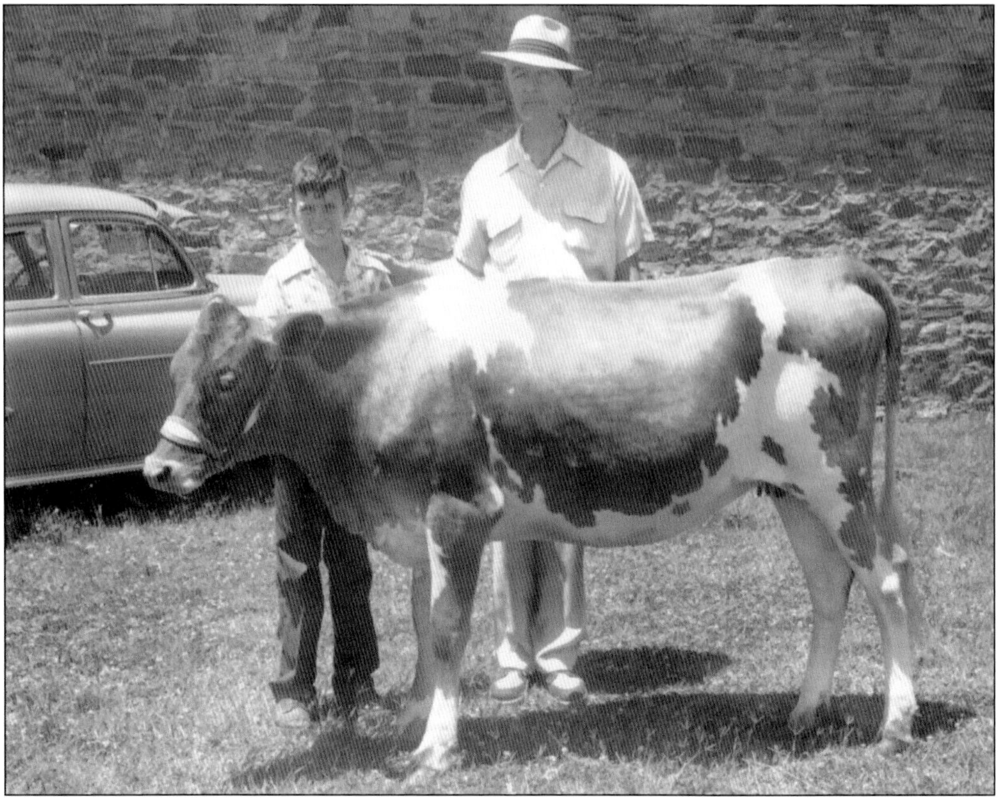

In 1952, several civic leaders invested in a Wagoner Chamber of Commerce program where youths were awarded dairy heifers to be fed and raised for a 4-H dairy show. This heifer was sponsored by Arch Lancaster of Wagoner County Abstract and given to Kenneth Peters. It took second place Guernsey in the junior yearling class. (Courtesy of Margie Semore.)

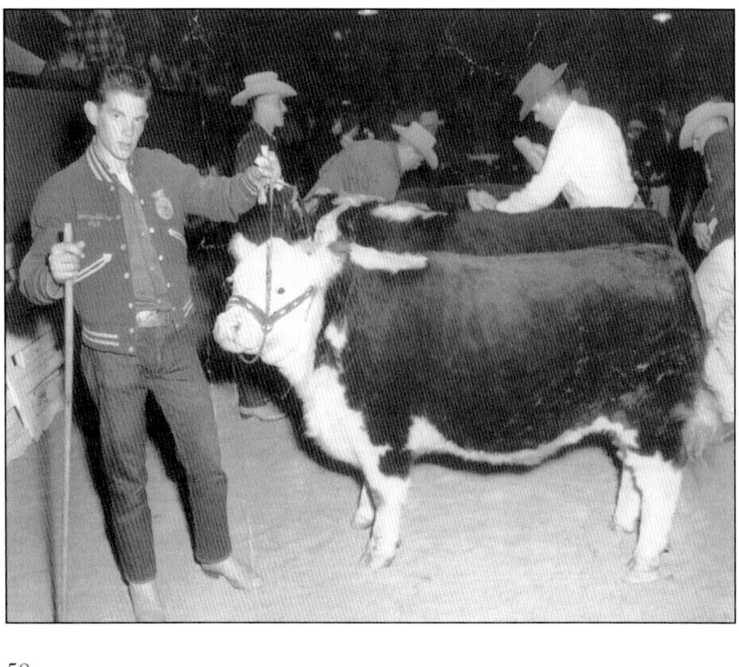

Winning livestock shows has been a tradition for Wagoner 4-H and FFA members. Here, Tommy Gilbert shows the reserve grand champion market steer at the 1961 Muskogee Junior Livestock show. (Author's collection.)

Five

The Lake Took Over Farms

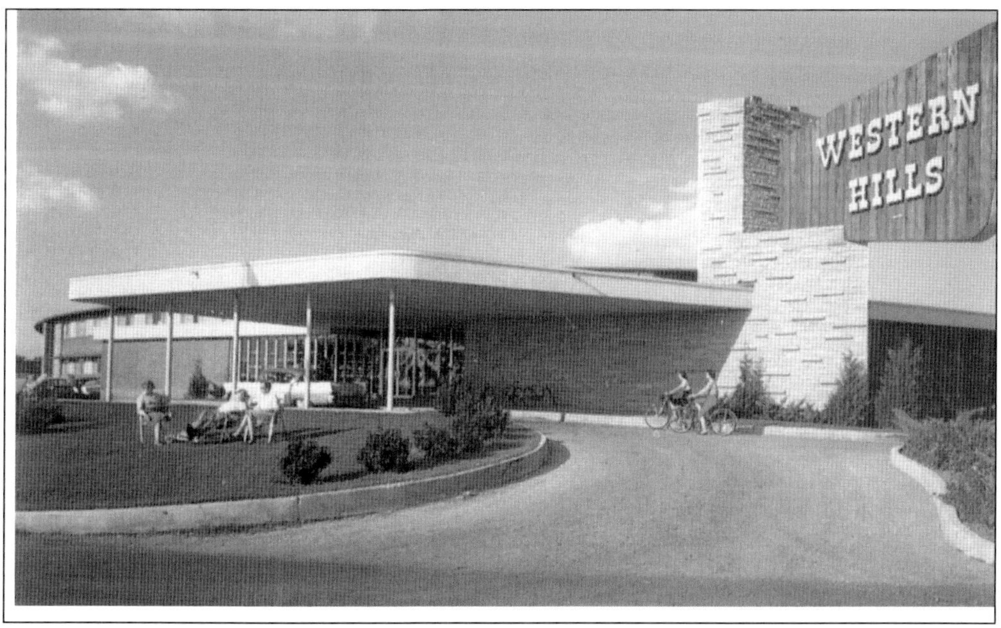

As Fort Gibson Lake was filling up, a number of resorts opened, including Western Hills State Lodge, located east of Wagoner off State Highway 51. The lodge was completely remodeled in 2015. (Author's collection.)

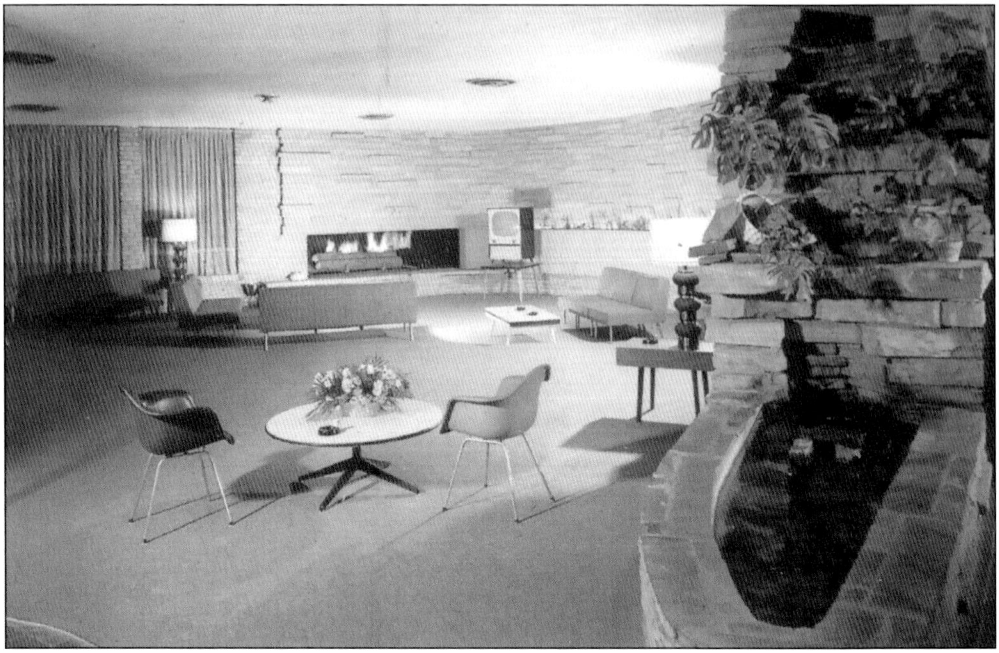

The lobby of Western Hills State Lodge was decorated with western, 1950s look. (Author's collection.)

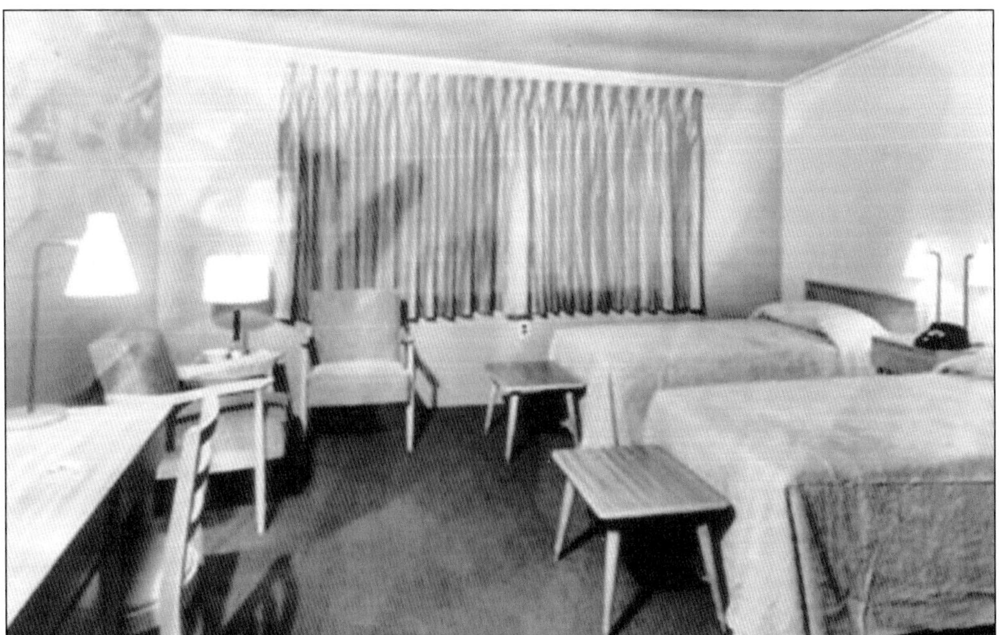

Rooms at the lodge were spacious and filled with the same 1950s look as the rest of the lodges. (Author's collection.)

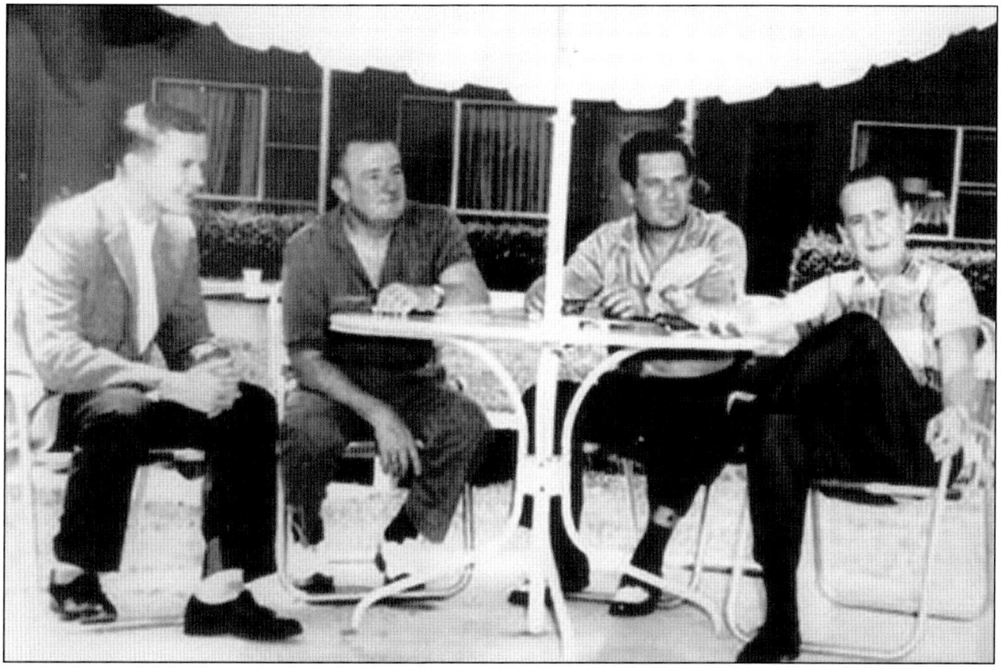

Red Foley, star of the *Ozark Jubilee*, made a visit to Western Hills in 1958. Shown here, from left to right, are Harold Martinson, Jim Nix, Judge Kirksey Nix, and Foley. Foley was on a personal appearance tour in Oklahoma. (Courtesy of Harold Martinson.)

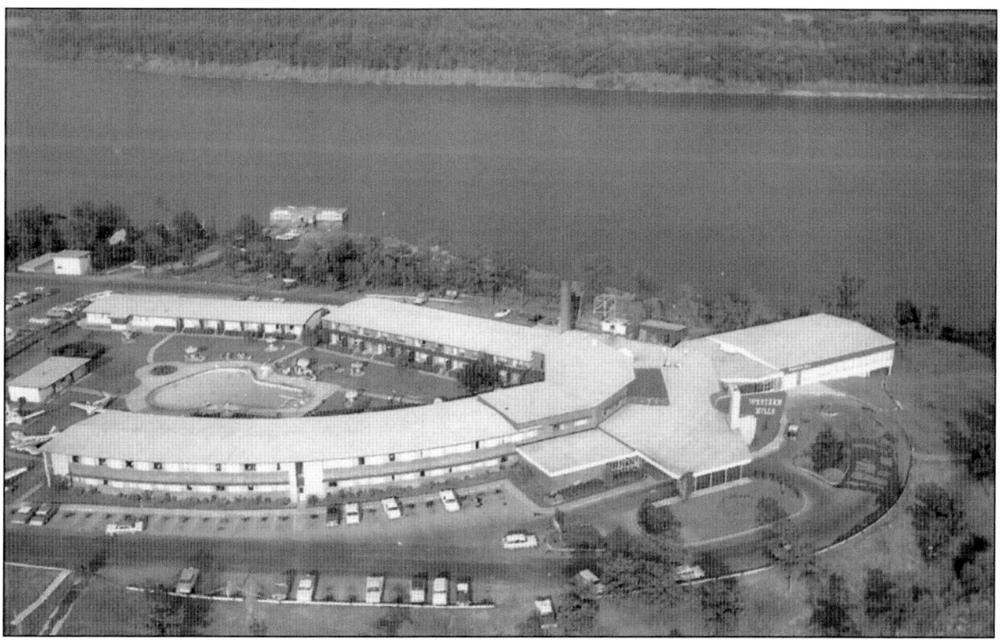

An aerial view of Western Hills State Lodge shows its proximity to Fort Gibson Lake. The lodge has been expanded to include a facility for large groups. (Author's collection.)

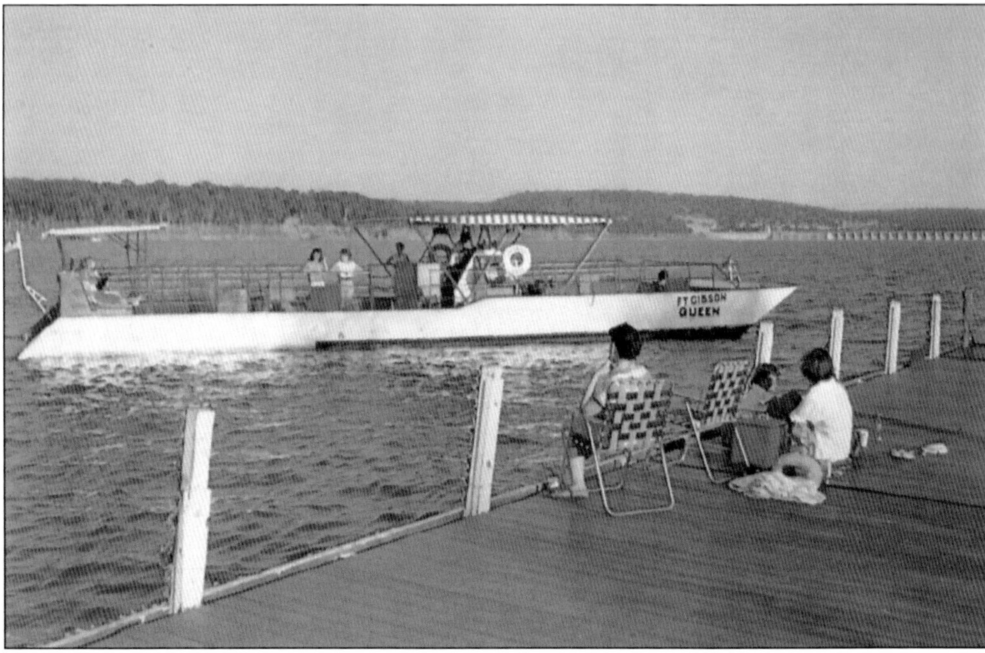

Western Hills and Sequoyah State Park offered more than just lodging; there were also activities such as horseback riding, boat rides, and water-skiing lessons. (Author's collection.)

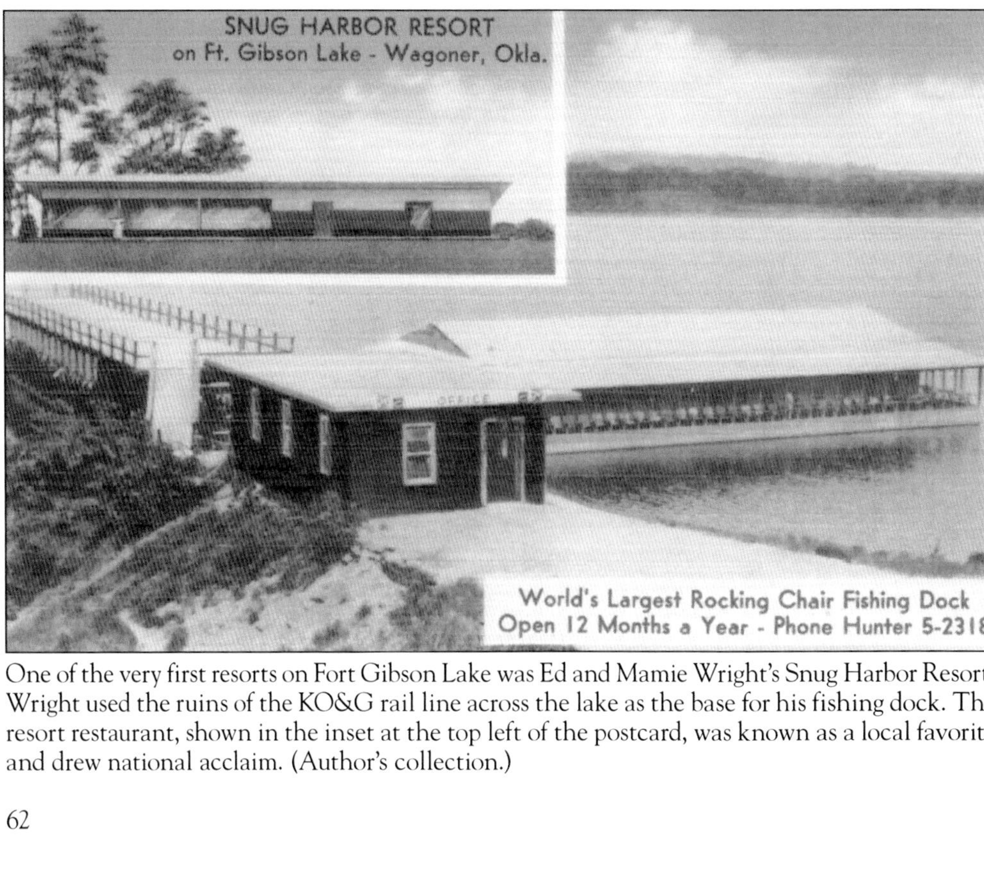

One of the very first resorts on Fort Gibson Lake was Ed and Mamie Wright's Snug Harbor Resort. Wright used the ruins of the KO&G rail line across the lake as the base for his fishing dock. The resort restaurant, shown in the inset at the top left of the postcard, was known as a local favorite and drew national acclaim. (Author's collection.)

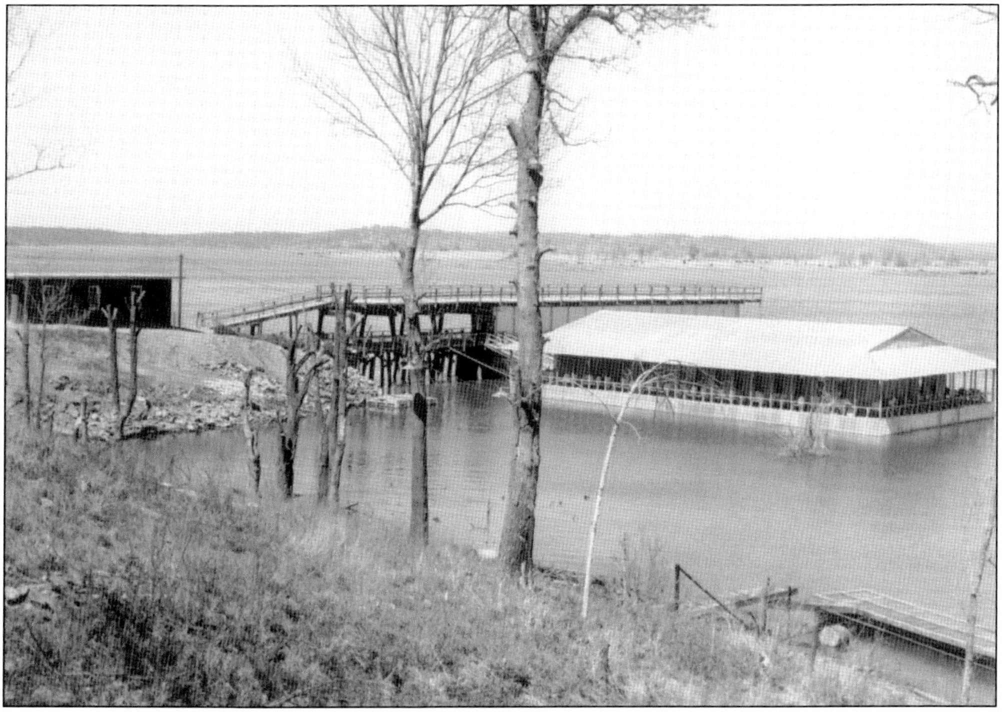

This image captures a very early picture of Snug Harbor fishing dock. The resort closed in the early 1970s. (Courtesy of Jerry Hickman.)

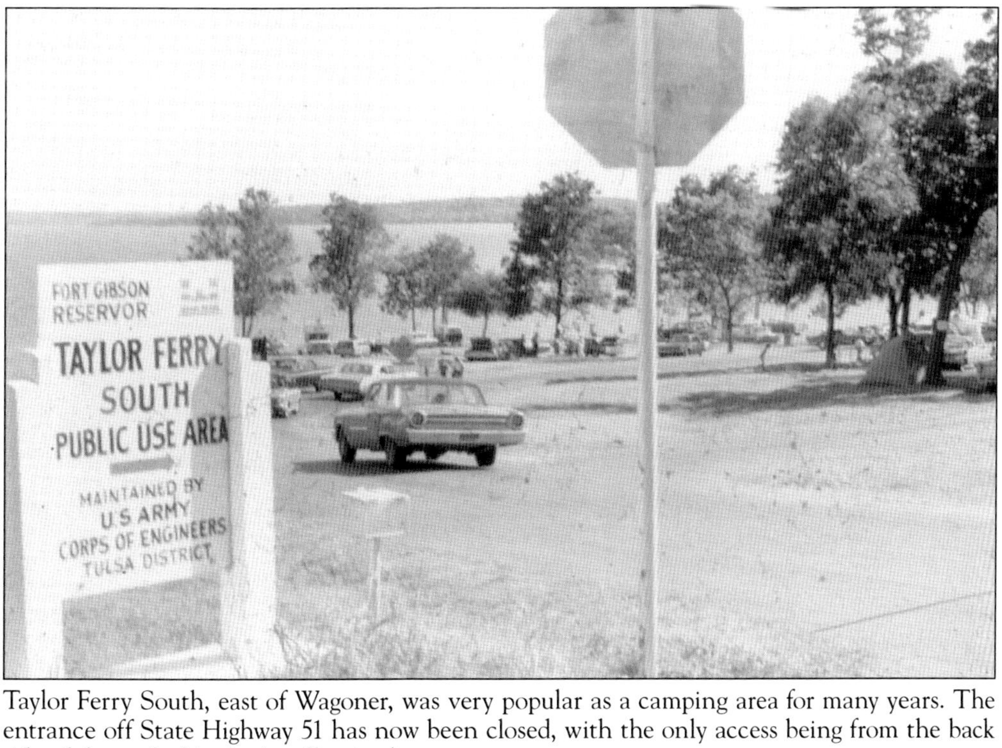

Taylor Ferry South, east of Wagoner, was very popular as a camping area for many years. The entrance off State Highway 51 has now been closed, with the only access being from the back side of the park. (Author's collection.)

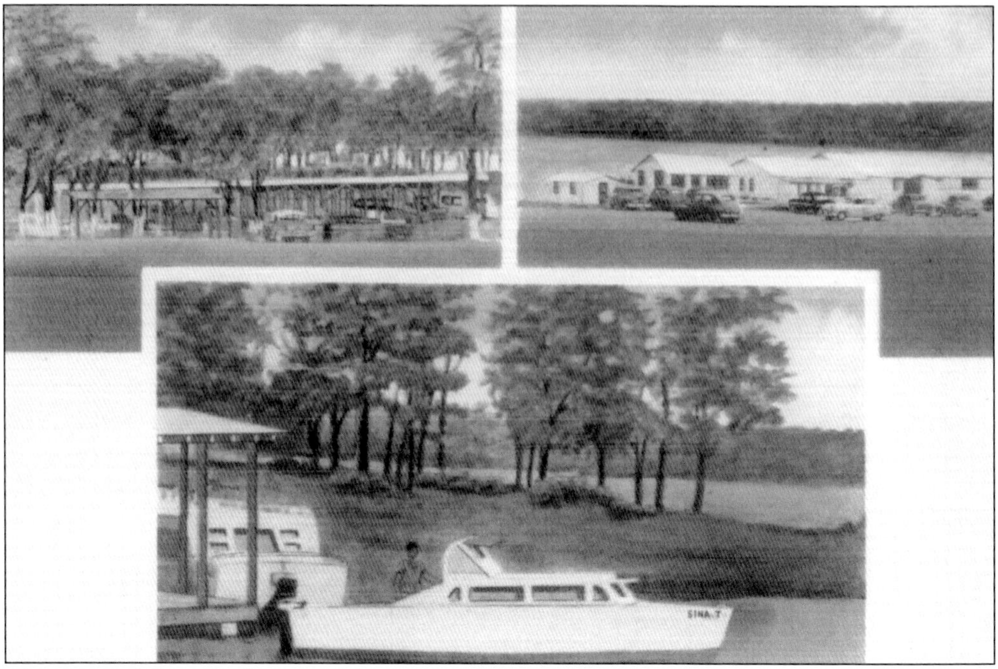

This postcard shows facilities available at Taylor Ferry Marina. The marina continues to offer cabins and fishing. The most popular of the facilities at the Taylor Ferry North area is the swimming beach. A little island near the beach is the ruins of an Indian mound. (Author's collection.)

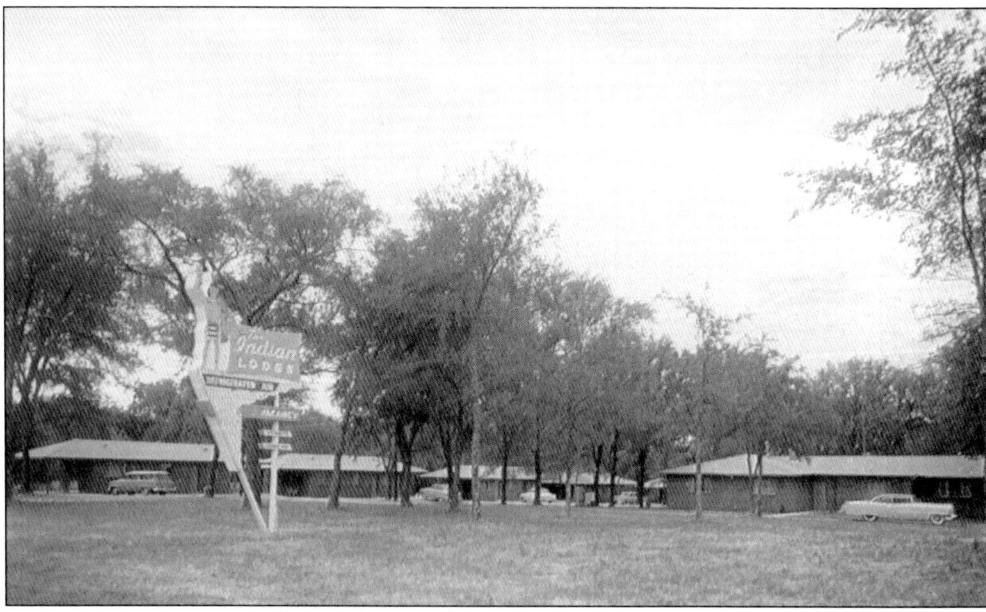

Located on State Highway 51, just west of Fort Gibson Lake, the Indian Lodge's neon sign still welcomes visitors to the lake. The motel was built by Charles and Thelma Landon shortly after they moved to Wagoner from Phoenix, Arizona, in 1954. The sign was installed when the first cabins—those to the east of the office—were built in 1955. The cabins to the west of the office opened in 1959, and a swimming pool was added in 1962. The motel is now open April–October and managed by the Landons' son, Scott. (Author's collection.)

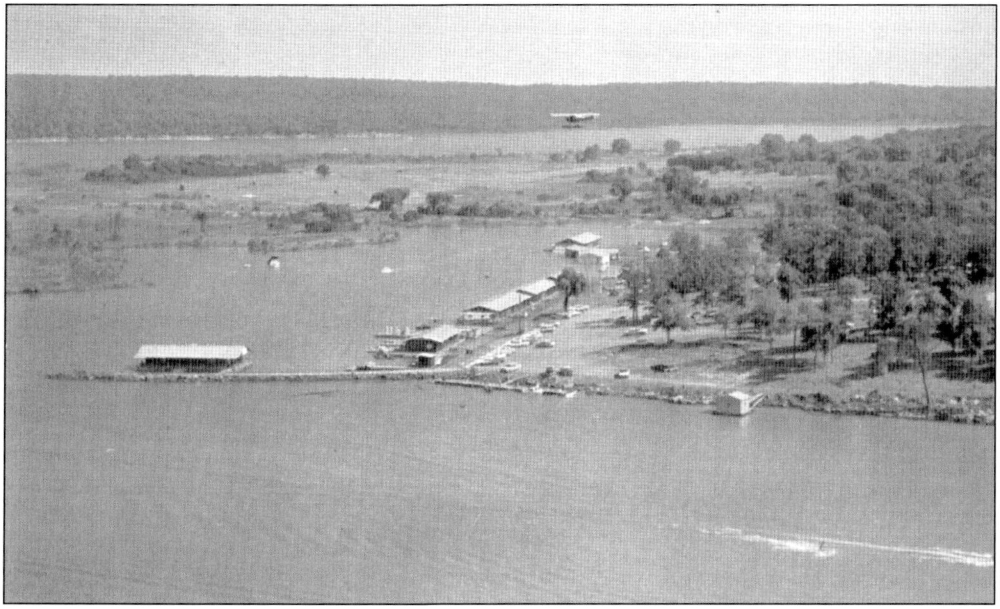

Carl and Golda Laner established Whitehorn Cove resort north of Wagoner in the late 1950s or early 1960s. The resort still operates and includes a restaurant, fuel sales, and fishing. (Author's collection.)

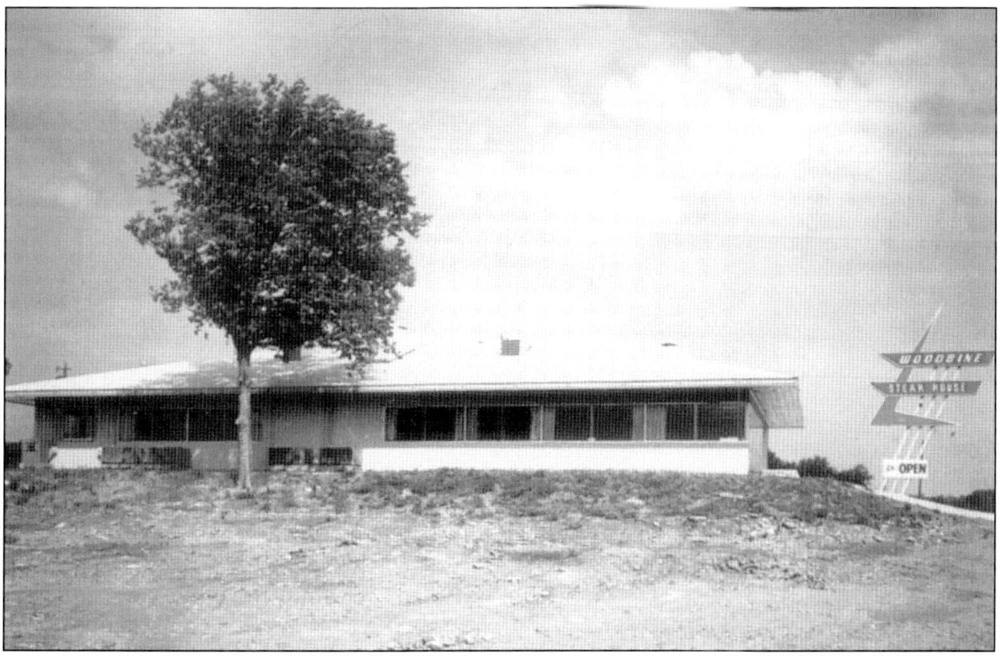

Woodbine Steak House was established on a bluff overlooking the lake. The restaurant was also known in its early years as Sleepy Hollow. It was a great place that quickly became a favorite for special events, such as prom night dinner. It later operated under several different owners and was vacant as of 2015. (Author's collection.)

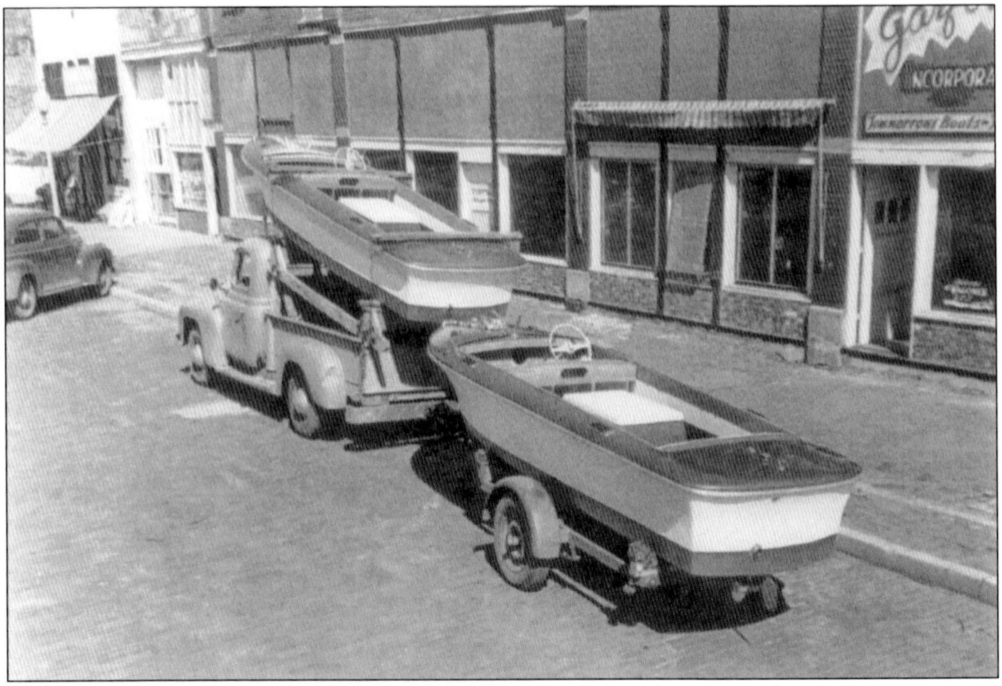

Garform Boat Co. announced in 1950 that it was moving its plant from Tulsa to Wagoner's old Axtell Hotel. The boat was developed by Gar Wood, an internationally known boat racer and designer. (Courtesy of the Cradow Smith collection.)

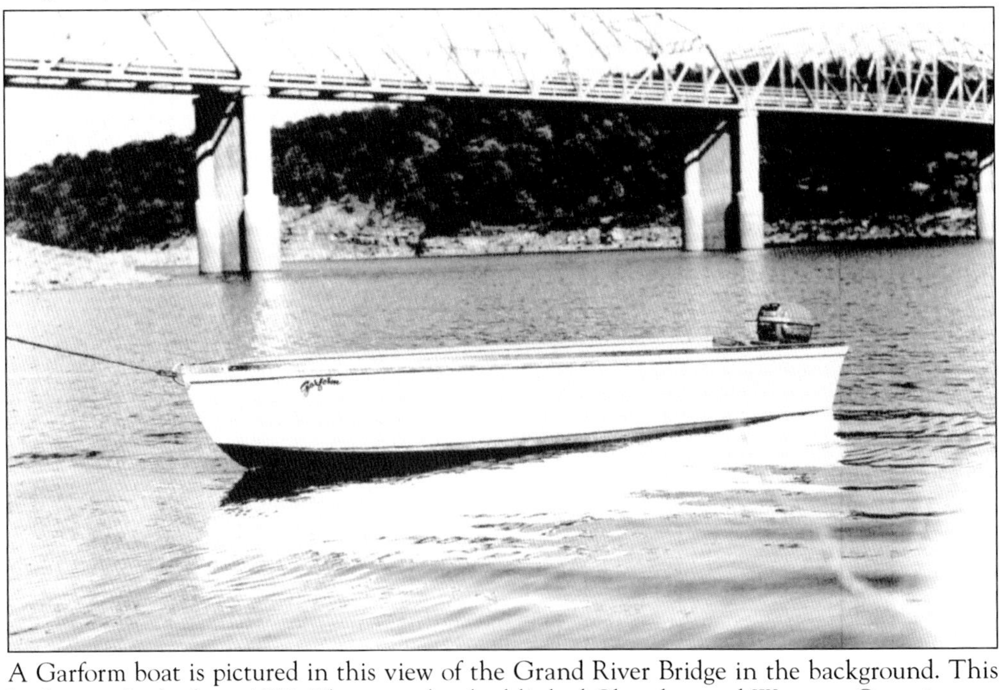

A Garform boat is pictured in this view of the Grand River Bridge in the background. This bridge was built about 1950. The span that had linked Cherokee and Wagoner Counties was moved several miles east and still serves as the 14-Mile Creek bridge. (Courtesy of the Cradow Smith collection.)

Six

Outlaws, Lawmen, and Those Who Protected and Served

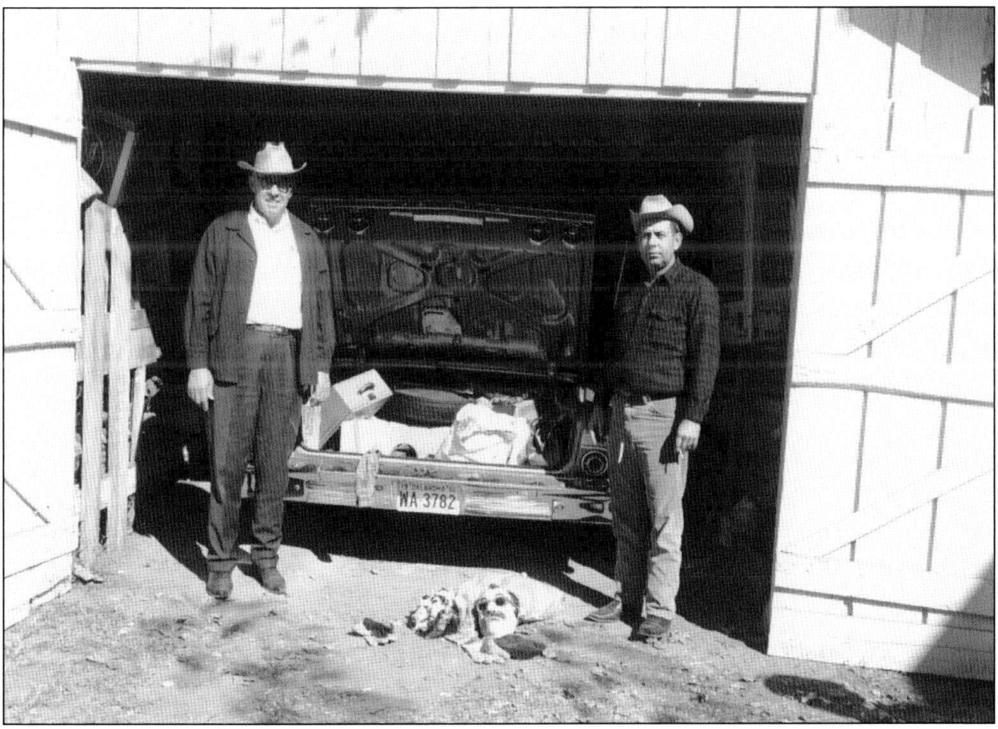

One of Wagoner's highest-profile criminal cases in the 20th century was one in which Wagoner pool hall operator Guy King was arrested and convicted in the 1966 armed robbery of a local woman. King was sentenced to 50 years and died in prison. Sheriff Ellis Garrison (left) and Wagoner police officer Bob Mahan discovered the car involved in the robbery in King's garage a short time after the holdup. Mahan went on to become sheriff and then county commissioner. (Courtesy of the Cradow Smith collection.)

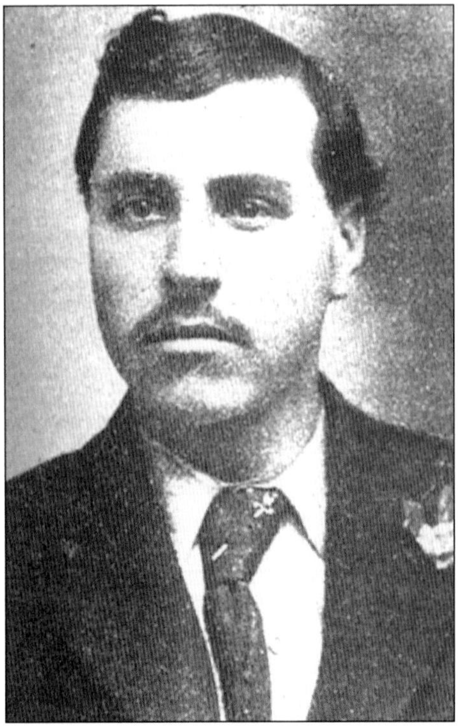

After their service as deputy marshals, the Crittenden brothers were killed in Wagoner on October 25, 1895. They were gunned down by Ed Reed, son of outlaw queen Belle Starr. Reed had been appointed deputy marshal in Wagoner by "Hanging Judge" Isaac Parker. (Author's collection.)

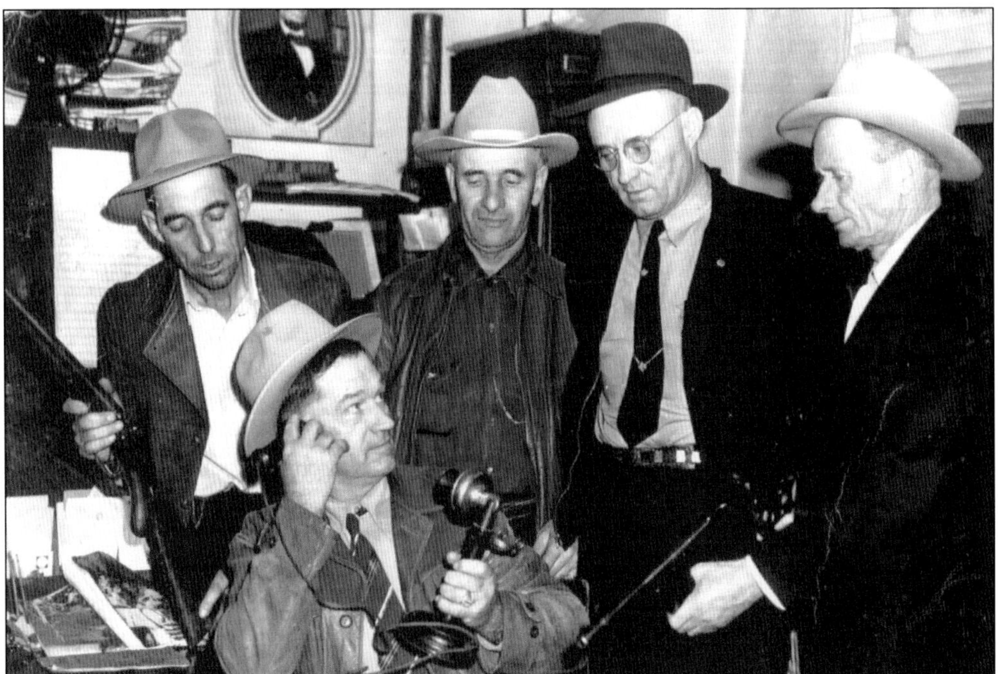

This photograph is believed to have been taken on November 19, 1945, the day notorious bank robber and murderer Matt Kimes came to Wagoner. Seated and on the telephone is Chester Hall, sheriff. Standing, from left to right, are Deputy Ross Nickle; Deputy Harry Coday; an unidentified officer, perhaps from the FBI; and Deputy Bob Woodward. (Courtesy of Bob Woodward.)

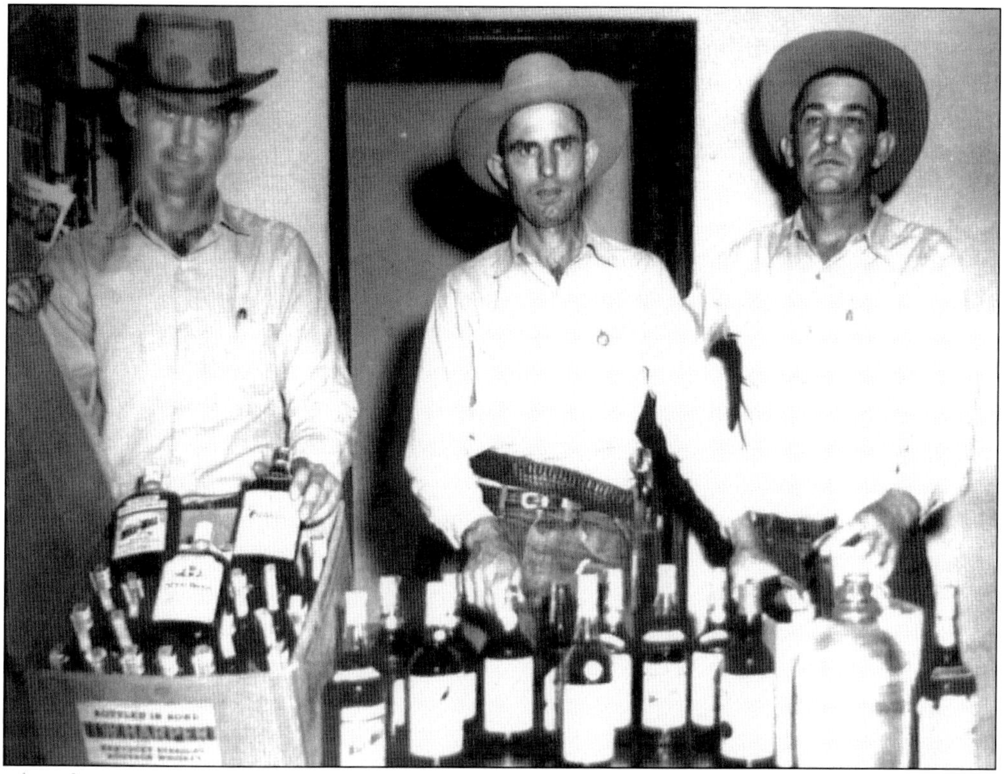

This photograph was taken in the 1950s during a roundup of bonded and moonshine bootleg whiskey in Wagoner County. Pictured are, from left to right, W.A. Trapp, deputy; Raymond Thomas, sheriff; and Noal Choate, deputy. (Author's collection.)

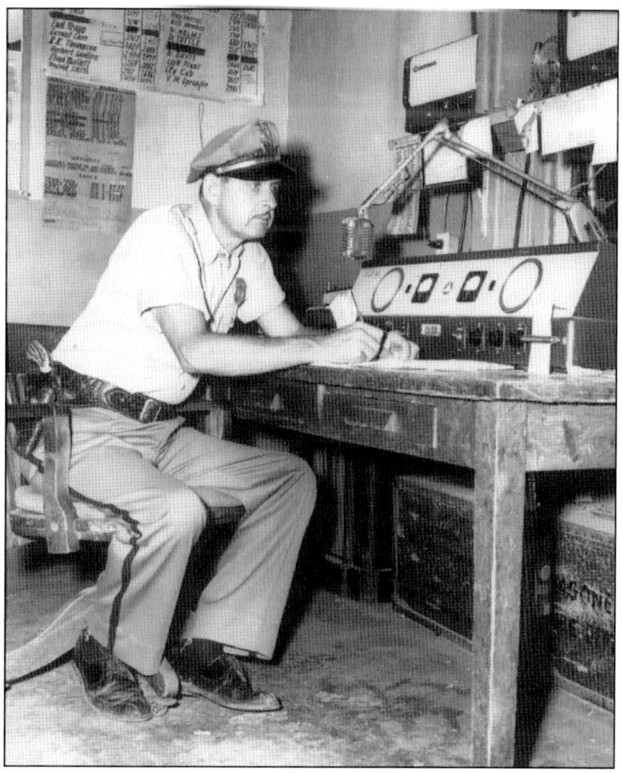

A.A. Goins was an early dispatcher at the Wagoner Police Department. The posters behind him were a quick reference for the telephone numbers of local wreckers, cafés (so meals could be ordered for prisoners), Oklahoma Highway Patrol officers, firemen, doctors, and the City Cab Co. (Author's collection.)

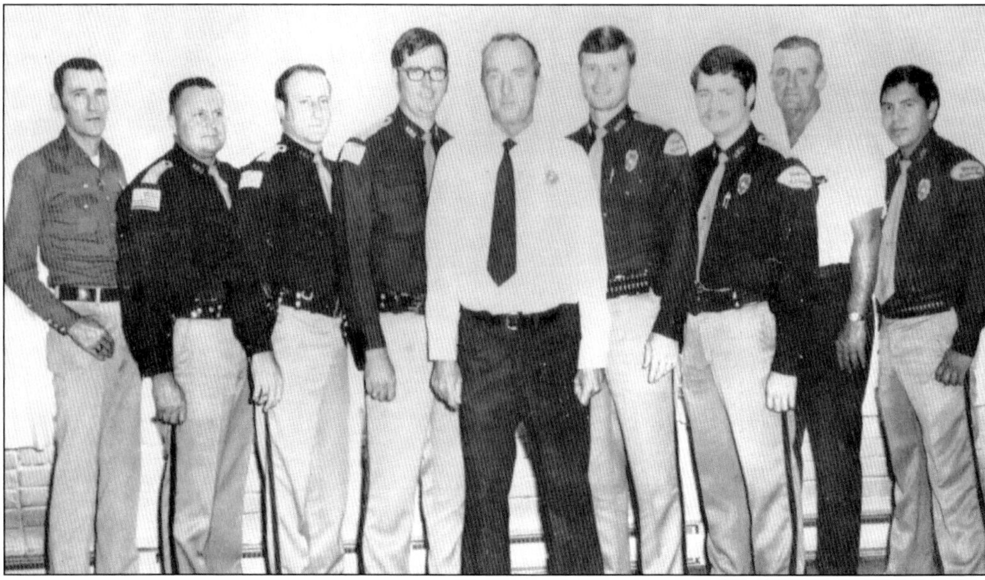

Raymond Olson became the Wagoner chief of police on May 1, 1966, and served for many years. Shown in this photograph are, from left to right, Leonard Gross, dispatcher; Leroy Champlain, Kenneth Brunson, and Marshall Wilson, patrolmen; Olson; Gary Henderick, Wayne Martin, John Mell, and Bobby Neugin, patrolmen. (Courtesy of the Cradow Smith collection.)

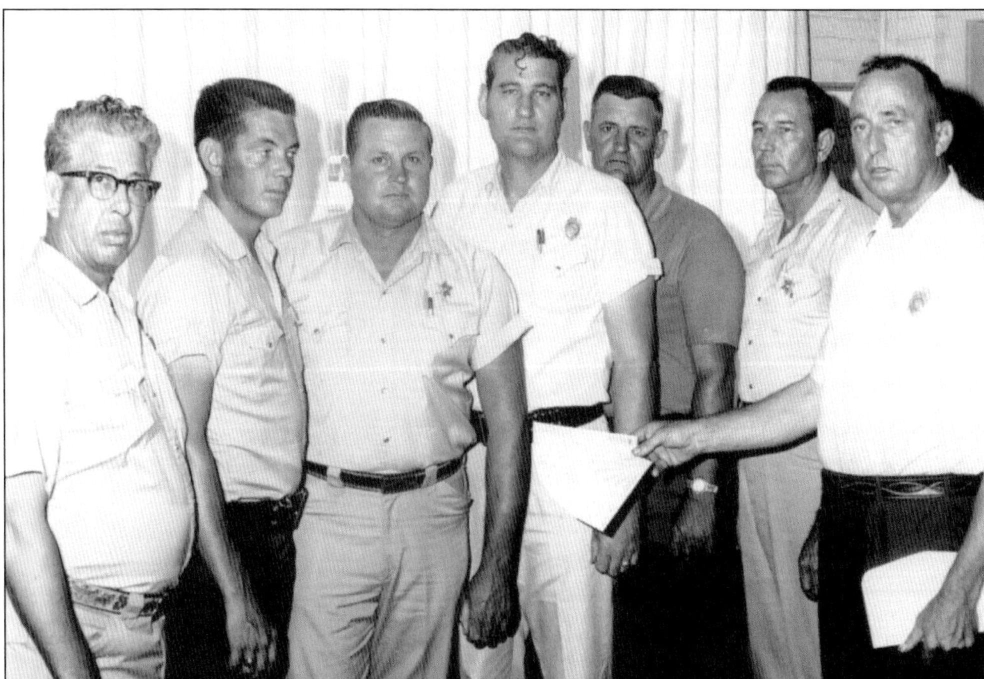

With Police Chief Raymond Olson (far right) are, from left to right, Patrolmen Winston Carey, Tommy Gilbert, Leroy Champlain, Dick Gross, Johnny Mell, and Gene Doughty. (Author's collection.)

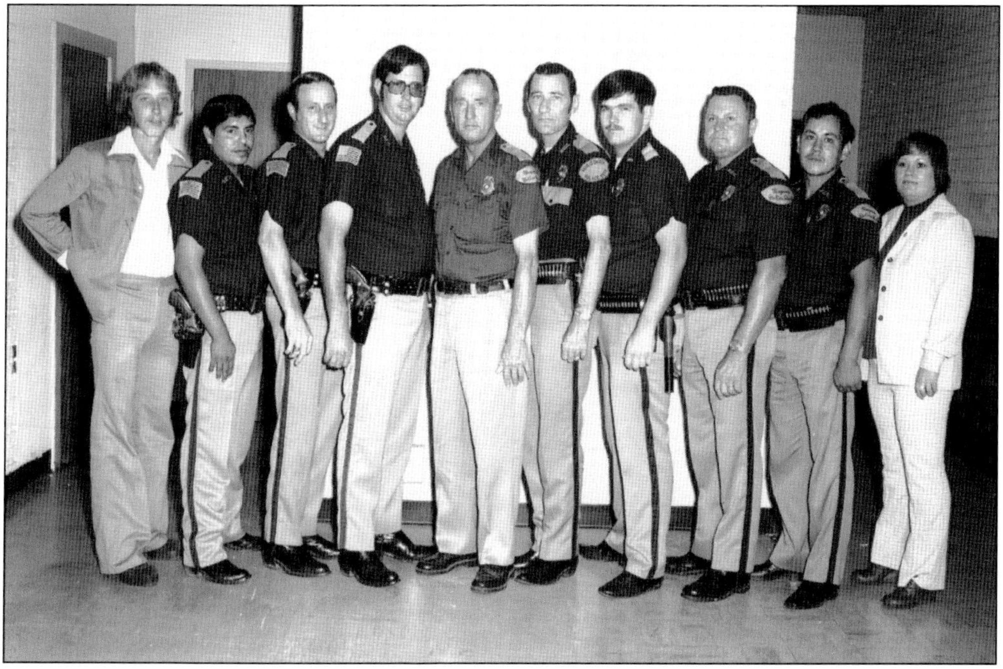

Wagoner police officers are seen here in probably the early 1970s, based on the leisure suit the man at far left is wearing. They are, from left to right, Steve Smith, Bobby Neugin, Kenneth Brunson, Marshall Wilson, Chief Raymond Olson, Mack Gross, Jack McCain, Leroy Champlain, Ernie Tiger, and unidentified. (Courtesy of the Cradow Smith collection.)

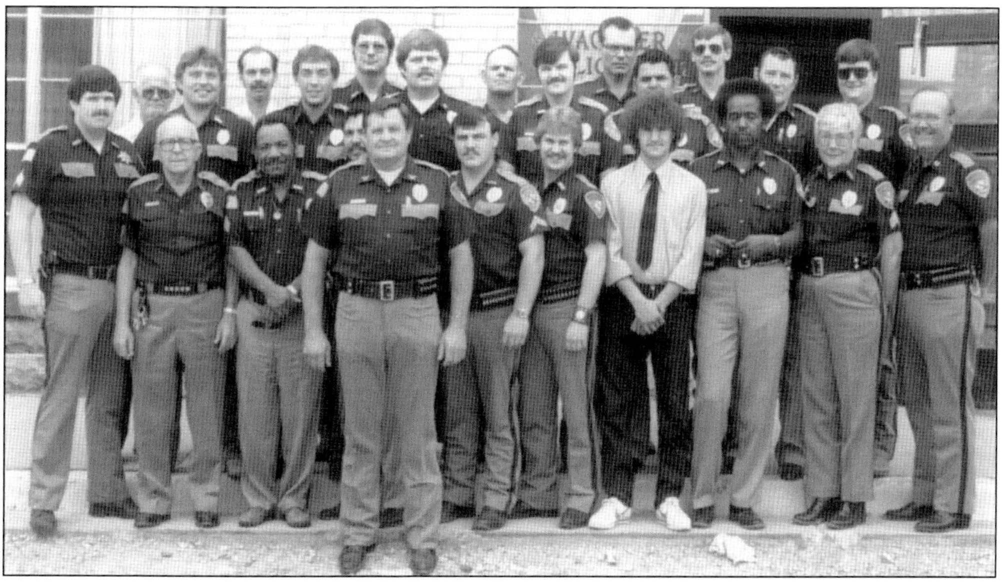

Wagoner, Coweta, and county officers and reserves are pictured here around 1983. They are identified as (front) Leroy Champlain, Wagoner chief of police, and, from left to right, (first row) Jack McCain, Leonard Freise, Elmo Randles, Bobby Neugin, Gary Rowe, Pat Mayes, Robert Jones, James Blandon, Skip Freise, and Elmer Shepherd; (second row) Fred Coleman, Danny Crabtree, Ralph Curry, Bobby Watkins, Stanley Gross, Guy Stickelmeyer, Jim Harris, Clyde Miller, Larry Mock, Frank Jones, Steve Hash, Leonard Gross, and Ron Ross. (Author's collection.)

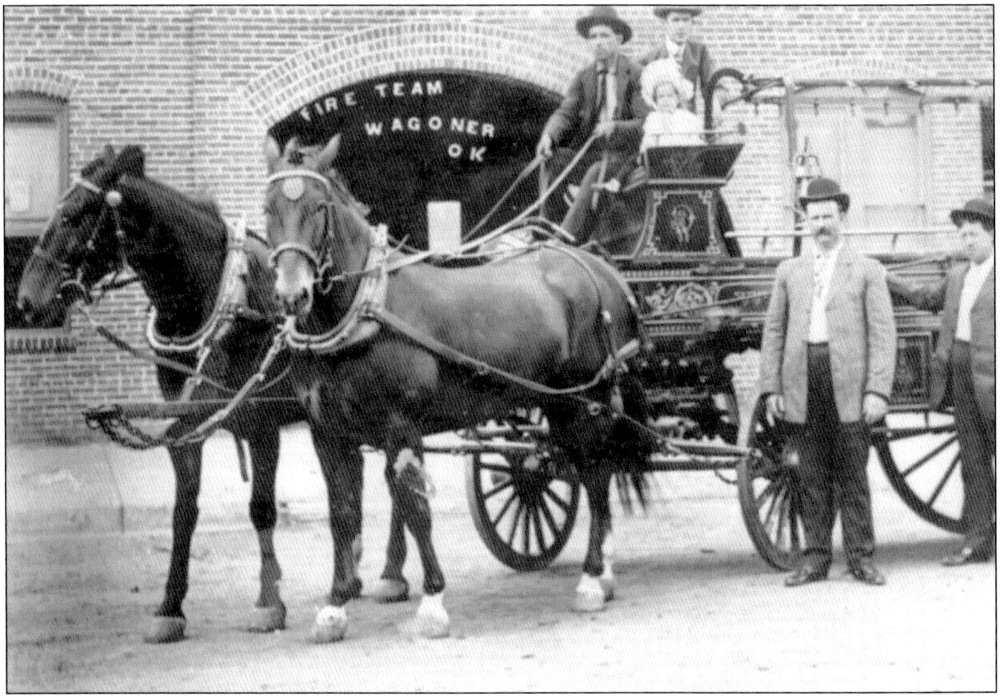

With Wagoner's downtown businesses first built of wood, having a fully equipped fire department was of utmost importance of this new prairie town. Here, fire horses Mack and Dan pose outside of the fire station on South Main Street around 1907. (Courtesy of Linda French.)

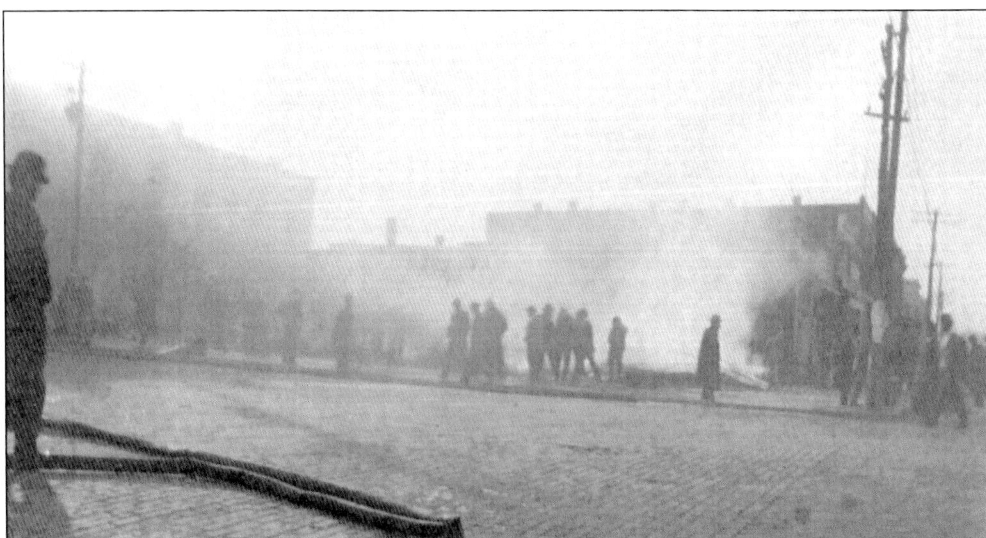

Fire destroyed half a dozen businesses on the southeast corner of Cherokee and Main Streets the morning of January 6, 1911. (Courtesy of Jerry Hickman.)

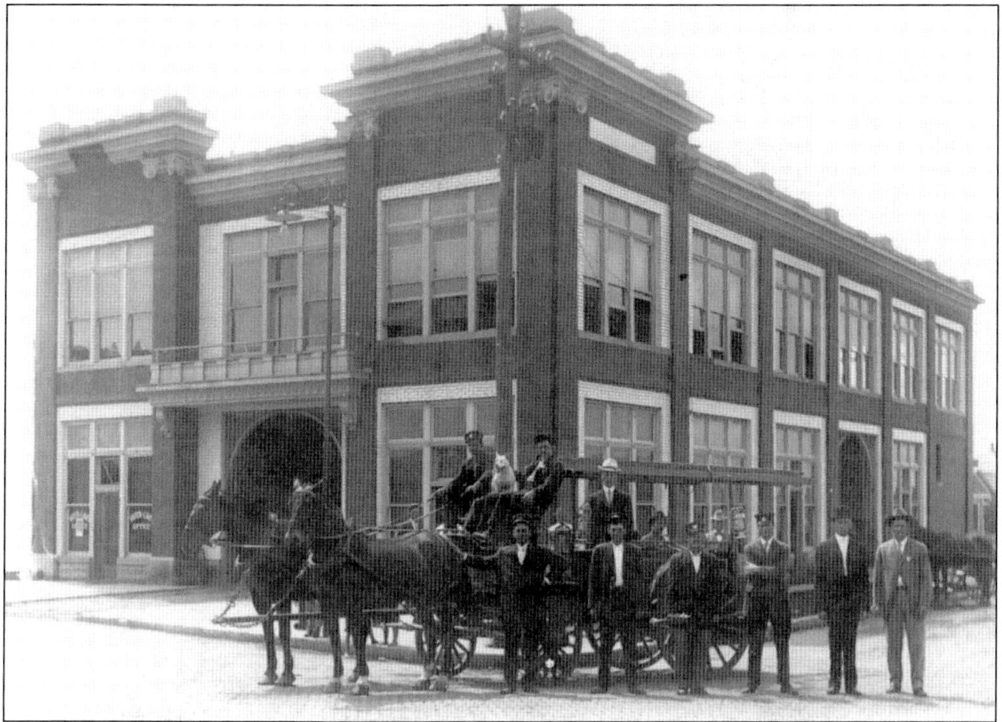

This 1912 photograph shows the Wagoner Fire Department's new horse-drawn equipment in front of the new city hall at Cherokee Street and Casaver Avenue. The fire department was housed in the center arch at the front of the building. (Author's collection.)

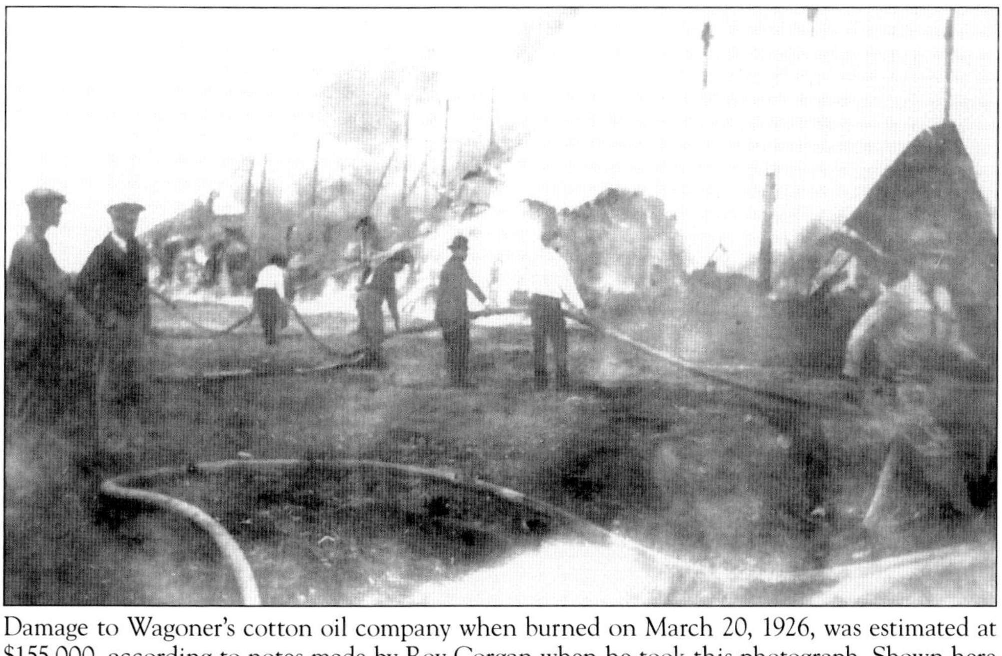

Damage to Wagoner's cotton oil company when burned on March 20, 1926, was estimated at $155,000, according to notes made by Roy Corgan when he took this photograph. Shown here is the cottonseed storehouse burning. (Courtesy of Jerry Hickman.)

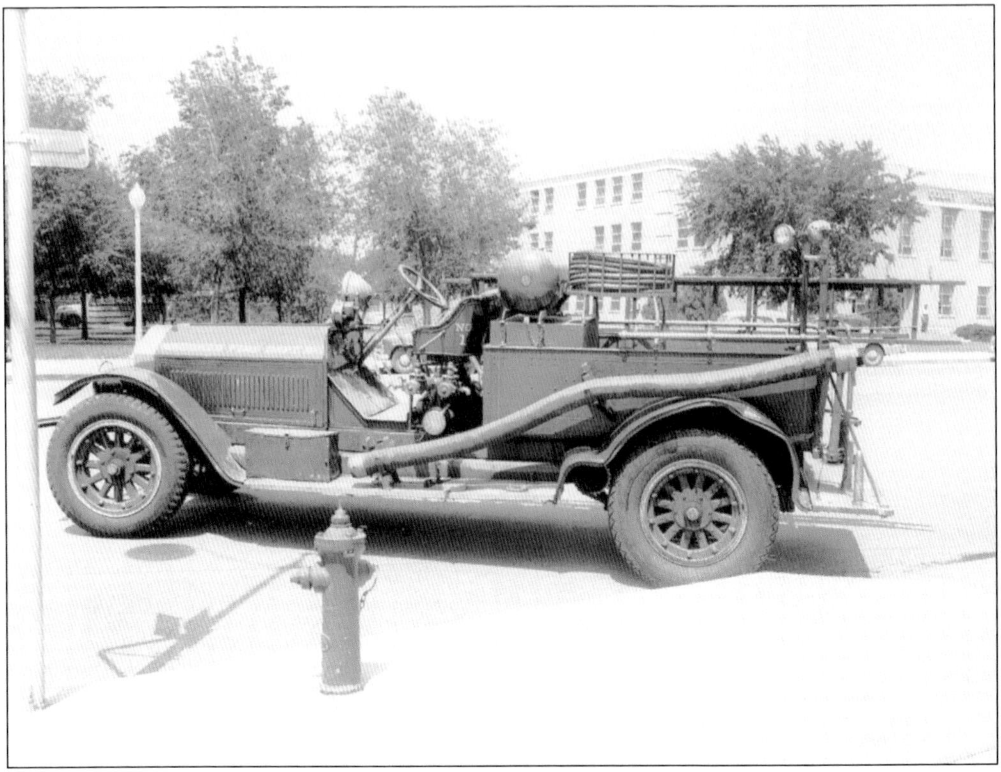

The city purchased this fire truck around 1914. (Courtesy of Jerry Hickman.)

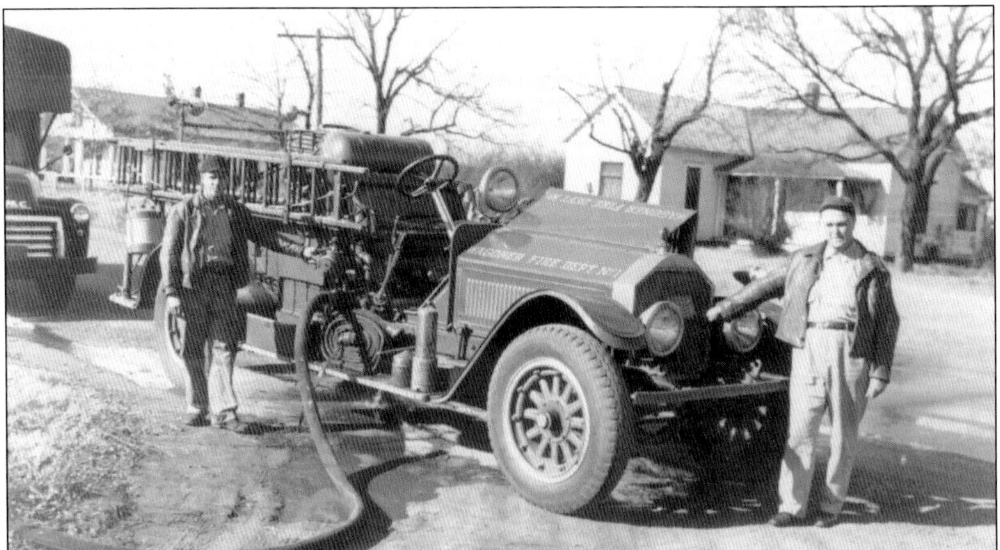

Cecil Beard was Wagoner's fire chief when the city bought this fire truck in 1947. (Courtesy of Bettie Gaylor Saccardo.)

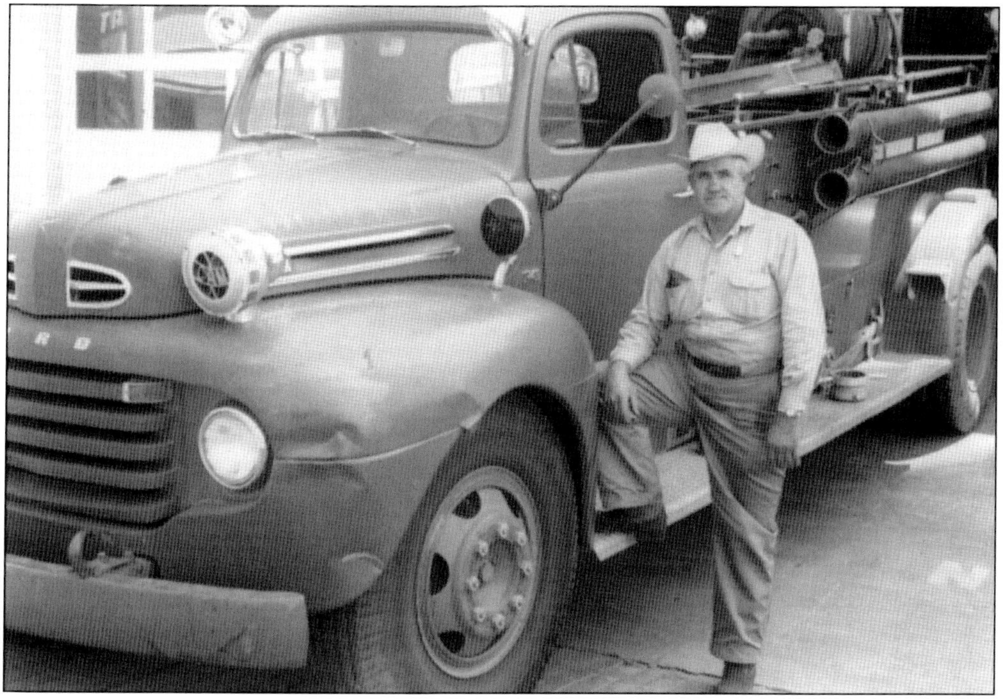

John Hays was a full-time fire truck driver for the Wagoner Fire Department, and before rural water districts were established, he had a business delivering water to farmers from a tank mounted on the back of his old Chevrolet truck. Hays came to Wagoner in 1916; his first job was with Leo Brumnett's butcher shop. He also later drove a school bus for Wagoner Public Schools and later worked for Nordam. Hays and his wife, Ethel, had nine children. He was born in 1912 and died in 1972. (Courtesy of the Hays family.)

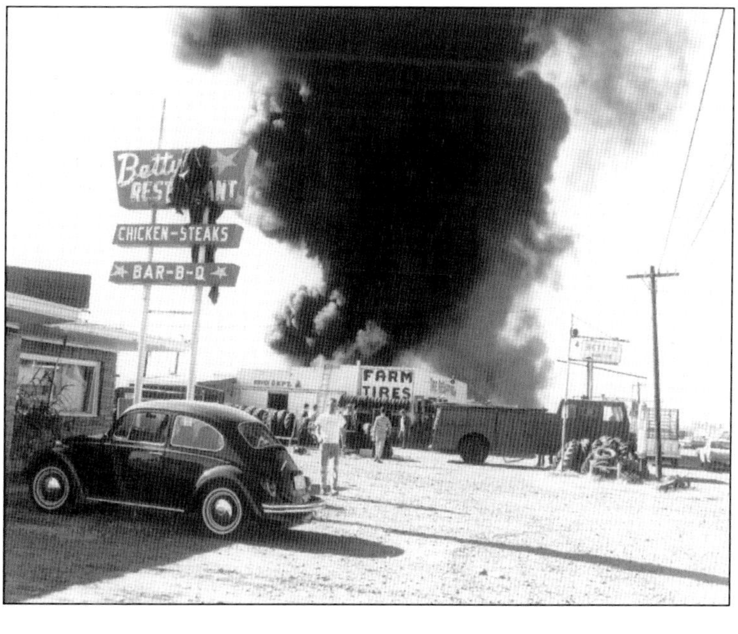

Chapman Tire Co., just west of Wagoner on State Highway 51, was destroyed in a 1967 fire that could be seen for miles around. A.D. "Red" Chapman, owner and operator of the firm, said the fire began when a grassfire started by the owner of the Hi-Ho Tavern, immediately to the west of the tire company, got out of control. Chapman estimated his loss at nearly $100,000. (Author's collection.)

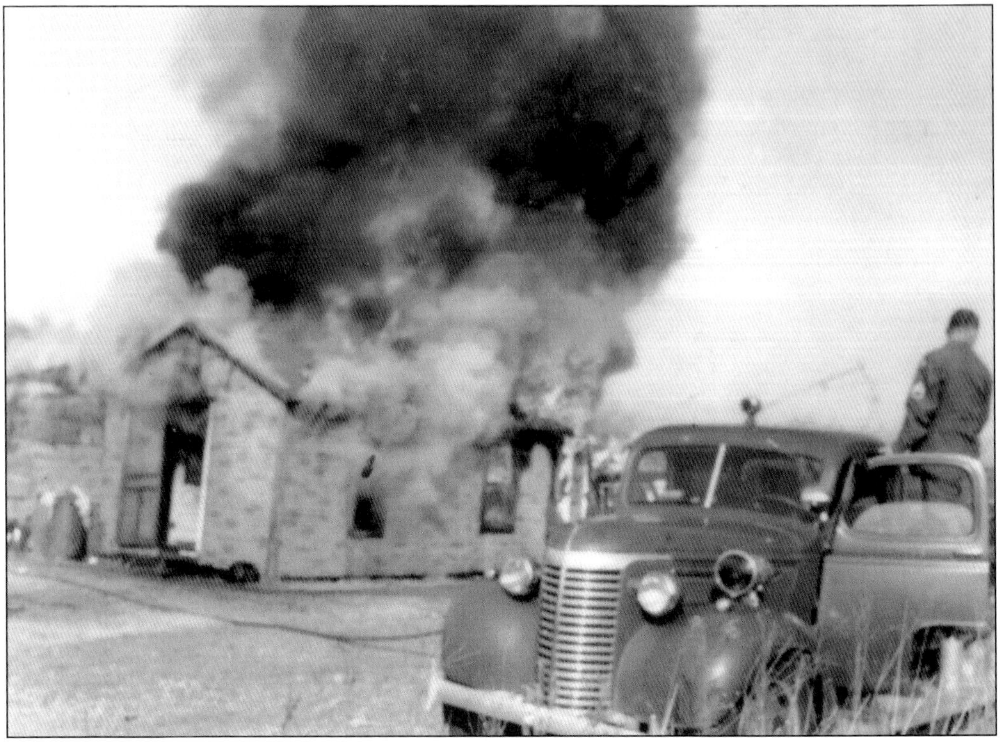

Firefighter Gerald McCuan works from the back of a truck while other firefighters man the hoses, trying to extinguish this blaze in December 1966. (Courtesy of the Wagoner Fire Department.)

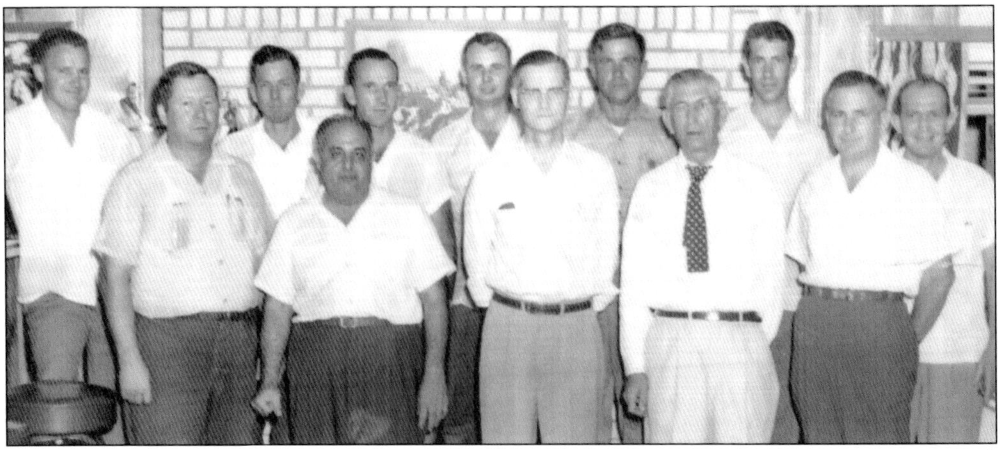

This photograph of the Wagoner Volunteer Fire Department was taken in the early 1950s. Pictured, from left to right, are (first row) Ernest Carr, Jim Kraker, Ed Smith, Paul Hersman, and Cradow Smith; (second row) Jack Smalley, Lloyd Dale, Charles Ralls, Jake Bradfield, John Hays, Howard Morrison, and A.C. Miller. (Author's collection.)

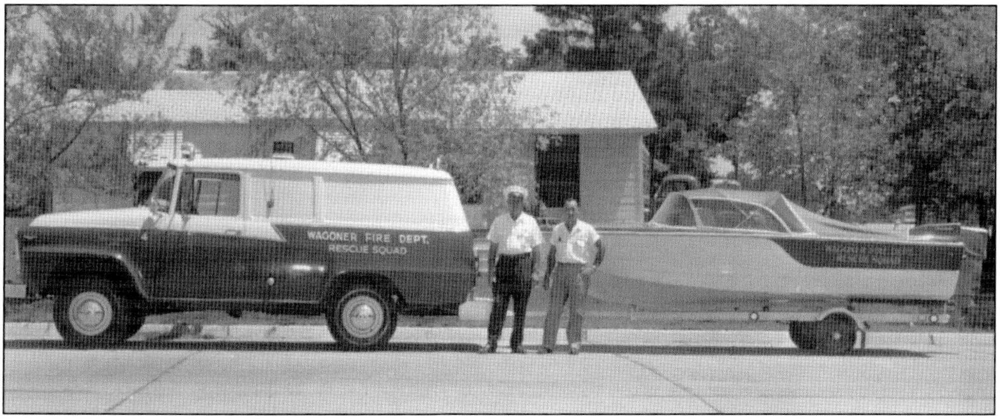

After Fort Gibson Lake was built, the Wagoner Fire Department's duties expanded to include lake rescues. Firefighters spent many hours soliciting donations to purchase a boat and truck to use in these new operations. Shown with one of the early-day units are firemen John Hays (left) -and Charlie Ralls. (Courtesy of the Cradow Smith collection.)

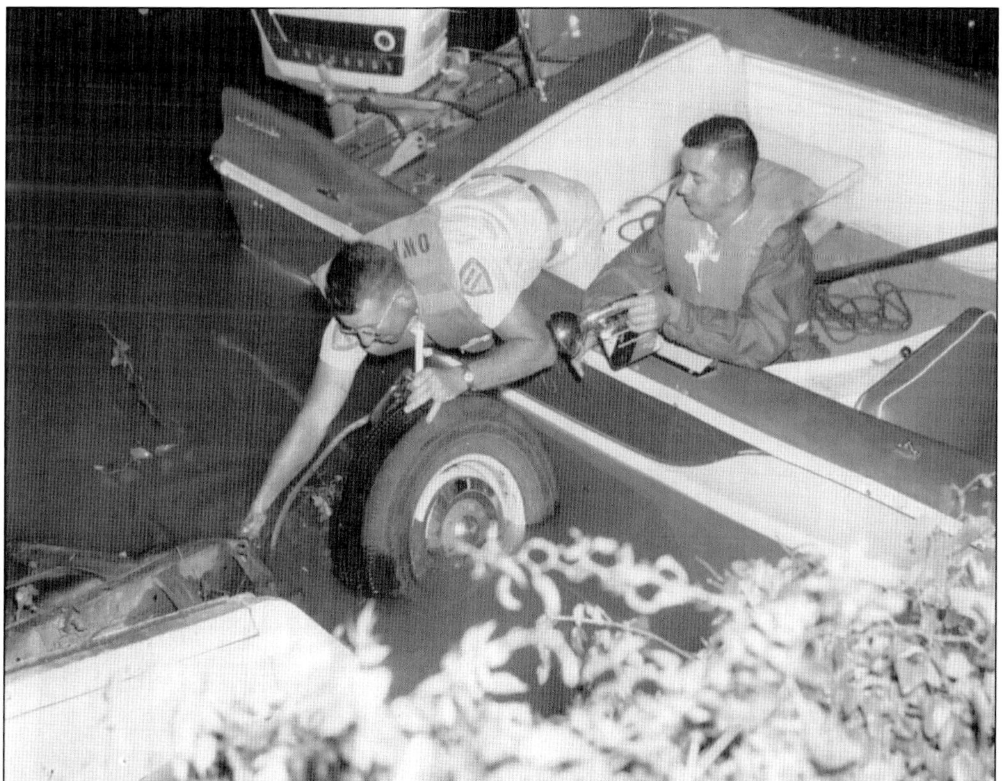

Fireman Gerald McCuan holds a flashlight for V.K. Thompson as he makes a rescue from the lake. (Courtesy of the Cradow Smith collection.)

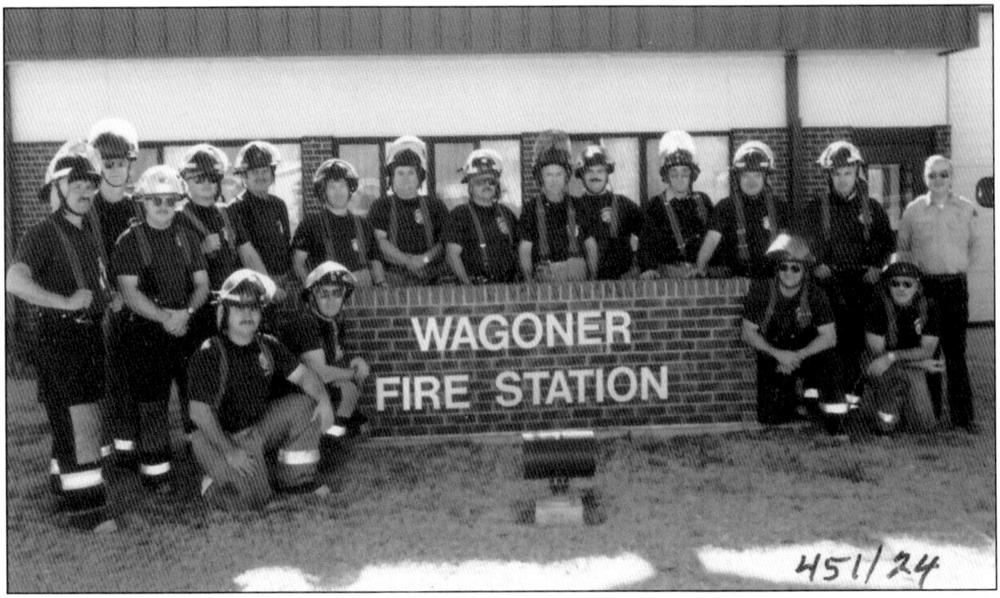

The Wagoner Fire Department today operates with a chief and eight full-time drivers, along with a cadre of volunteers. (Courtesy of the Wagoner Fire Department.)

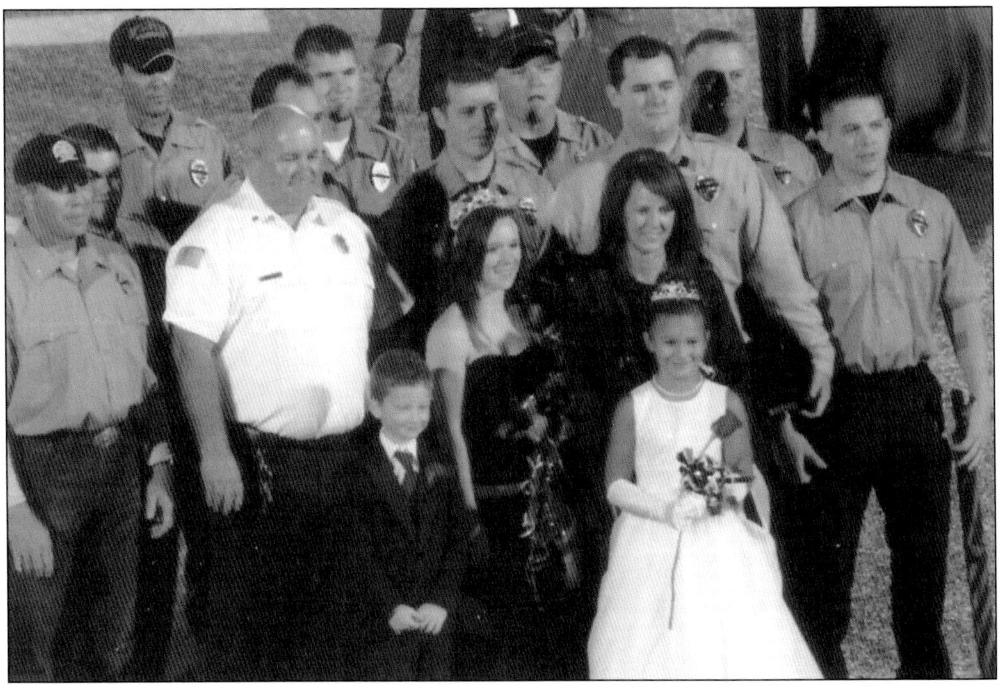
Assistant Fire Chief Mark Wofford died just days before his daughter, Molly, was to walk in the 2014 Homecoming Queen Ceremonies at W.L. Odom field. Members of the Wagoner fire department stepped up to take her father's place as Molly was crowned queen. The firefighters include, from left to right, Jeff Hamilton, Brett Bardell, James McMahan, Brice Martin, Jarrad Edwards, Rusty Harris, J.W. Berry, Dalton Self, Roger Schilling, and Nick Fulk. At front are Kael Humphries and Kendra Condict; next to Molly is Chief Kelly Grooms; her mother, Teresa Wofford, is to her right. (Courtesy of David Frost.)

Seven

Bulldogs Forever

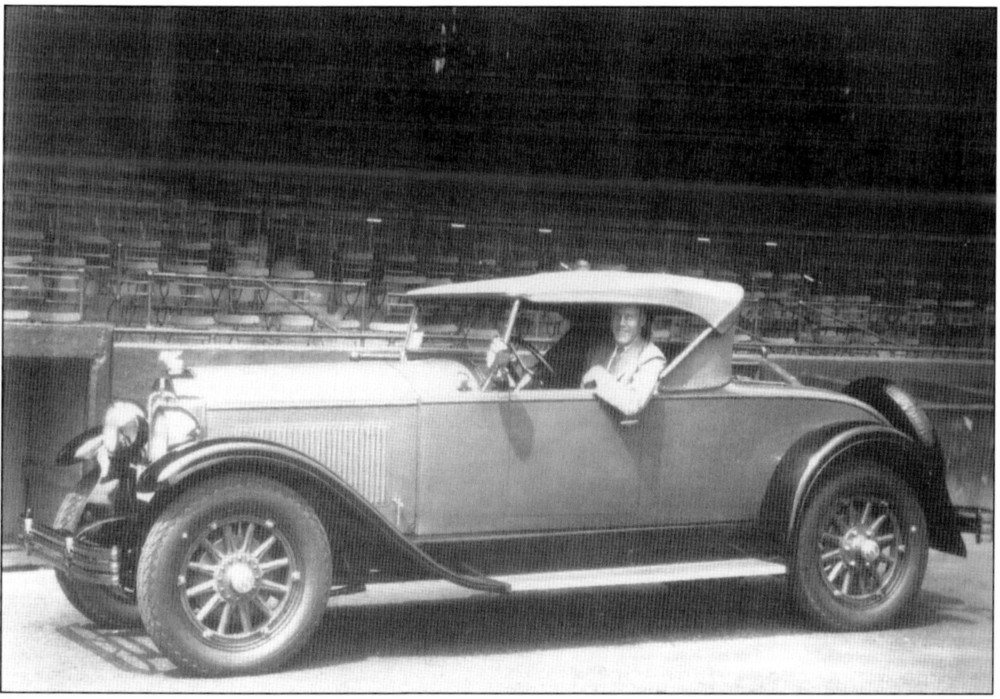

Wagoner's Willis Hudlin is seen in the touring car he bought shortly after his arrival in Cleveland to pitch for the Cleveland Indians in 1926. The car was red and black. Hudlin dropped out of Wagoner High School, where he had been an outstanding athlete, to accept the $25,000 Cleveland contract. The Wagoner High School baseball field has been named in honor of Hudlin. (Courtesy of John Dale Hancock.)

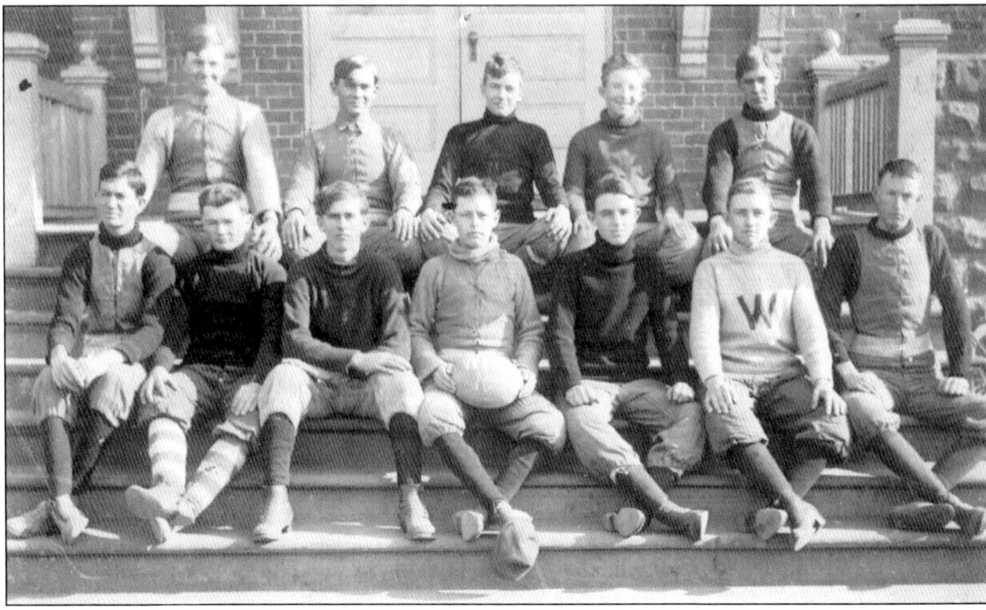

Wagoner High School's first football team is seated on the steps in front of the school in 1910. Pictured are, from left to right, (first row) unidentified, Frank Stocklasa, Lawrence Rutherford, Ray Moreland, John Hunt, Ted Sullivan, and Kent Ruble; (second row) Glenn Jones, Roy Stocklasa, Owen Watts, Ernest Clow, and unidentified. (Courtesy of Shirle Lamb Williams.)

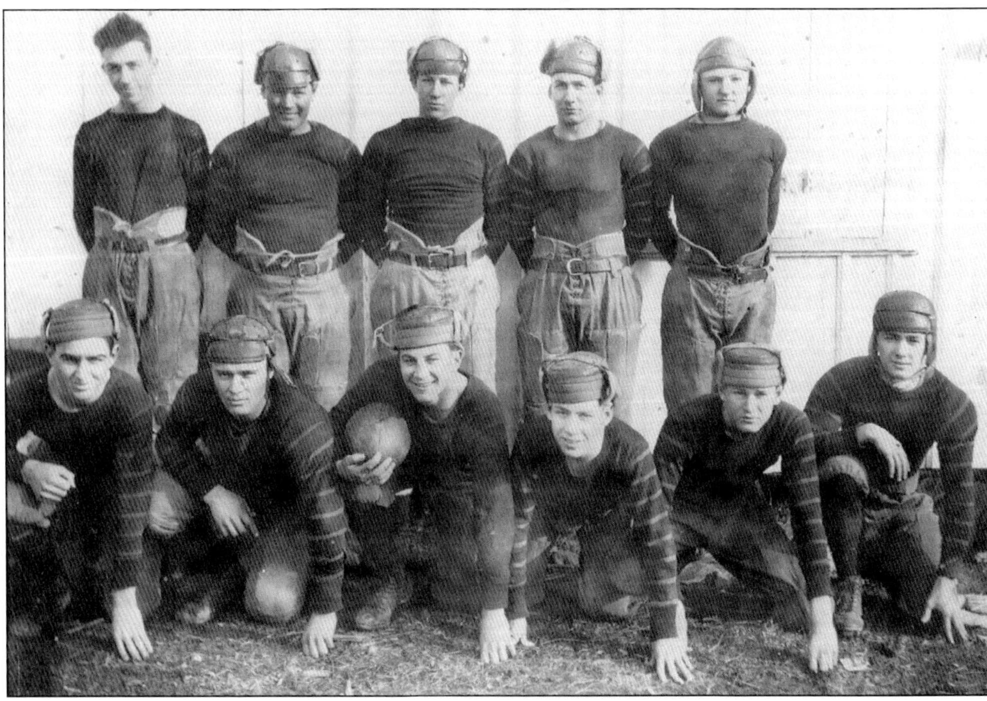

Wagoner High School's 1921 football team sported new leather helmets. Pictured, from left to right, are (first row) Hugh Posey, Oliver Kingham, Darrell Moss, Scotty Goddard, Earl Brown, and Marlin Goddard; (second row) Chester Olmstead, Buddy Bogard, Charles Lamb, George Bennett, and George Wassom. (Courtesy of Shirle Lamb Williams.)

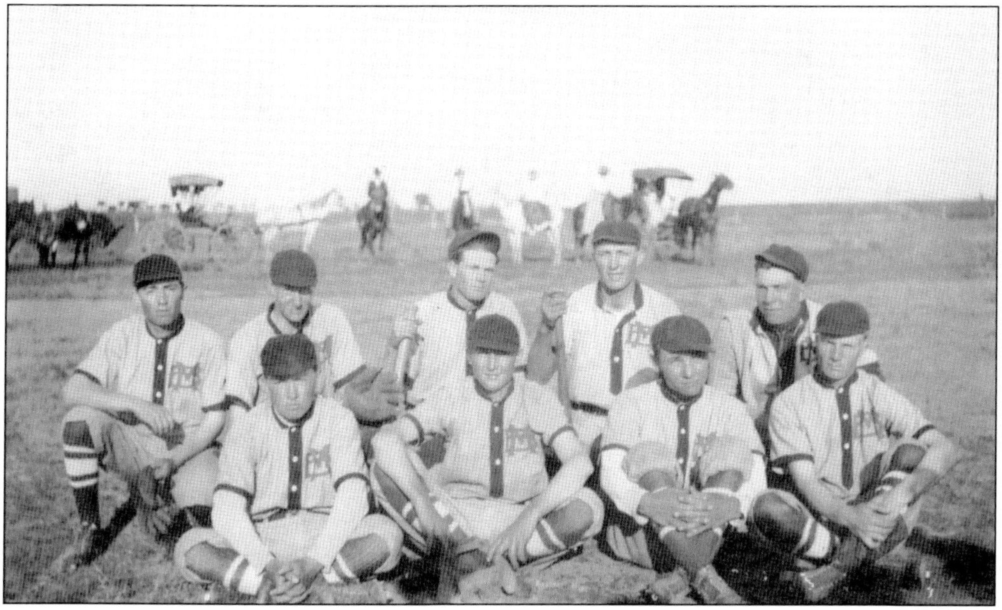

The members of the baseball team for Blue Mound School, just west of Wagoner, proudly sport their uniforms from around 1910 or 1912. They are, from left to right, (first row) Ern Freund, Ray Williams, Carl Williams, and Shirley Shafer; (second row) Dirl Nickel, Gene Shafer, Stanley Shafer, Curt Williams, George Williams. (Author's collection.)

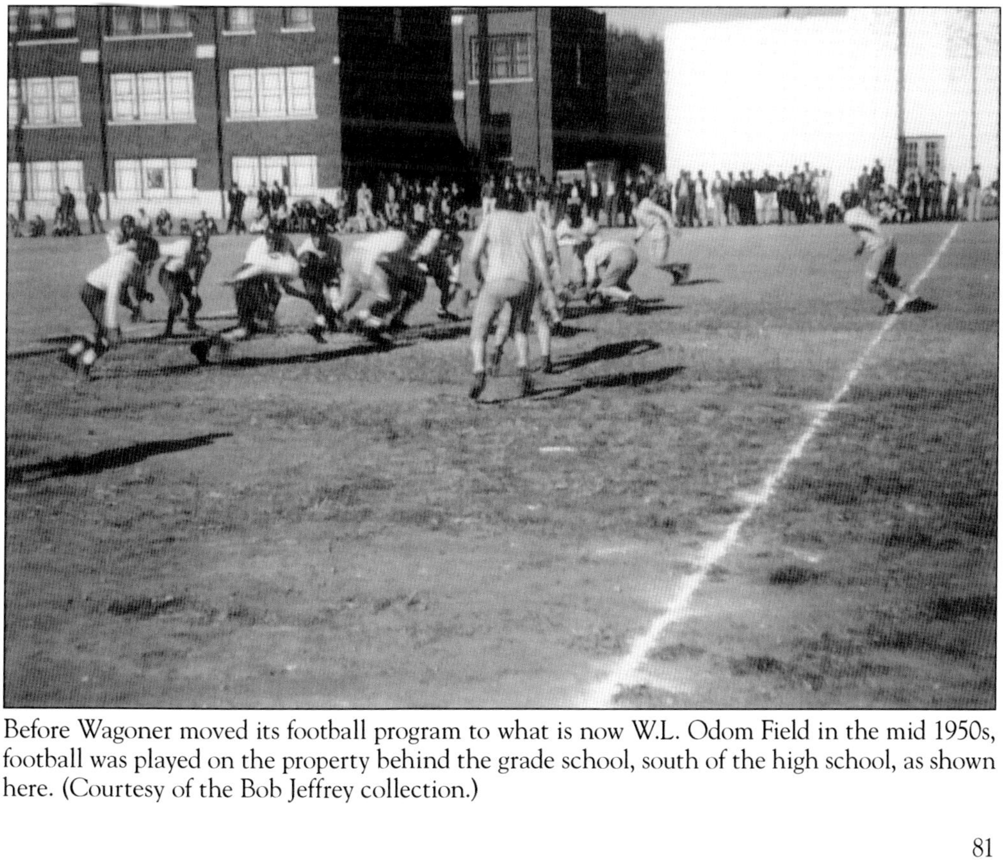

Before Wagoner moved its football program to what is now W.L. Odom Field in the mid 1950s, football was played on the property behind the grade school, south of the high school, as shown here. (Courtesy of the Bob Jeffrey collection.)

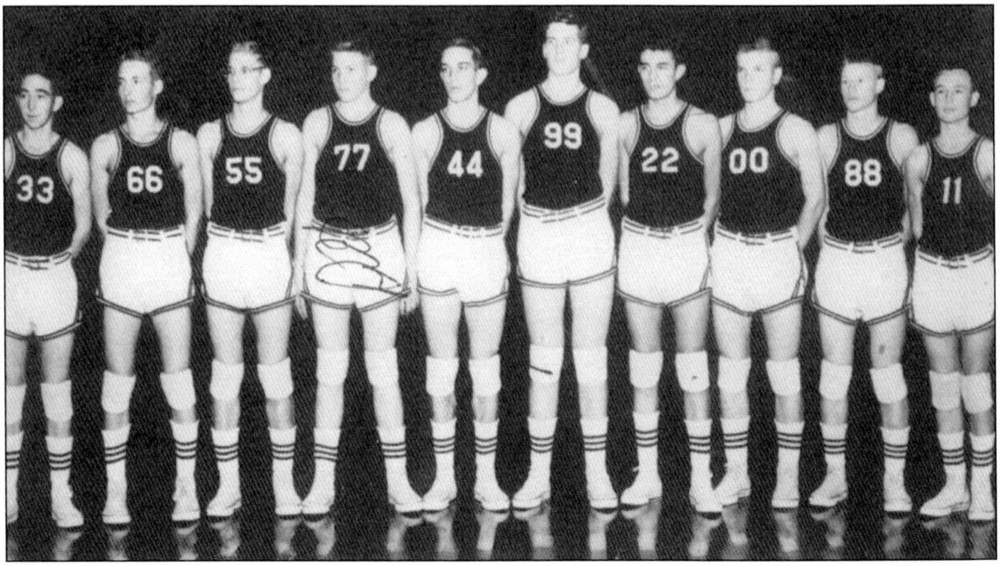

Shown here is Wagoner High School's 1954 basketball team, coached by a Mr. Hughes. The players are, from left to right, Jim Baker, Kenneth McDaris, Dewey Talley, Dick Brown, Farrell Rosson, David Holloway, Jim Durant, Jesse Page, Henry Talley, and Kenneth Henson. (Author's collection.)

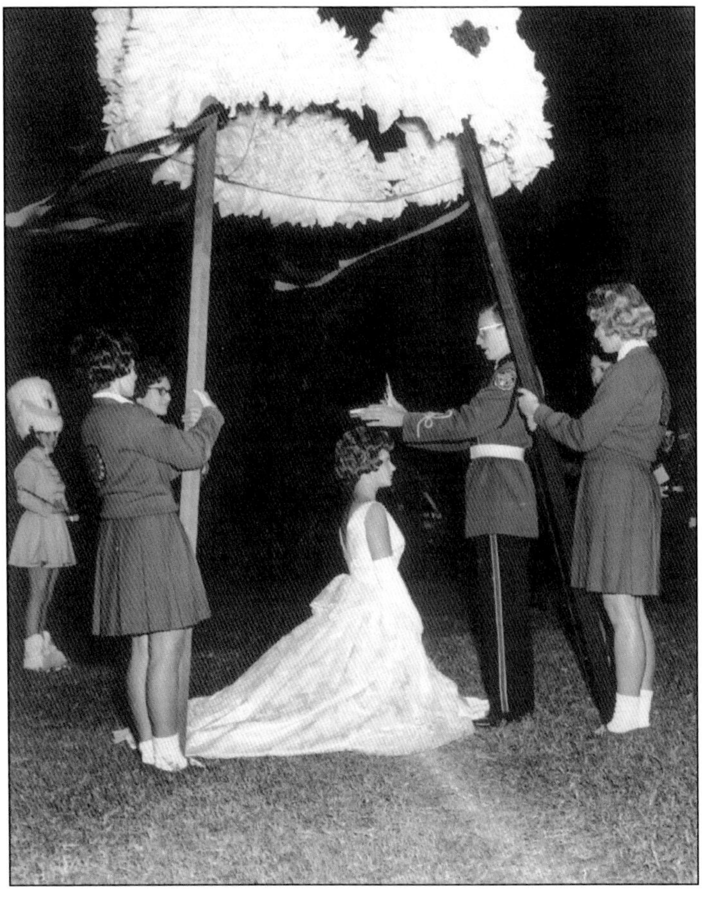

Joyce Johnson is crowned 1962 Band Queen by Richard Hickman. Surrounding them are, from left to right, Wanda Lee, Barbara French, Pat Wright, and Wanda Kay Neel. (Courtesy of the Cradow Smith collection.)

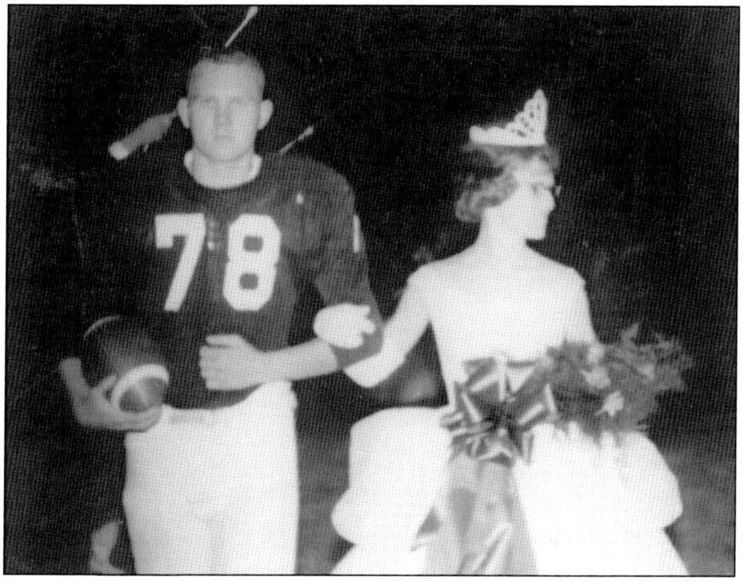

Barbara French was crowned Wagoner High School football queen in 1963. She was escorted by David Carr, whom she later married. Both are now deceased. (Courtesy of the Cradow Smith collection.)

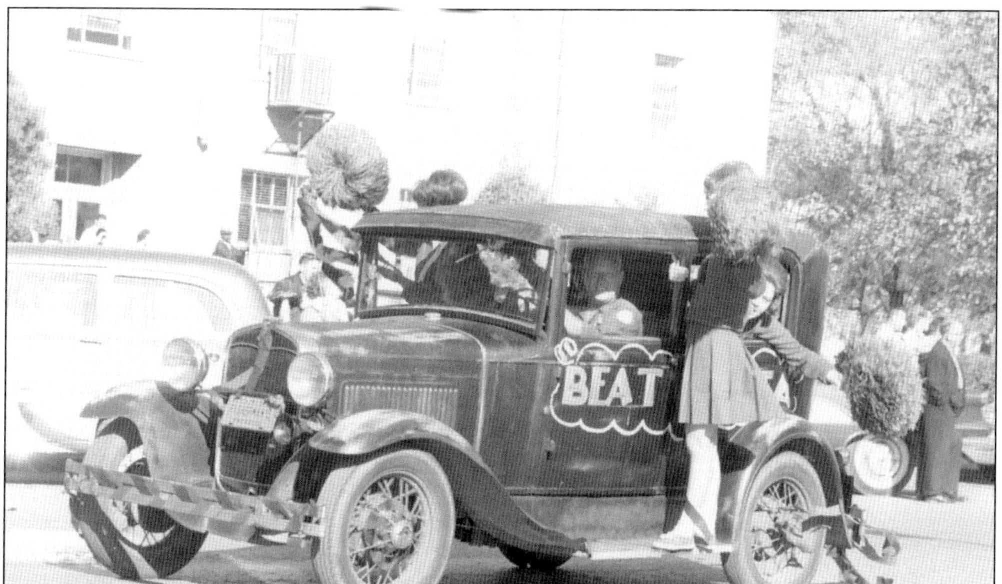

John Gephart's Model A was used in high school parades for years. Linda Spence is the cheerleader looking out the back window. Other cheerleaders for this school year were Wanda Neel, Barbara French, Libby Gephart, Lois Davenport, and Linda Smith. (Courtesy of Jerry Hickman.)

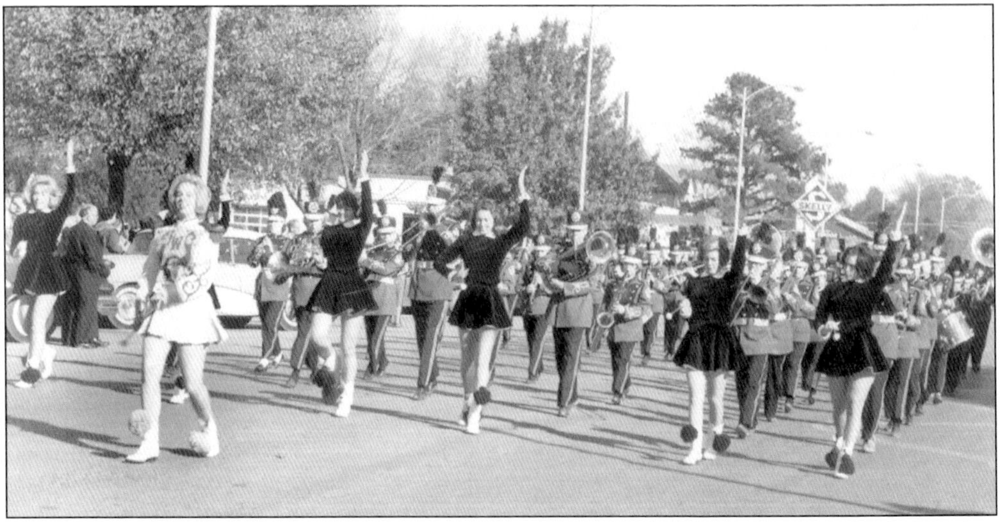

The Wagoner High School band struts its stuff in the 1963 football homecoming parade. Twirlers are, from left to right, Karen Kyle; Susan Stauss, majorette (Jacque Childress is right behind her, but not seen); Cheryl Fuller; Patty Scott; Kathy Bradfield; and Susan Whiteturkey. Jerry Hickman is right behind Kathy Bradfield, playing the trombone. Don Potter at far right with the drum. Terry Cunningham is the second person behind Patty, playing a saxophone. Larry Walker is directly in front of her. JD Ross is between Patty and Cheryl. Maribeth Geurin is just to the left of Cheryl with the French horn. (Courtesy of the Cradow Smith collection.)

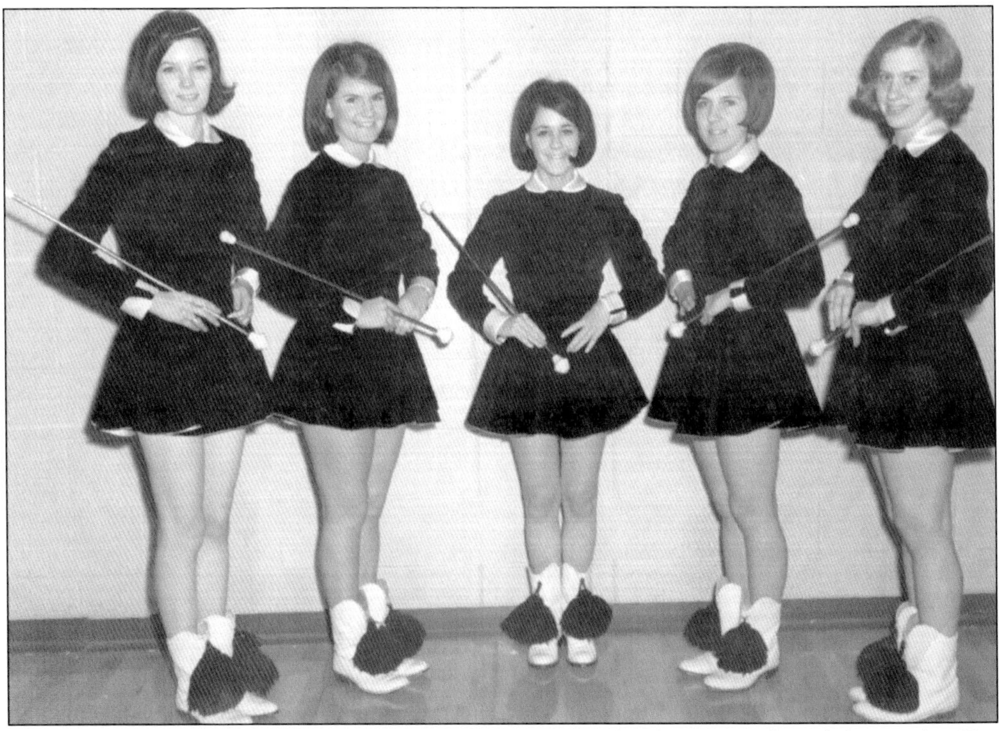

Wagoner High School senior twirlers for the 1966–1967 school year are, from left to right, Kay Martin, Janice Harvey, Judy Childress, Sue Collins, and Mary Kay Brown. (Courtesy of the Cradow Smith collection.)

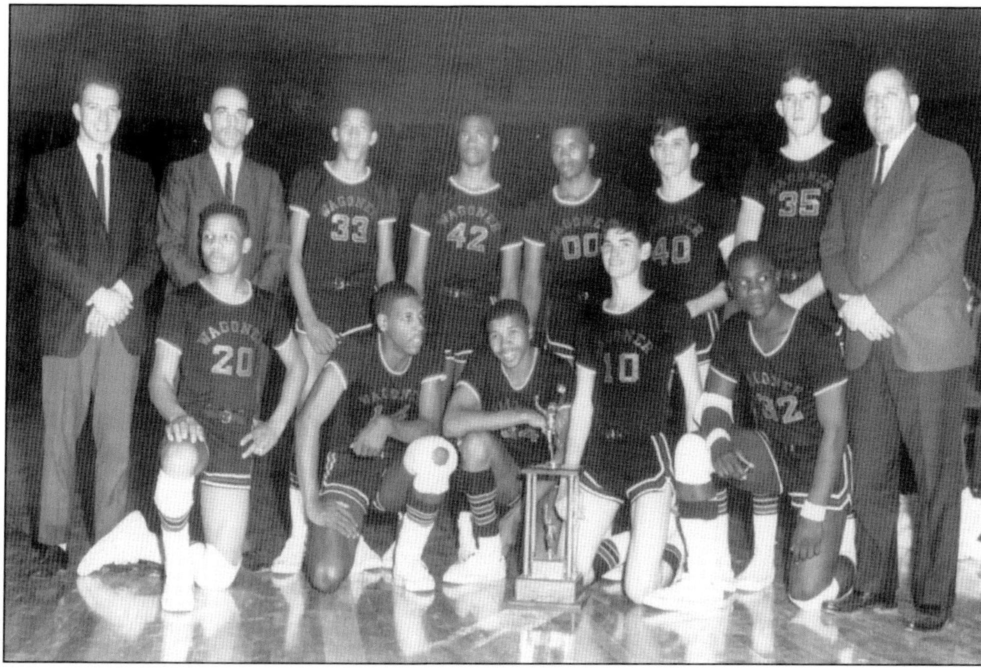

In 1966, Wagoner's basketball team won the state championship. Players and coaches are, from left to right, (first row) Kenneth Harris, Curtis Ford, Johnny Gibbs, Harry Henderson, and Roy Barnett; (second row) Bill Benham, Farrell Rosson, Johnny Williams, Elijah Releford, Thomas Stephens, Jimmy Murphy, Jim Henderson, and Bob Irvin. (Courtesy of the Cradow Smith collection.)

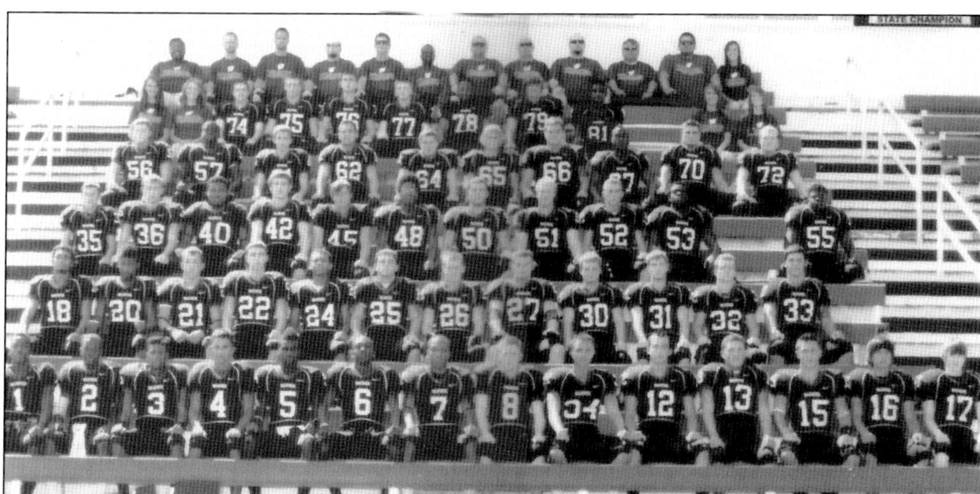

While the Wagoner Bulldog football team came close to winning the state championship several times over the years, it never quite accomplished the task until 2011, when the "Dawgs" took the gold ball with a score of 23-0 over Clinton. The Bulldogs repeated the state championship in 2014, when they defeated Oologah 45-21. (Courtesy of Wagoner Public Schools.)

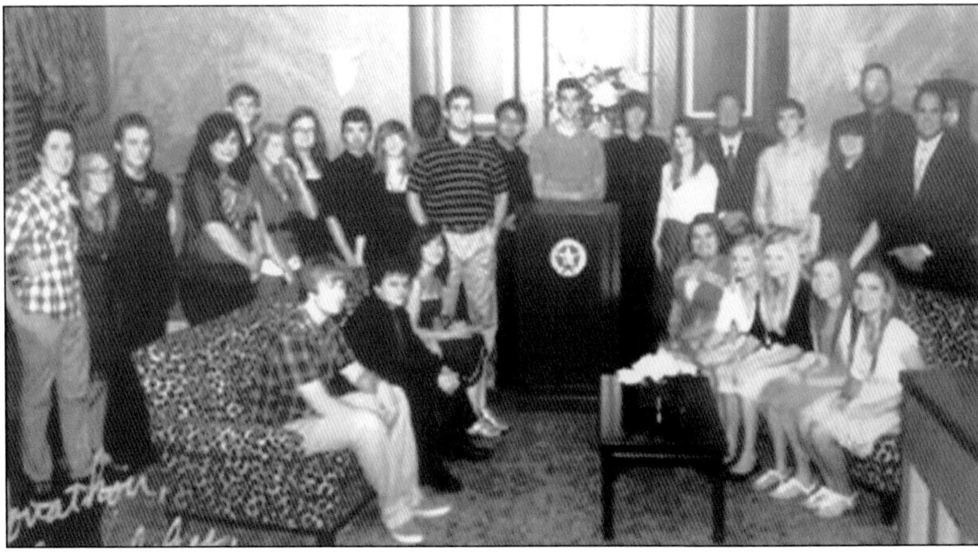

The Wagoner High School Jazz Band received recognition at the state capitol in 2012 for its state championship win. With the band members in this photograph is State Rep. Wade Roussselot, who is standing at far right. (Courtesy of the Kathy Laner Frost.)

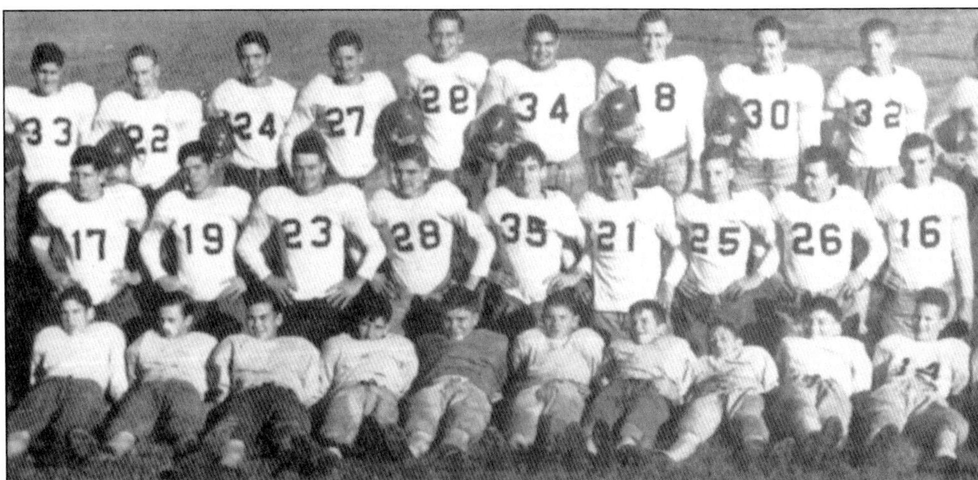

The Wagoner High School Bulldogs football team made it to the state finals in 1945 and while the high school yearbook shows Wagoner as cochampion that year for Class B, official state records show the championship went to Woodward in a forfeited game. Wagoner's team had a flu outbreak just before the final game. In the team photo are, from left to right, (front row) Walter Odom, Joe Hayes, Bill Culpepper, Marshall Callaway, Harvey Craig, Dennis Crabtree, Jim Martin, Joe Cobb, Louis White, and Charles Gilmore; (second row) Carl Dorr, Bill Cannon, Floyd Jones, James Lancaster, Dick Hereford, Henry Sandlin, Howard Miller, Louis Arnold, and Marvin Osmus; (third row) Bill Mitchell, Ray Looper, Eugene Wing, Ray Ferguson, Joel Rutherford, H.W. Irby, Dale Zachary, James Coventon, Ben Fisher, and Don Shanahan. (Author's collection.)

Eight

Our Hometown

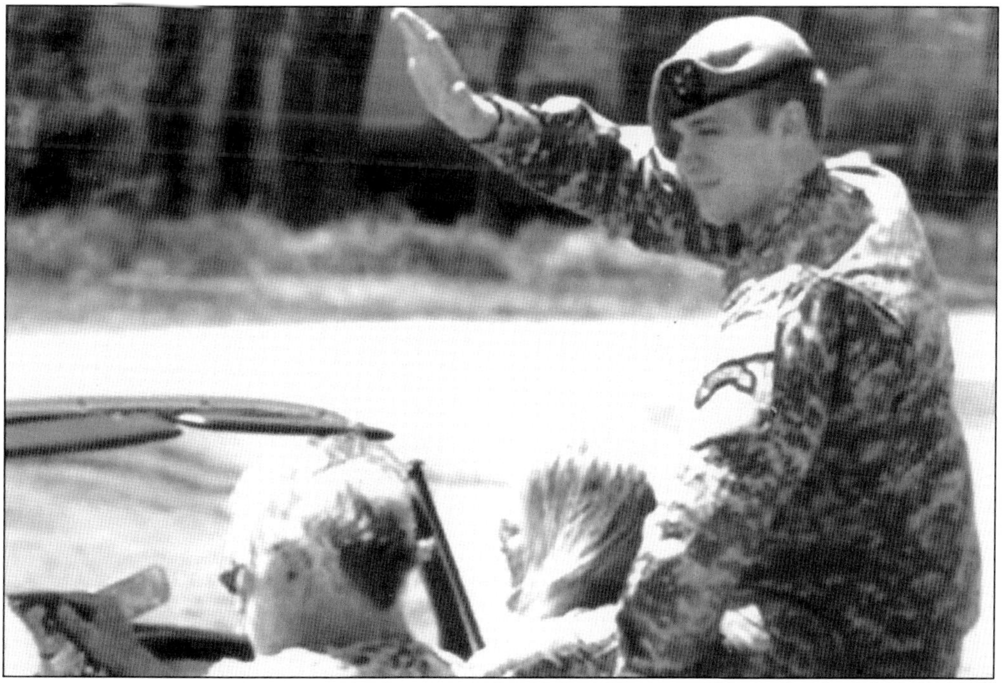

Army Ranger Kyle Emmons waves to the crowds lining Wagoner's streets on his return home from Afghanistan in April 2014 after being wounded. He lost his right leg below the knee, and sustained injuries to his left leg, left arm, and his left eye when an improvised explosive device (IED) went off. (Author's collection.)

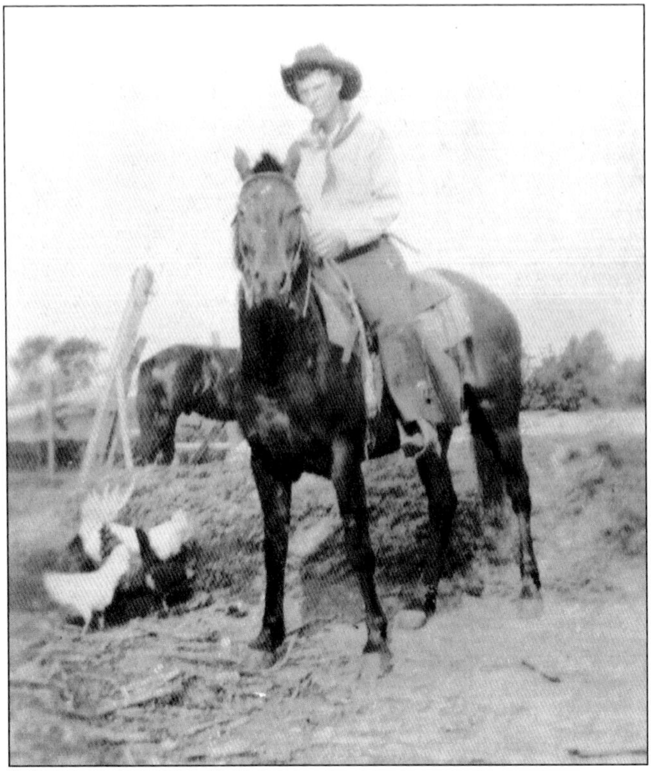

If his mother had not intervened, Allen Bays of Wagoner could have been a big movie star. Tom Mix "discovered" Bays at a rodeo and had him all but signed to a contract. His mother was furious when she found out and hired attorneys to get the contract voided, says granddaughter Linda Lancaster. (Courtesy of Linda Lancaster.)

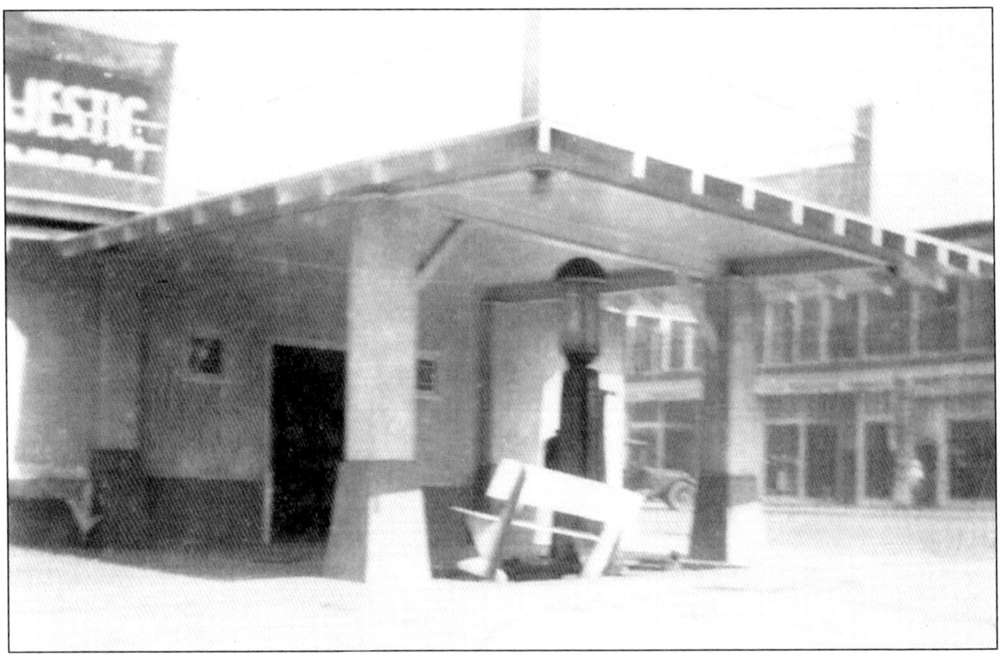

Remnants of this old service station at the southwest corner of Cherokee Street and Casaver Avenue still stand, now housing a bail bond office and other businesses. The old Majestic Hotel can be seen at far left of photograph and Gorin Mercantile is across the street. (Courtesy of Margie Semore.)

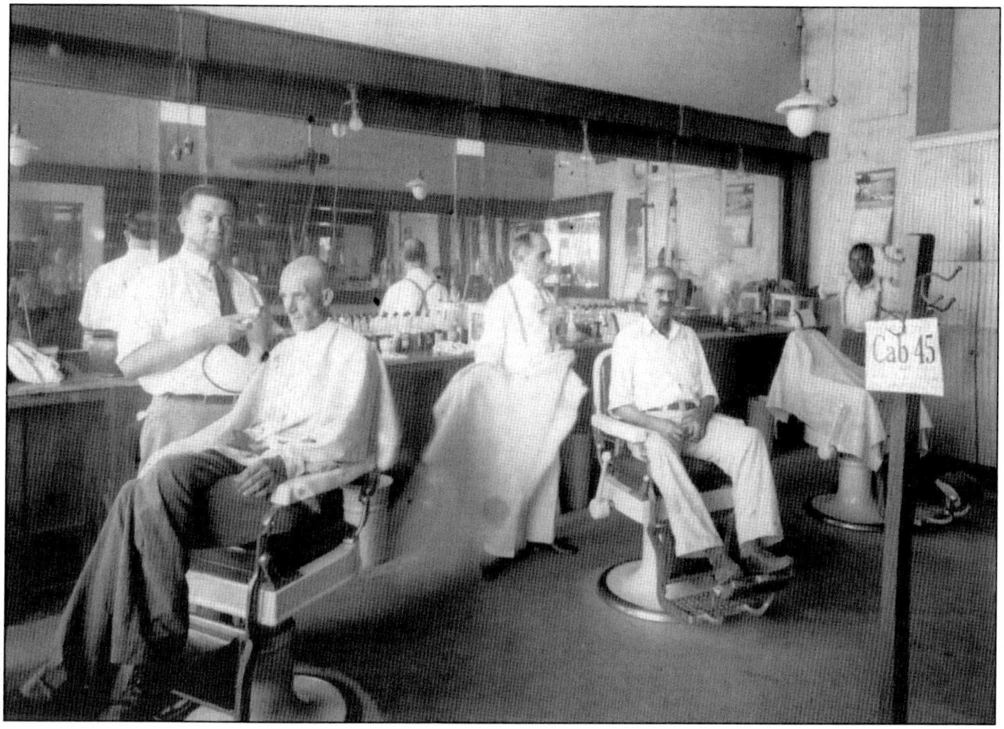

Jess Cochran, with clippers in hand at the front chair, began working in the Majestic Barber Shop on Cherokee Street in the late 1930s. Cochran's customer in this photograph is a Mr. Campbell. Henshaw is the second barber. Henshaw's customer is Henry Woods. The porter is John Henry Smiles. (Author's collection.)

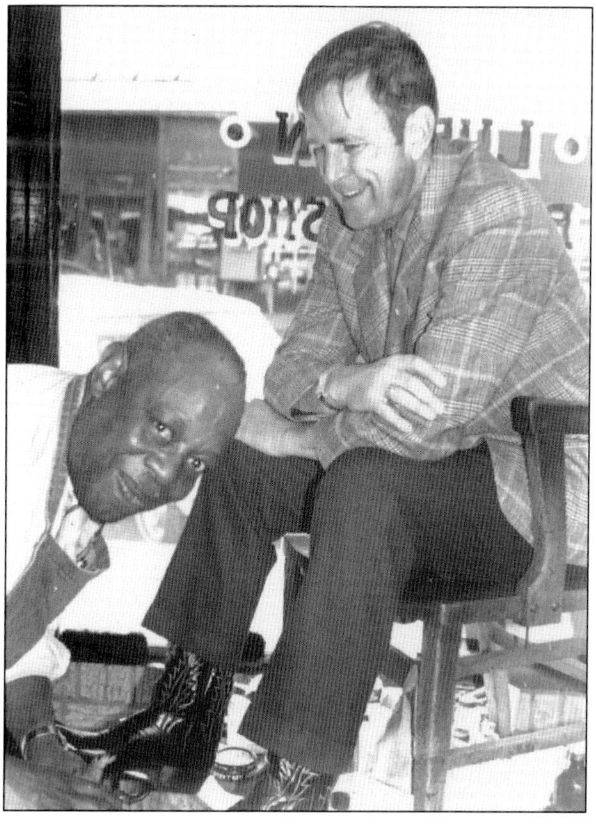

Everyone, including the governor, liked getting his or her shoes shined by Birty Booker. Here, Oklahoma governor Dewey Bartlett gets his boots shined by Booker at Luellen's Barber Shop on South Main Street. Booker shined shoes in Wagoner for more than 50 years. (Author's collection.)

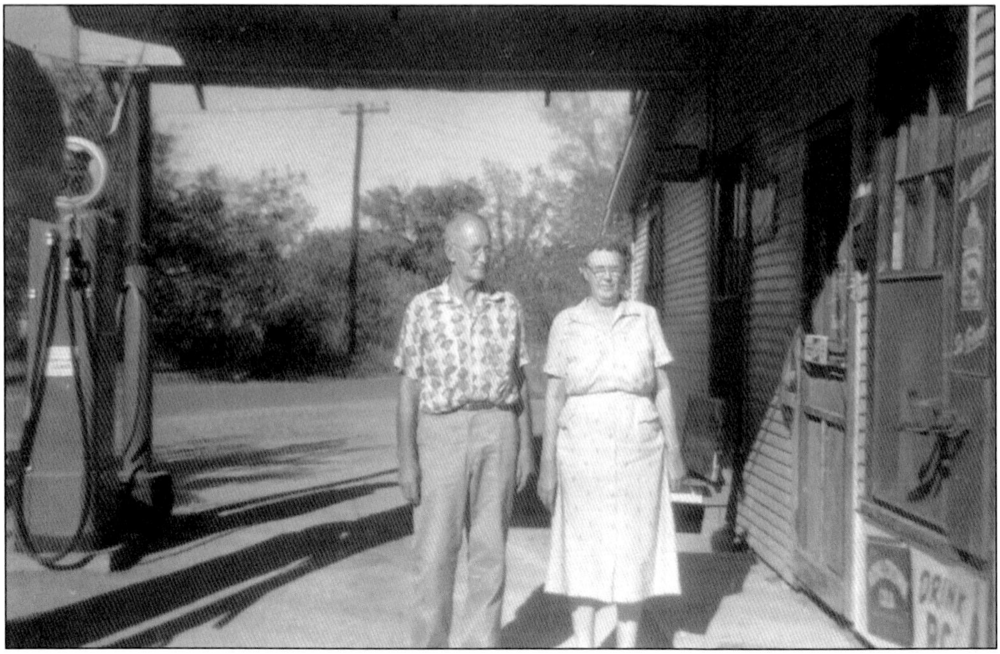

Walter and Susie Lee operated State Street Grocery at Northeast Ninth and State Streets for many years. This was a favorite place for children from the neighborhood to shop for a soda or penny candy and was located right on the Jefferson Highway, making the store a convenient stop for motorists. (Author's collection.)

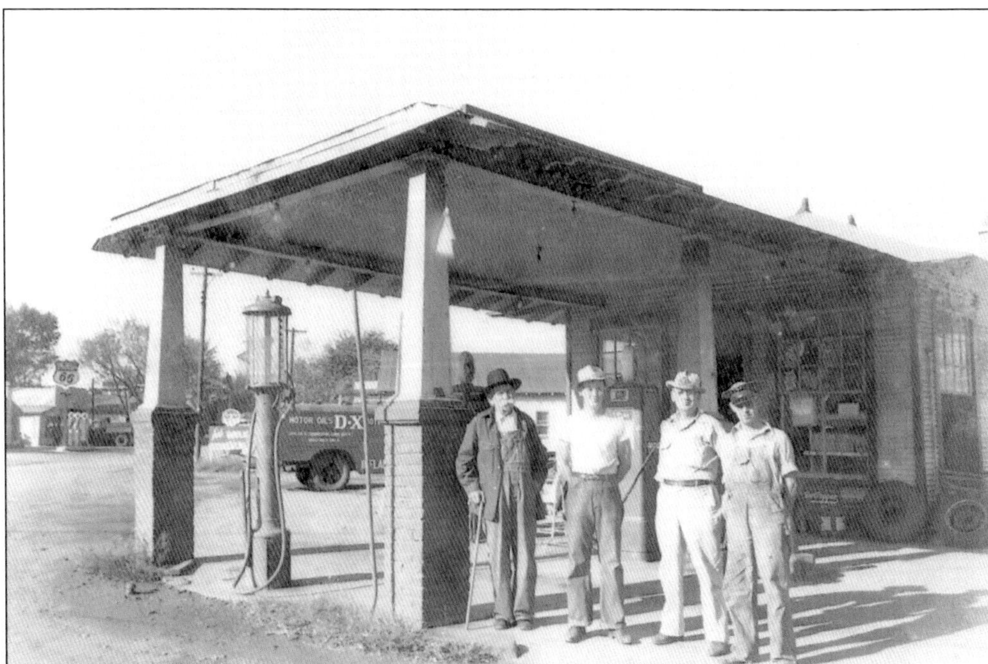

This station at the northeast corner of Church and State Streets was also on the Jefferson Highway. It is a D-X station in this photograph. Shown here, from left to right, are Ben Fisher, Floyd Walker, C.B. Cunningham, and Price Wiley. (Courtesy of Jerry Hickman.)

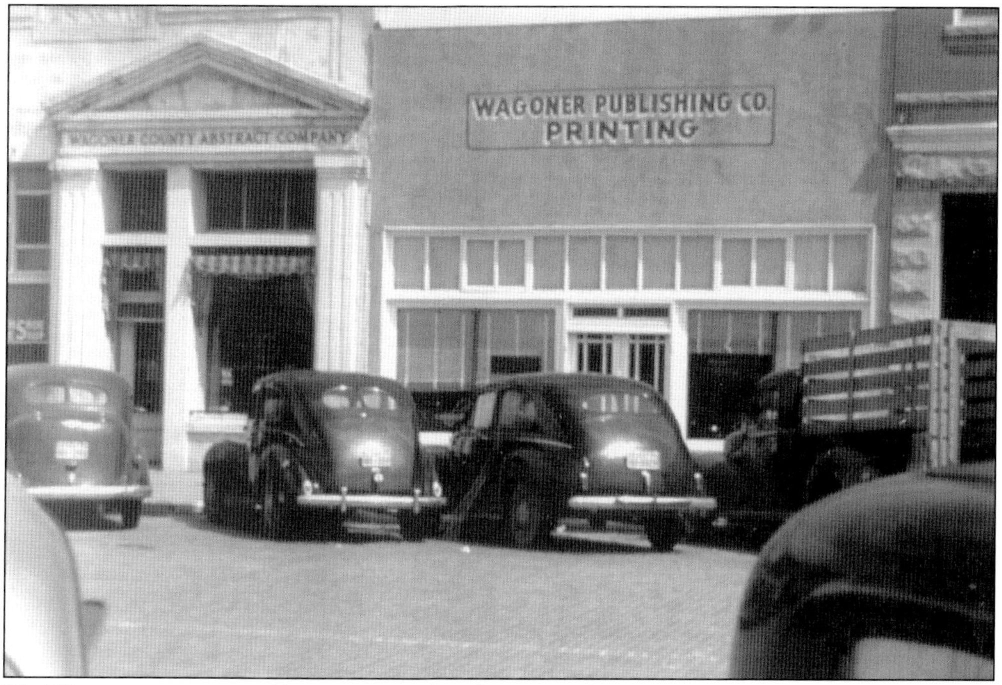

The Wagoner newspaper office, on West Cherokee Street, has greatly remolded its facade since this 1940s photograph. Wagoner County Abstract still operates in the building on the left. (Courtesy of the Bob Jeffrey collection.)

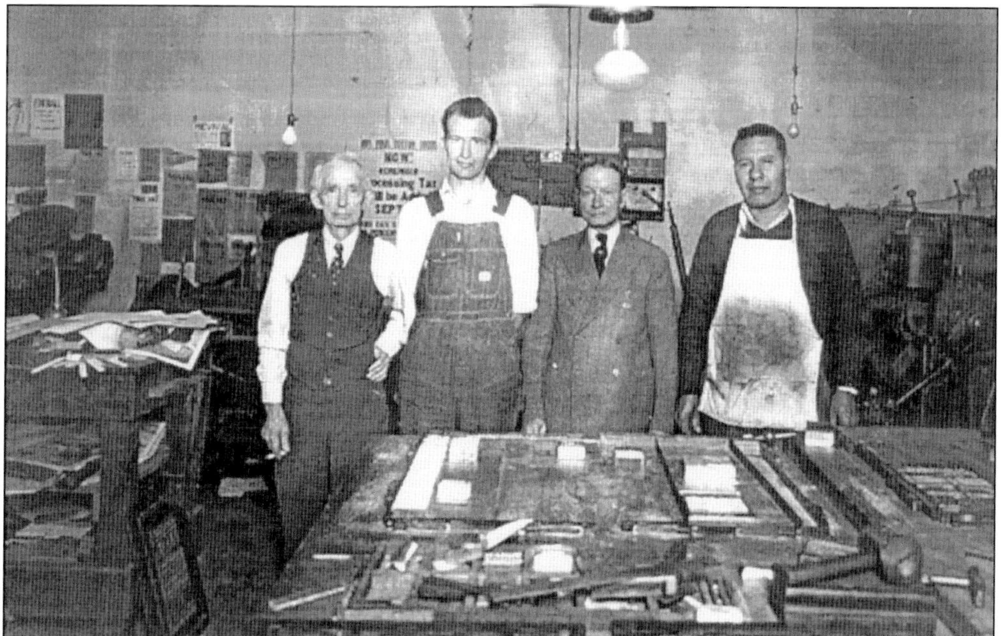

The *Wagoner Tribune* and *Record-Democrat* were published in the 1940s by the Wagoner Publishing Co. Shown in the type-setting area here are, from left to right, Gant Harris, *Tribune* editor; Hughlin Baker, linotype operator; Jim Biggerstaff, *Record-Democrat* editor; and D.F. "Chief" Bruner, composing room foreman. (Courtesy of Barbara James.)

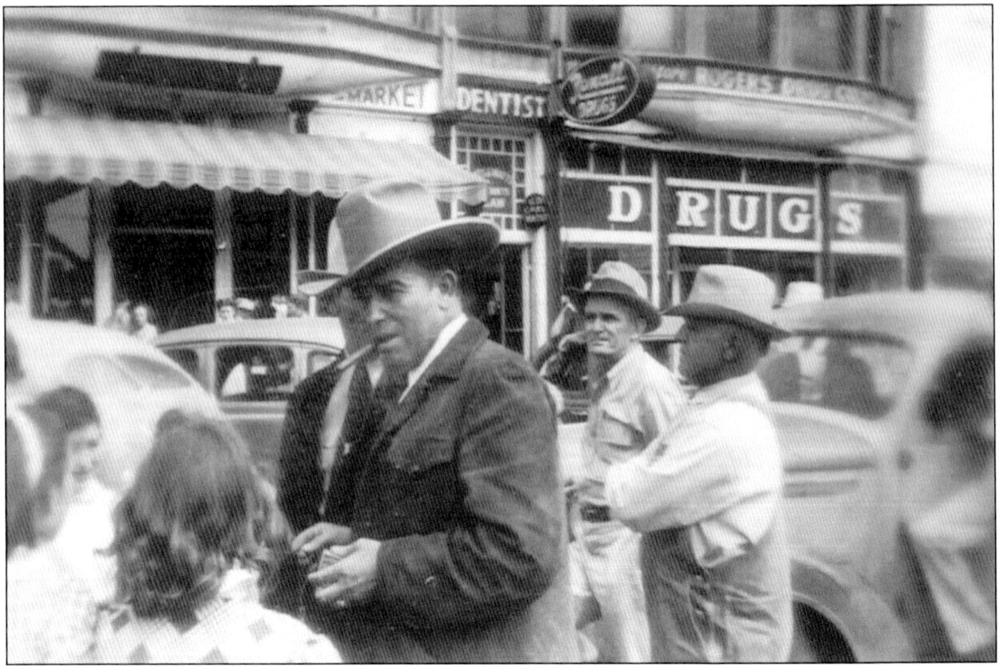

Bob Wills, leader of Bob Wills and the Texas Playboys, visits with fans in front of Rogers Drug (now American Bank) in the late 1940s. (Courtesy of Shirle Lamb Williams.)

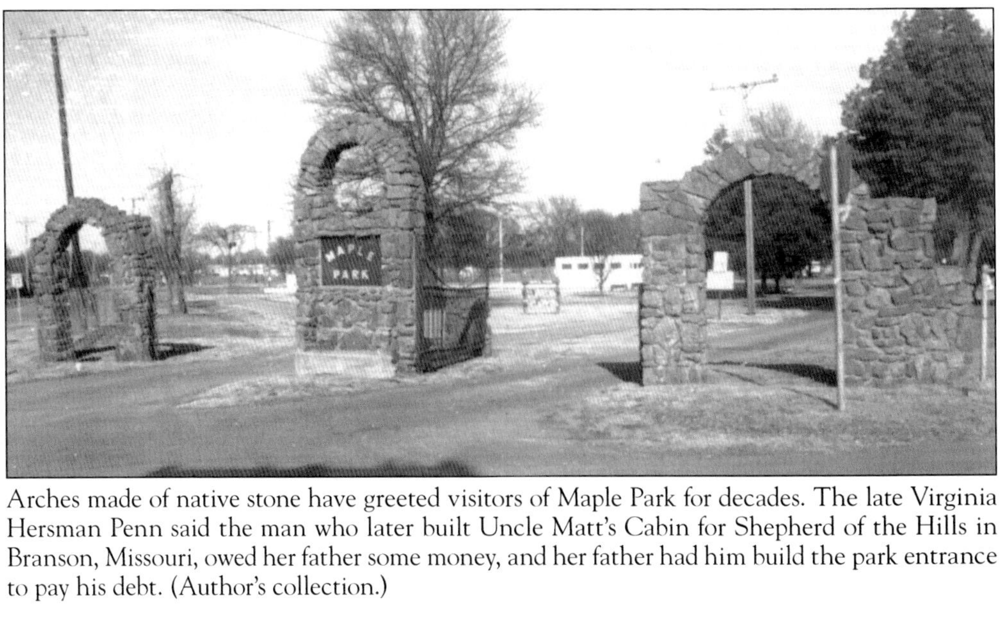

Arches made of native stone have greeted visitors of Maple Park for decades. The late Virginia Hersman Penn said the man who later built Uncle Matt's Cabin for Shepherd of the Hills in Branson, Missouri, owed her father some money, and her father had him build the park entrance to pay his debt. (Author's collection.)

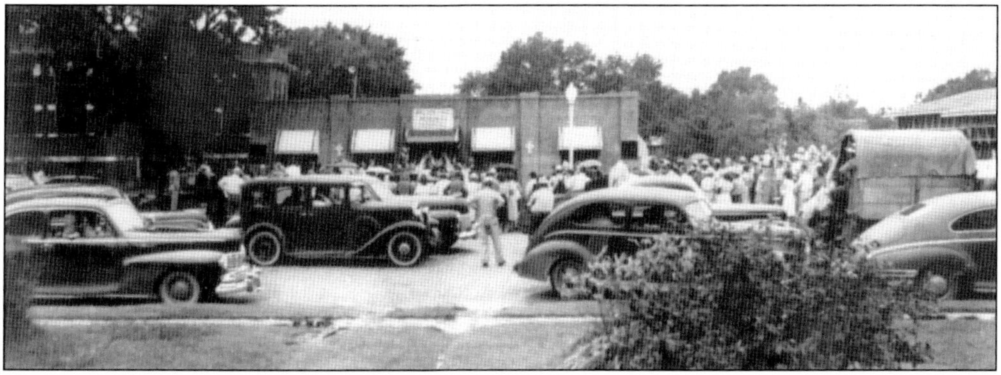

A hospital and a little motel opened as the Walden-Page Memorial Hospital in the early 1950s on East Cherokee Street, where Jackson Family Clinic is located in 2015. Jackson's office is in the old hospital. The west parking lot is where the motel was. It was built to house families of hospital patients. Helen French took over operation of the hospital when it became Wagoner Hospital. (Courtesy of Jerry Hickman.)

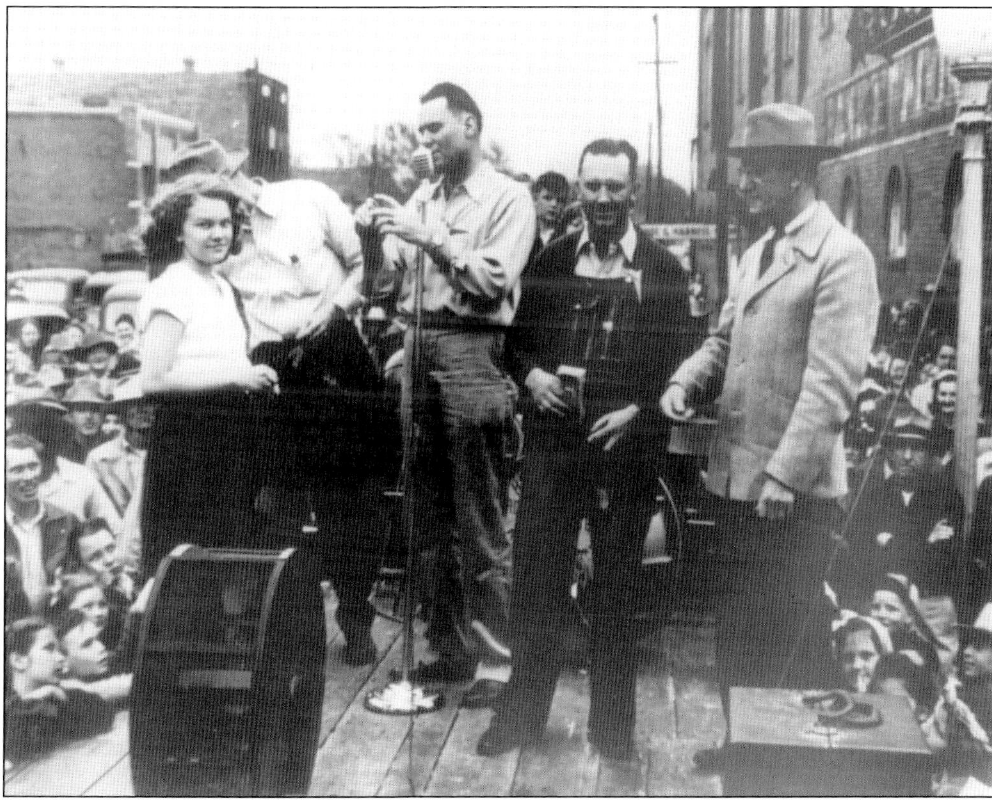

John Rice brought his family to town one Saturday in about 1950 to sell their cream and eggs, do a little shopping, and so forth. They, like so many, had no extra spending money. But they stayed in town for the Saturday afternoon drawing promoted by Bob Jeffrey, shown at the microphone. Rice ended up winning the $100, and felt that he was suddenly rich, at least for a little bit. Rice is second from left. (Courtesy of Billie Damet Rice.)

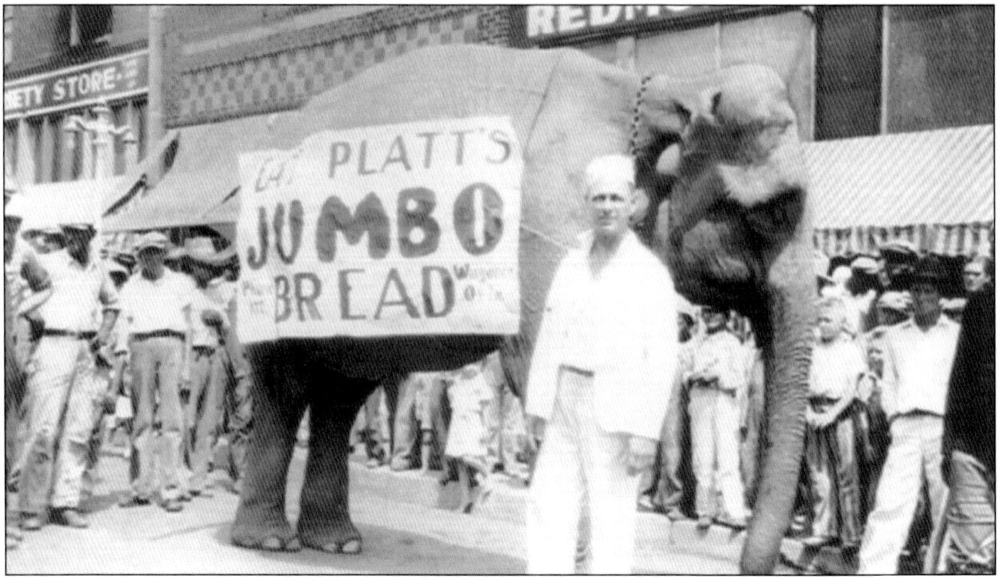

This photograph from the 1920–1930 era shows R.R. "Pop" Platt, owner of Platt's Bakery on West Cherokee Street, with an elephant advertising Platt's Jumbo Bread. The photograph was taken in front of Redmon's Studio on South Main Street. The sign has the bakery's phone number, 172, at left, and "Wagoner, Okla." at right. (Author's collection.)

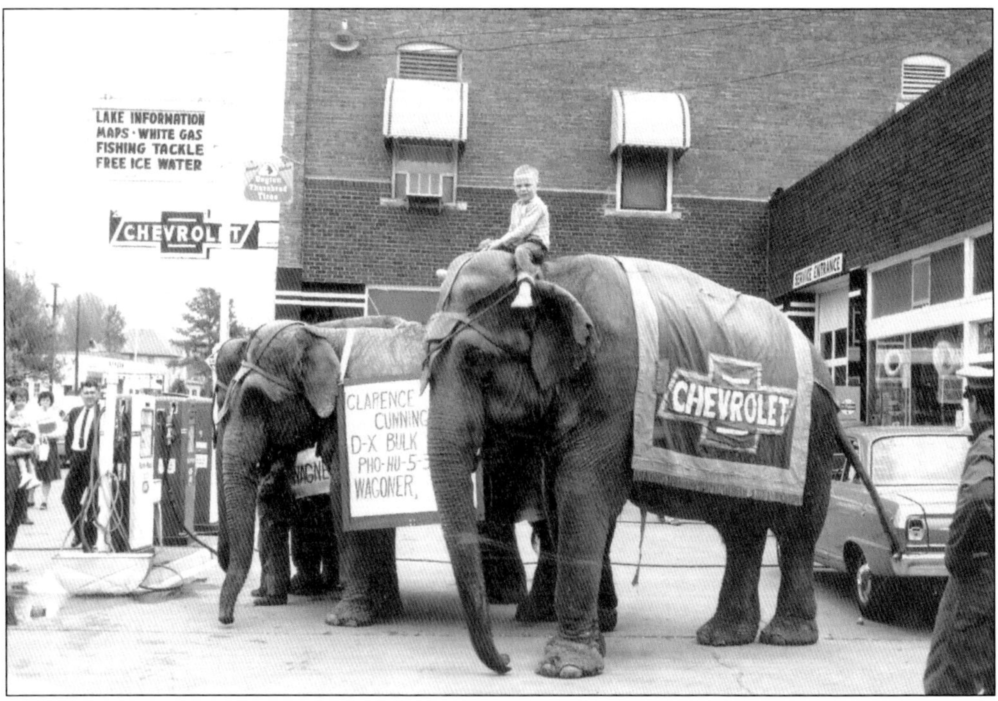

Greg Smith must have felt like he was sitting on top of the world when he got to ride this elephant in front of the family business, Grand Chevrolet. Notice the second elephant is sporting an advertisement for Clarence Cunningham's D-X bulk distributorship. A third elephant also advertises a business, but its sign cannot be read in this photograph. (Courtesy of the Cradow Smith collection.)

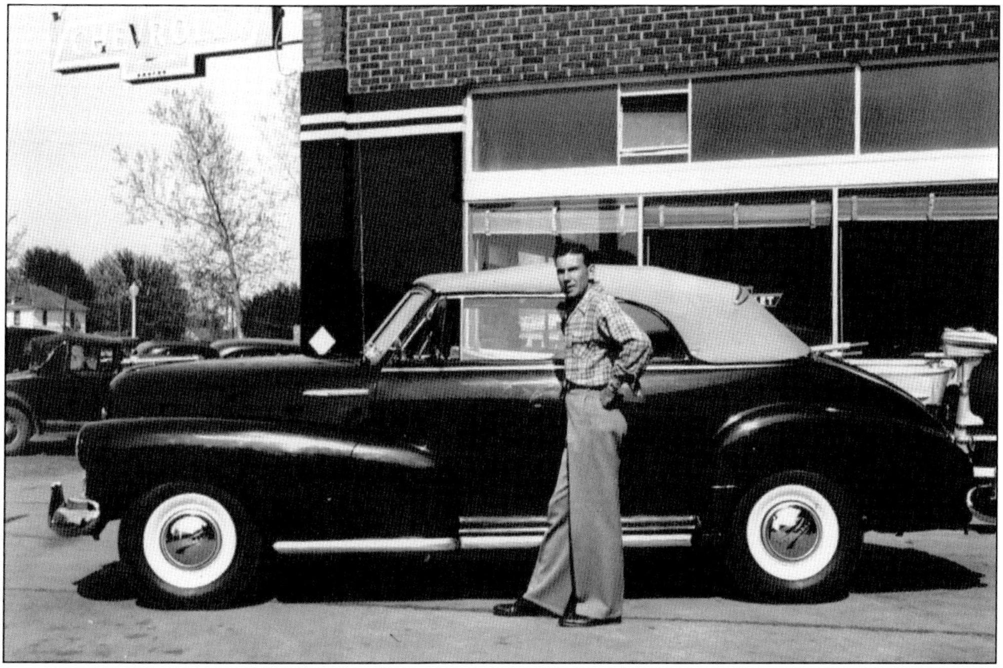

E.O. Smith shows a late 1940s Chevrolet convertible in front of Grand Chevrolet. (Courtesy of the Cradow Smith collection.)

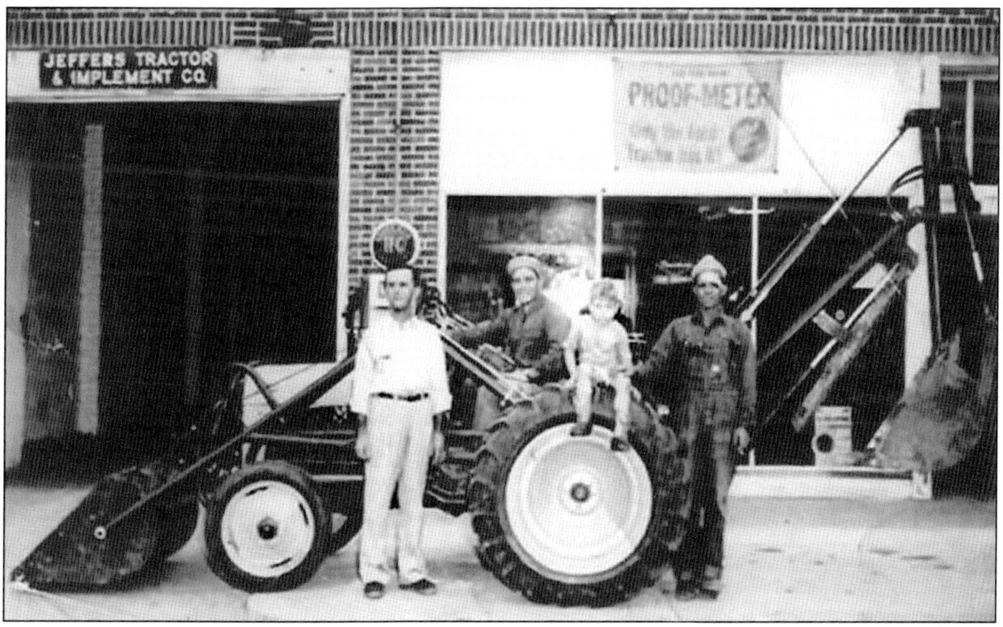

Delbert Killins sits in the driver's seat of a new Ford 8N tractor his father, Andy Killins, far right, purchased from Jeffers Tractor and Implement Co. on North Main Street in the 1950s. The dealership owner, Oscar "June" Jeffers, is at far left. Sitting on the tire is Joe Killins. (Courtesy of Jerry Hickman.)

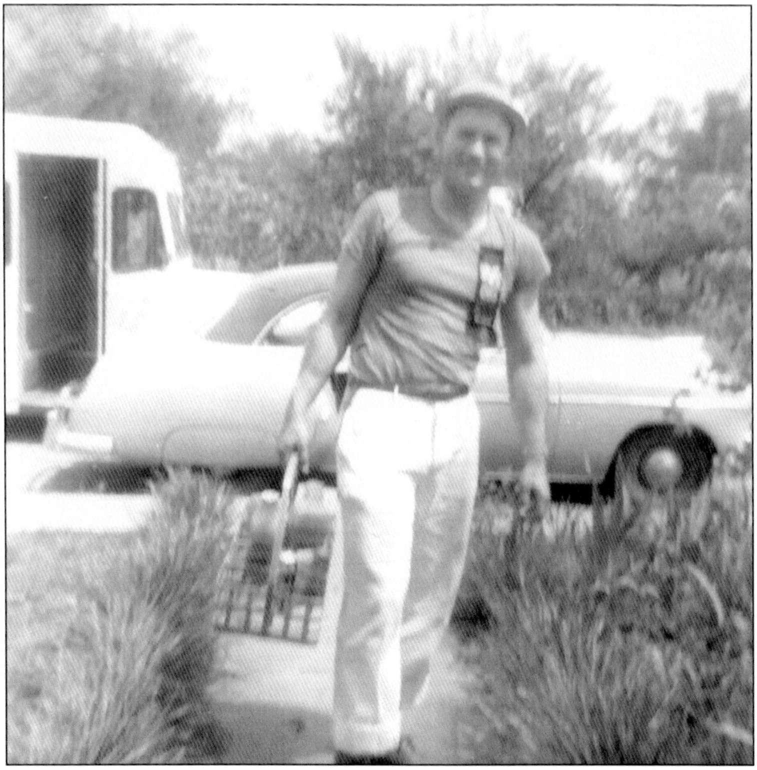

Lowell Lawson, who for many years delivered Meadow Gold milk to homes throughout Wagoner, is shown in this 1959 photograph. (Courtesy of Madeline Mesplay.)

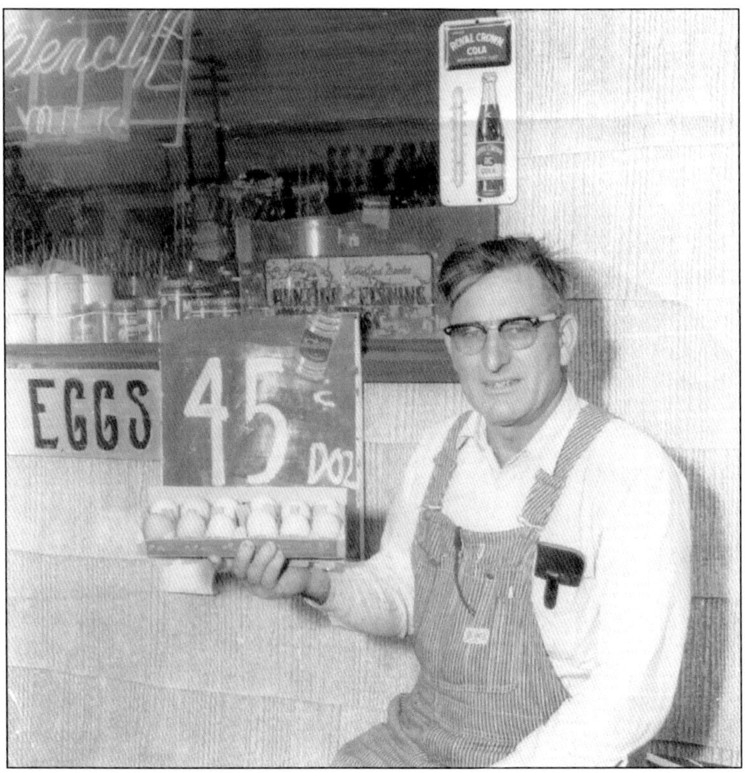

Raymond French sits on a bench in front of his Flat Rock Grocery on US 69, north of Wagoner at the Mayes County line. (Courtesy of Mary Hall.)

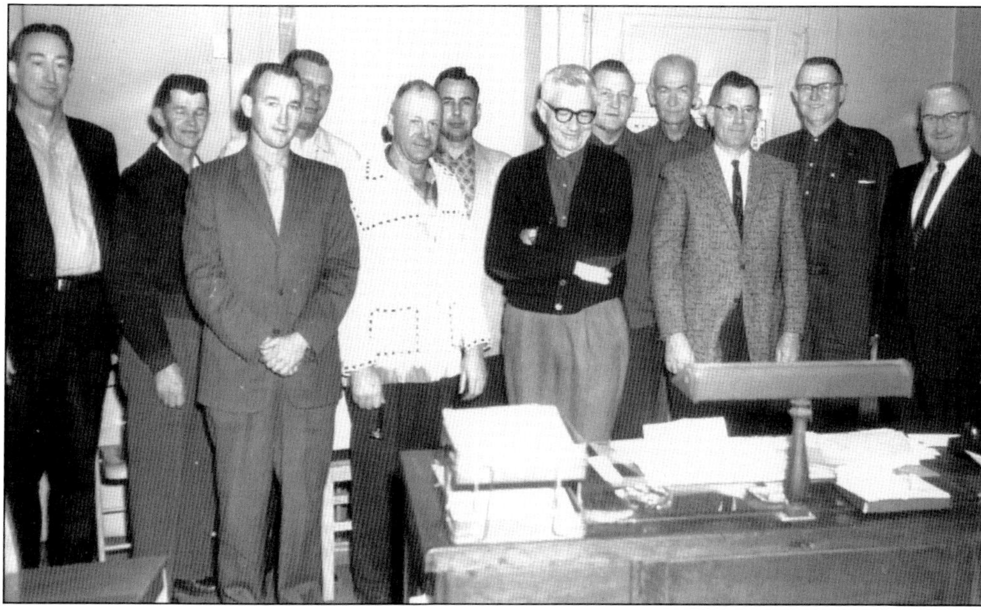

The Wagoner Chamber of Commerce board of directors in 1964 includes, from left to right, Charles Jeffers, Johnny Johnson, John Sleeper, John W. Russell Jr., Roy Lee, Cradow Smith, Frank Spence, L.A. Moore, Arch Lancaster, Walter Harvey, Cliff Dorsey, and H.H. Coats. (Author's collection.)

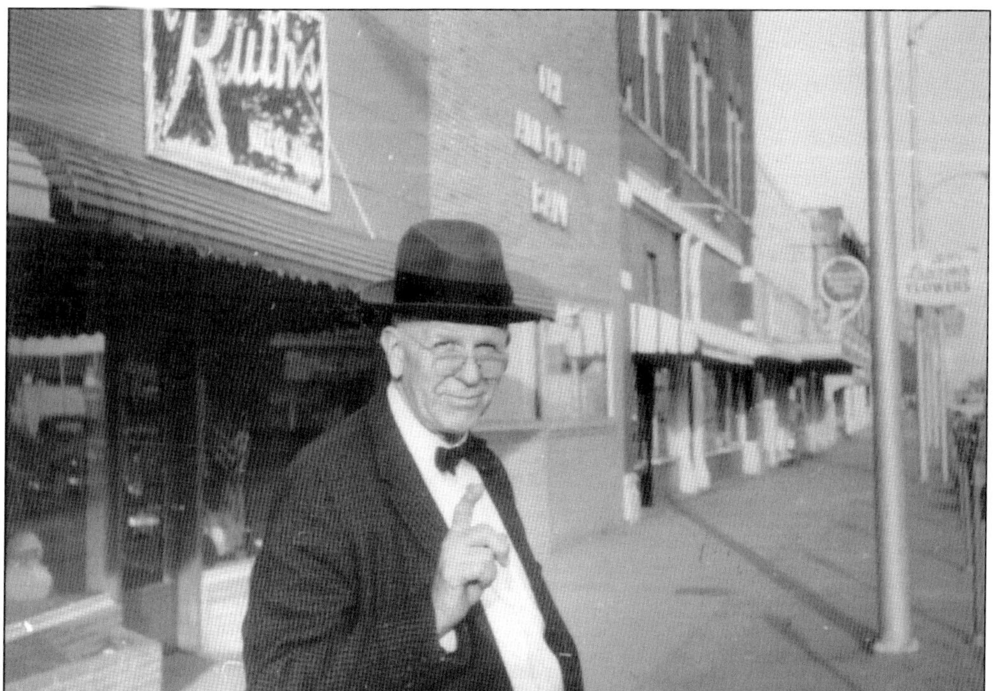

Charlie Rogers, who owned Rogers Drug from 1927 to 1972, came to Wagoner from Hulbert. His drugstore was located in the Cobb Building and had walnut shelving and a marble-topped soda fountain. (Courtesy of the Harvey Hunter collection.)

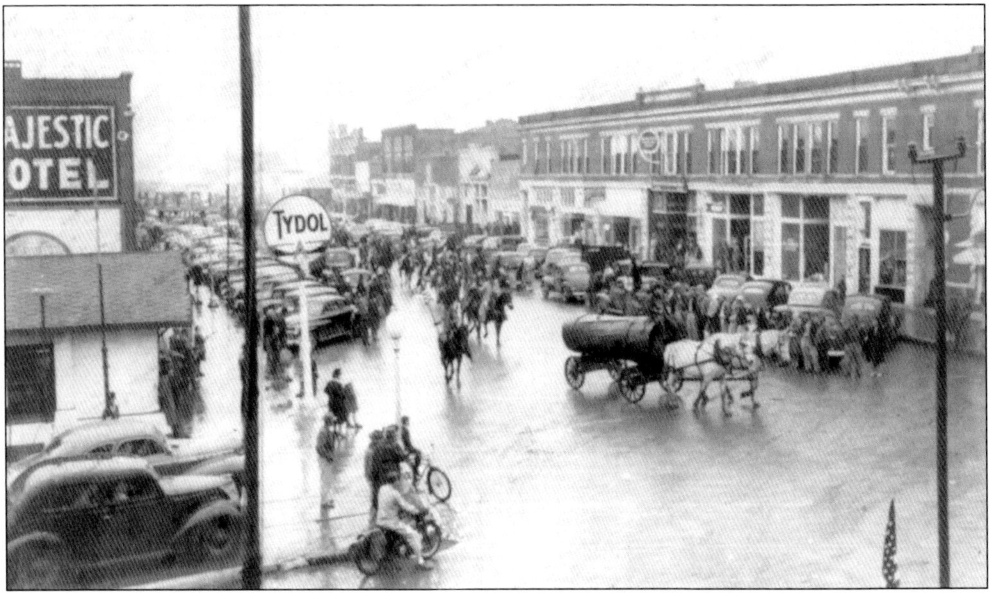

A parade on November 21, 1947, moves east on Cherokee Street at its intersection with Casaver Avenue. (Author's collection.)

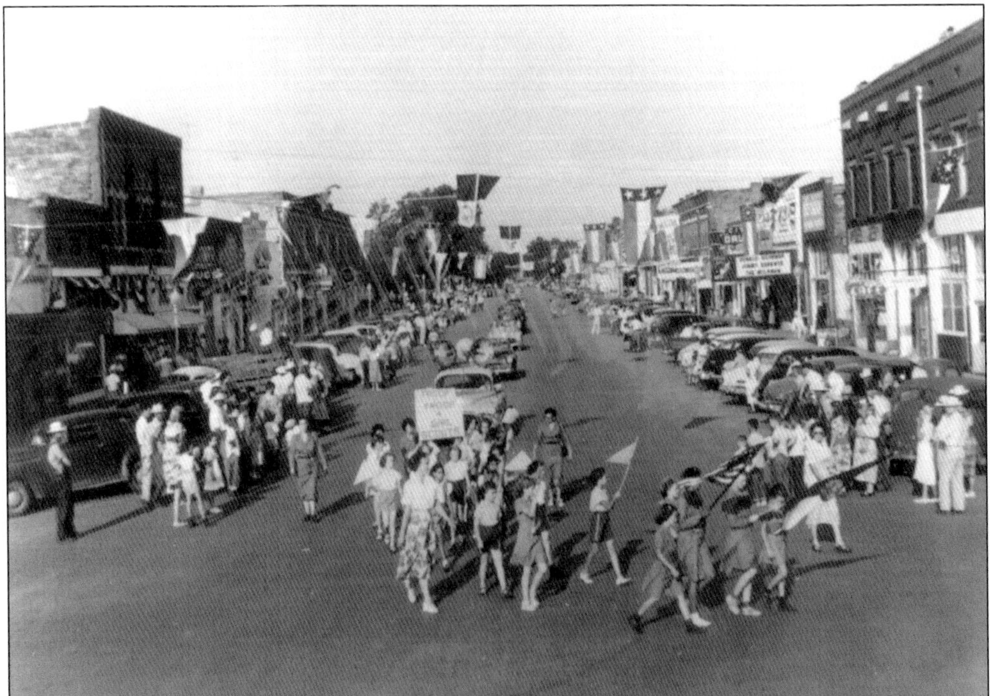
The marquee on the Cozy Theater advertises the showing of *The Milkman*, which dates the photograph to 1950. The group turning the corner from East Cherokee Street onto South Main Street is filled with Girl Scouts. (Author's collection.)

This view in this parade photograph looks south on Main Street. The Hotel Wagoner is at the far left. With horses headed in both directions, it is difficult to tell in which direction this parade is moving. (Author's collection.)

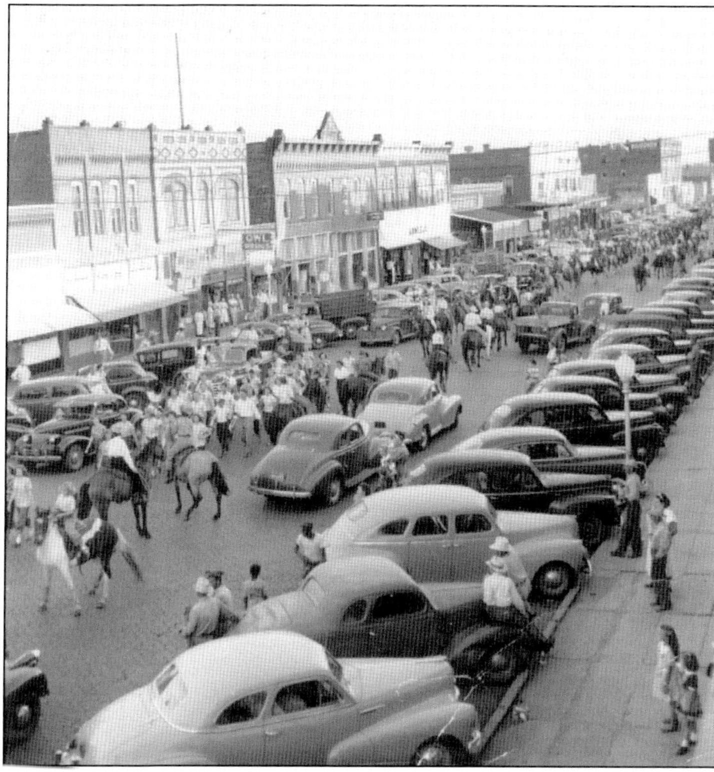

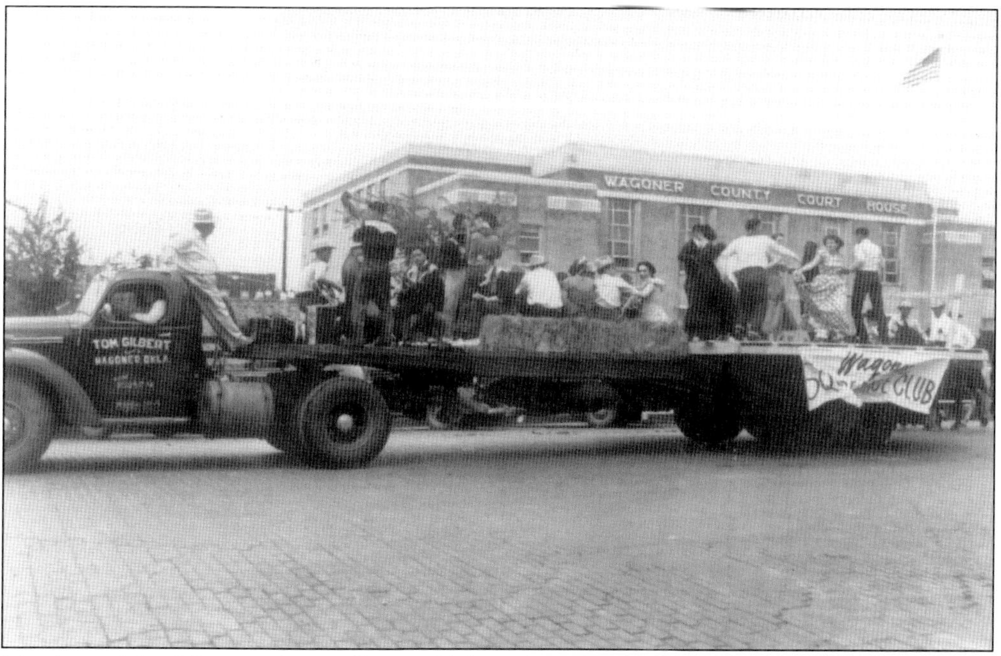

Members of the Wagoner Square Dance Club perform on the back of this trailer in a Wagoner parade. Tom Gilbert drives the truck he provided for the float. The man leaning against the cab is Ben Allen. No one else is identified. Notice that Cherokee Street still has its brick streets at this time. (Author's collection.)

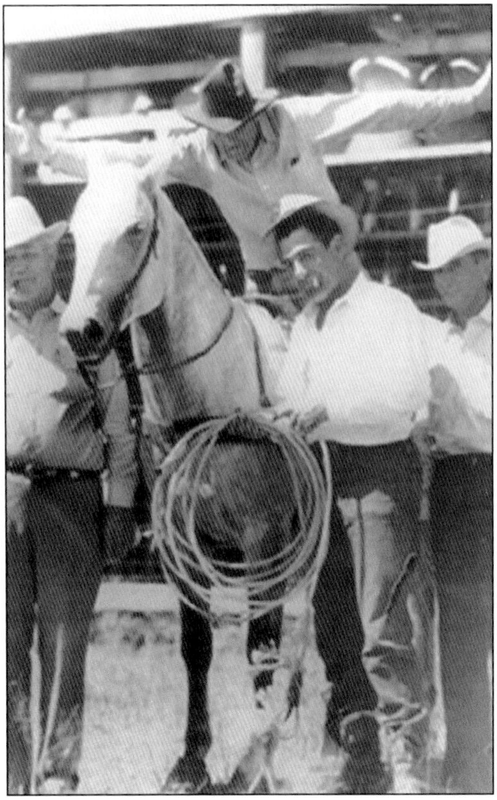

Ted Yochum of Wagoner was a nationally known bulldogging champion in the 1930s. He also was a spokesman for Camel cigarettes, his likeness appearing in magazines and on billboards. Here, Yochum and some friends mess around at a rodeo arena. On the horse is Curt Williams; Charlie Jernigan is at far left; Yochum is at center; and Tony Parsons is on the right. (Author's collection.)

Bill Lancaster, at the podium, was mayor in March 1973, when ground breaking was held for Wagoner's Prestolite plant. Pictured here are, from left to right, Gov. David Hall; Paul Grisham, Jim Smith, and Jim Boyd, all from Prestolite's Decatur, Alabama, plant; Lancaster; unidentified; Dick Newkirk, district engineer for the Oklahoma Department of Transportation; Jimmy Williams of Prestolite; and unidentified. (Courtesy of Jerry Hickman.)

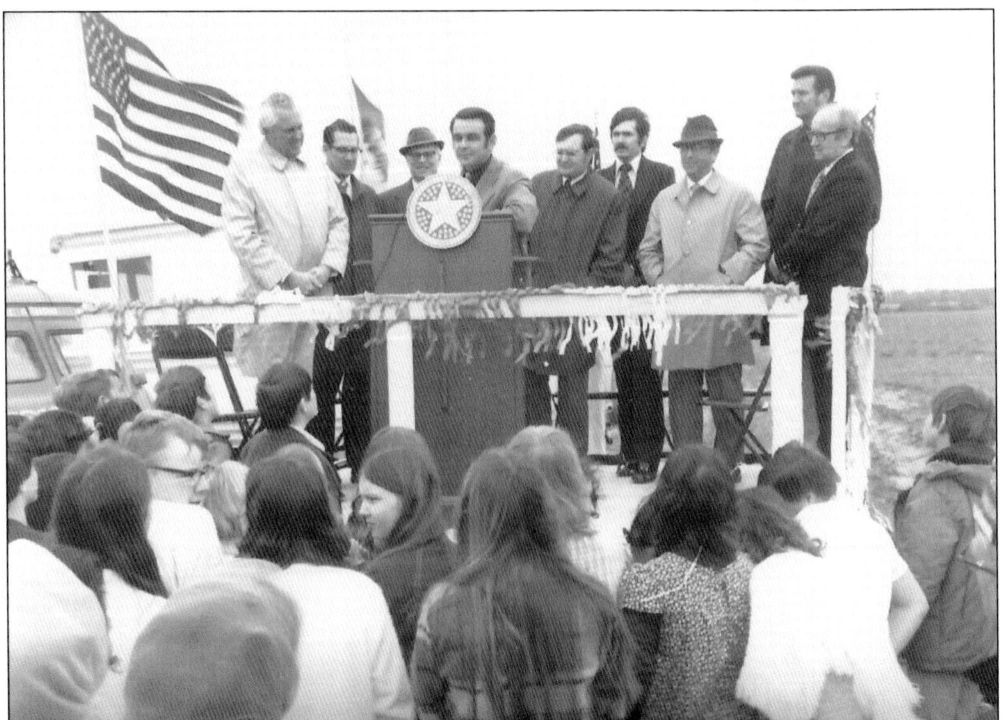

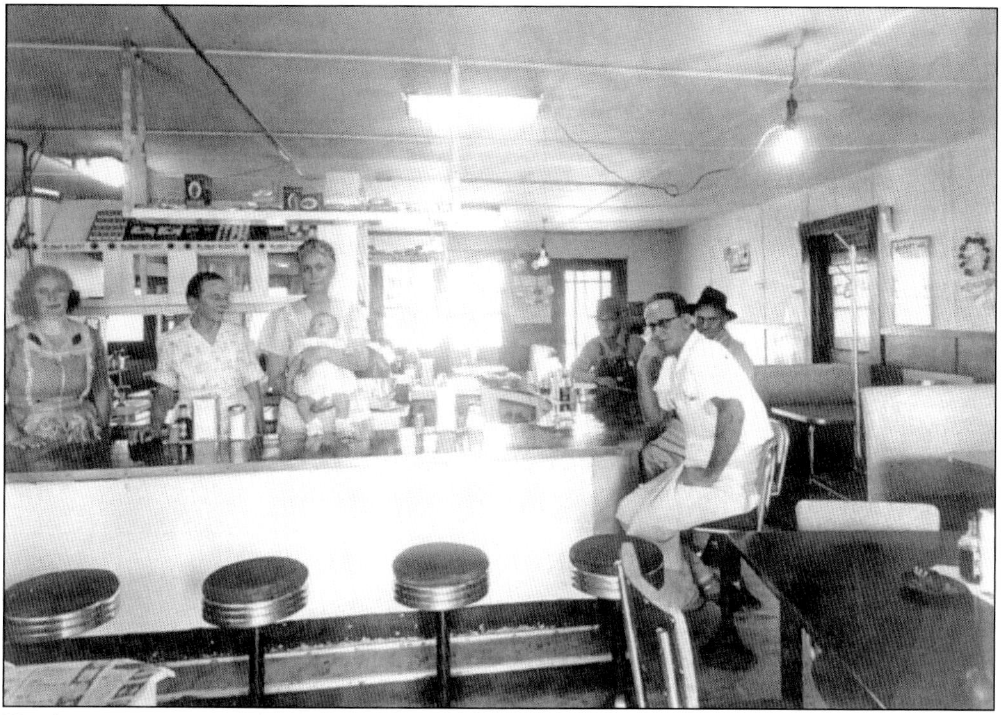

Hamburgers were 10¢ and a plate lunch was 50¢ at Todd's Café on Church Street. The Continental Trailways bus depot and tag agency also operated out of the building at times. Behind the counter are, from left to right, unidentified, ? Gilley, and Clevlie Broaddus, holding her firstborn grandchild, Mike Bunney. At the counter, from front to back, are Todd Broaddus, Lige North, and Glen Bunney. The café was sold around 1964. (Courtesy of Ella Pearl Lancaster.)

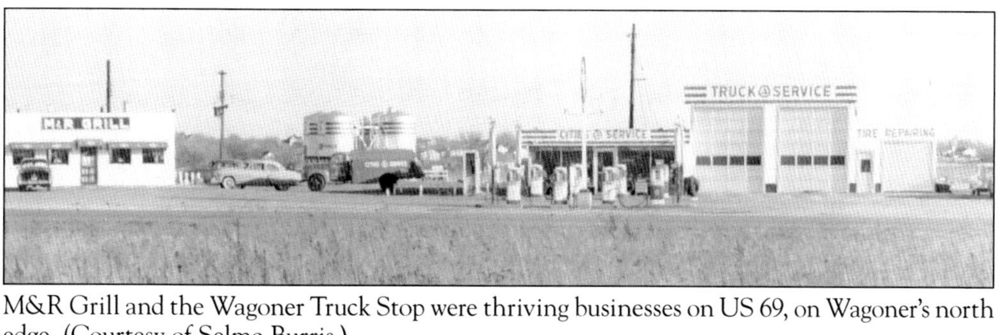

M&R Grill and the Wagoner Truck Stop were thriving businesses on US 69, on Wagoner's north edge. (Courtesy of Selma Burris.)

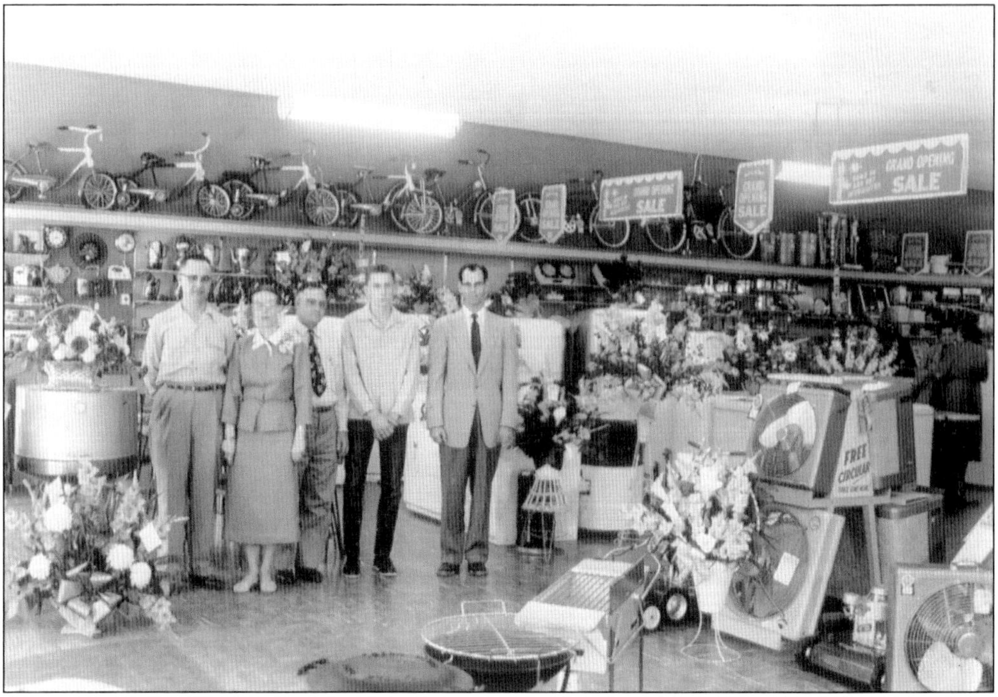

Pete and Lil Stauss (left) pose for this picture in 1956 at the grand opening of their new Western Auto store at 215 East Cherokee Street; it was located in the east end of John Sleeper Agency and west end of Wagoner County Abstract today. Lilo Zinn is second from right. (Courtesy of Janelle Semore.)

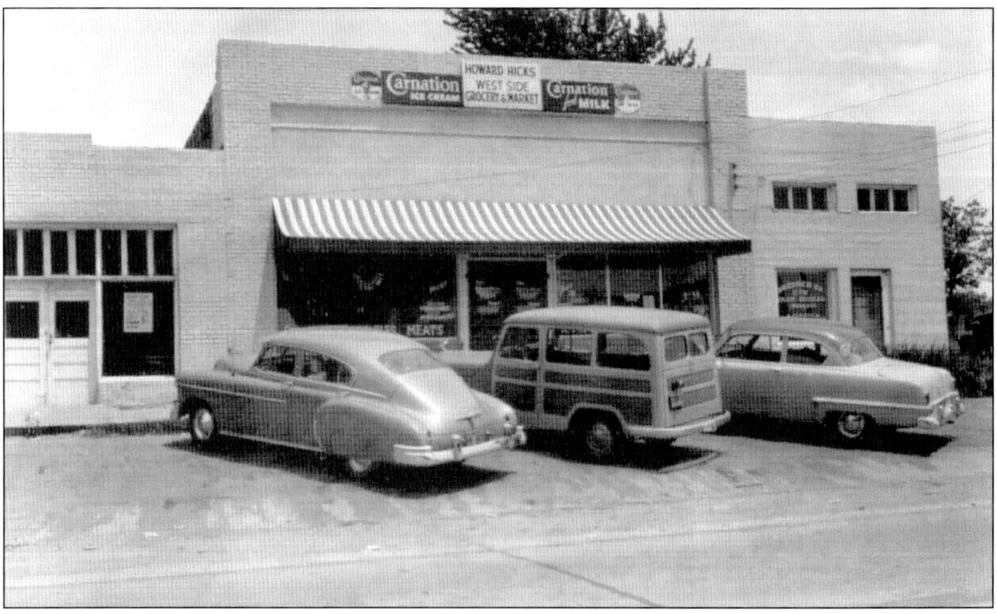

Howard Hicks opened his Hicks Westside Grocery in 1949 and operated it for 20 years before his health forced him to close. It was on West Cherokee Street, in the area occupied by Terry Jones Shopping Center in 2015. Hicks specialized in meat cutting, but the store offered a full line of groceries and items such as feed and kerosene. (Courtesy of the Cradow Smith collection.)

Pro Rodeo Hall of Fame calf roper Barry Burk (right) and his family lived west of Wagoner when he was a student at Wagoner High School. Shown here at Burk's home are Barry and his brother, Roy. Upon graduation from Wagoner High School, Barry had earned three college scholarship offers: football at Oklahoma State University, basketball at Northeastern Oklahoma State University, and rodeo at Hardin-Simmons University. He chose the basketball offer at NEOSU, but the rodeo spirit was too strong in his blood, and he was back on the road to a professional rodeo career. Roy went on to have a very successful stint at Northeastern State University and later coached football. (Author's collection.)

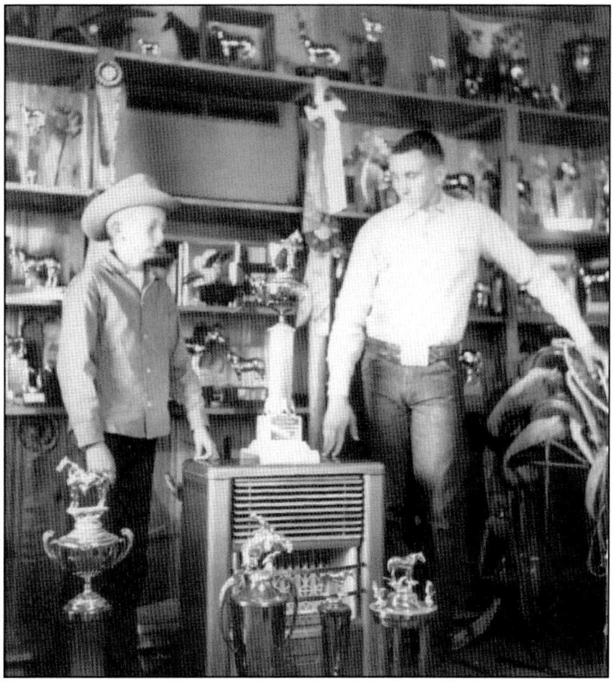

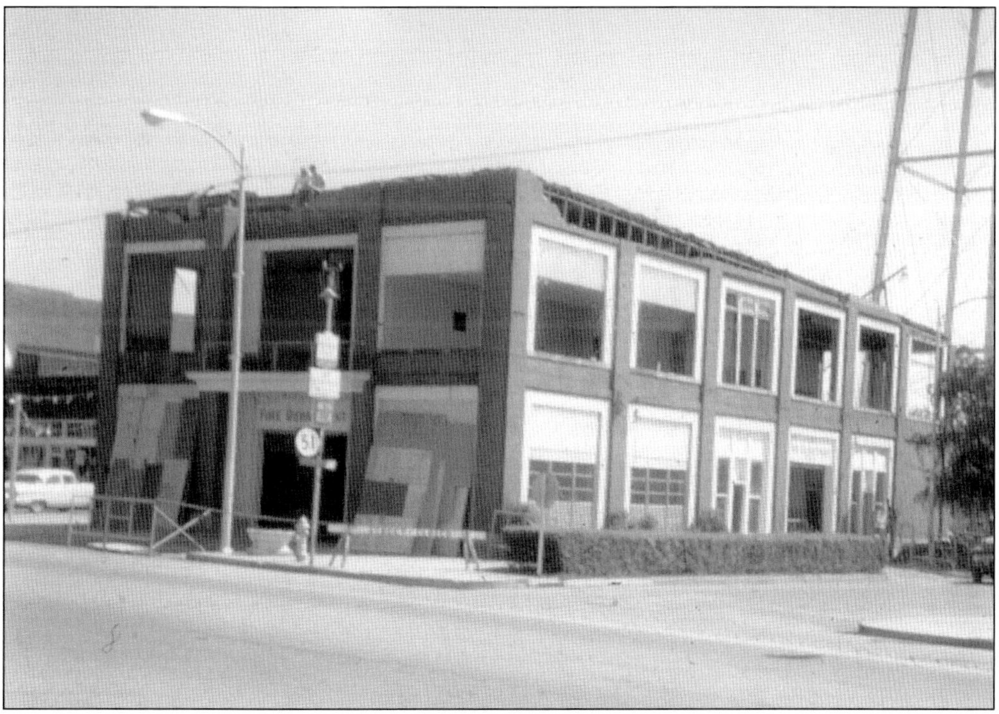

This structure was built in 1910 as Wagoner City Hall, the top story was removed in the 1960s, and light yellow brick was added to make the building's color coordinate with the county courthouse across the street. The building served many years as home of the clerk's office and police and fire departments. When the top floor was removed, a brass fire pole from the second to the ground floor was removed and placed in a private residence in Wagoner. (Author's collection.)

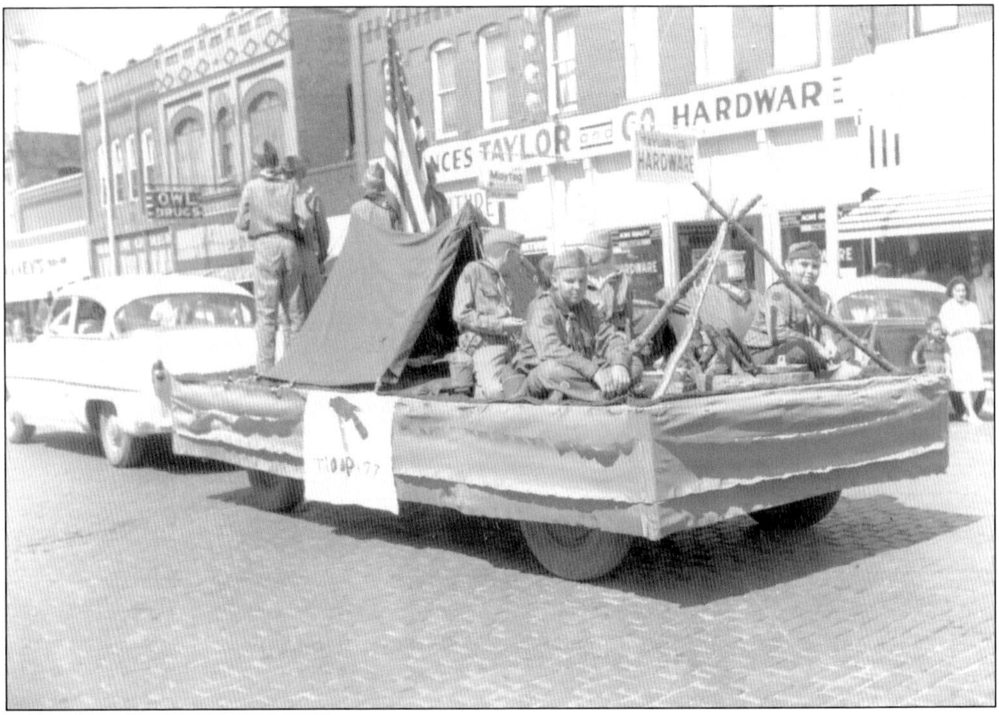

Wagoner Boy Scout Troop 177 members are shown on a float in one of the early Lake Festival parades. They are northbound on South Main Street. Those facing the camera are, from left to right, Bob Dickson, Dale Dugger, and Bill Nicholas. (Courtesy of Jerry Hickman.)

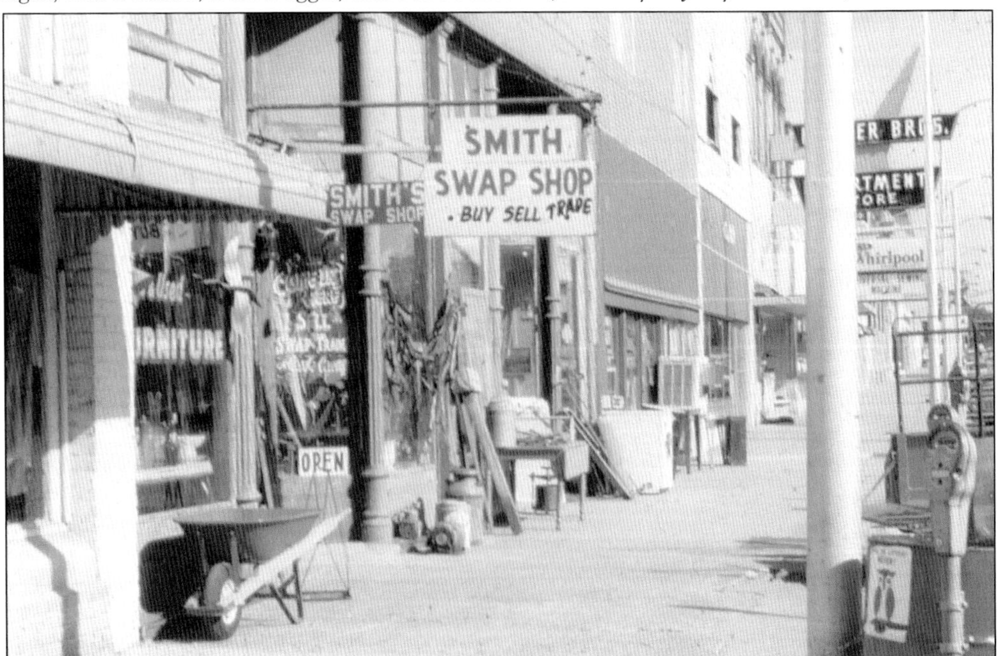

Wagoner still had parking meters (at right) when this photograph was taken. The view is looking north on South Main Street. (Courtesy of Ruby Bebout.)

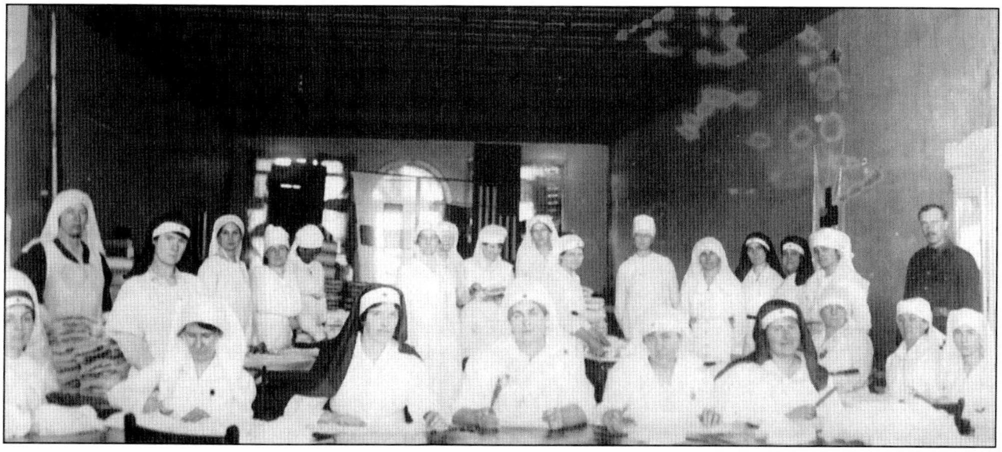

Wagoner Red Cross workers seen here in the 1920s include, from left to right, (front row) Mattie Lamon, Signa Hatfield, Mrs. ? Sharp, Olive Miller, Dula B. Shroyer, unidentified, Irene Sharp, Mrs. Terry Parkinson, Mrs. Mercer Gibson, and Nena Thompson; (back row) unidentified, Pearl M. Searcy, Pauline Palmer, Mrs. Merle Goddard, Mrs. A.J.W. Ahrens, Mrs. G.D. Carl, Mrs. ? Haworth, Clara Whaley, Mrs. Jim Wilson, Jennie Crowder, Mrs. Welch Wagoner, Mrs. Charles G. Watts, Anna Cook Hamer, Hattie Bates, unidentified, and Hubert Knight. Those in dark veils are instructors. (Courtesy of Margie Semore.)

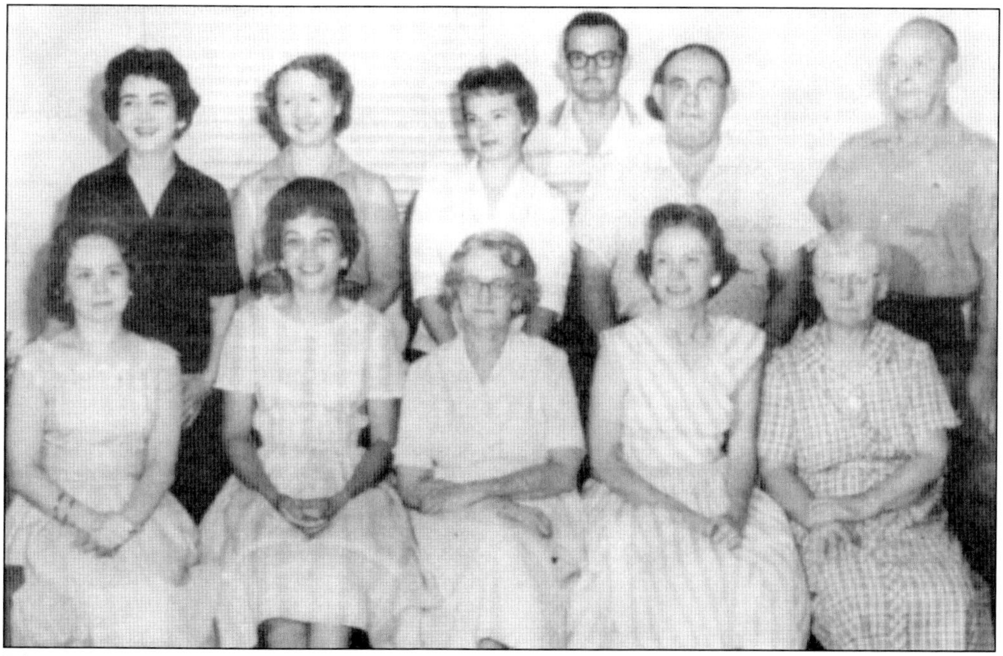

The Wagoner Department of Public Welfare staff in 1961 is made up of, from left to right, (first row) Ida Lee Stuart, senior clerk; Evelyn Easterling, stenographer; Mary L. Gregory, caseworker; Sue Ann Graham, caseworker; and Norma N. Johnson, caseworker; (second row) Ruth E. Wilson, county director; Geraldine Gilley, caseworker; Janelle Semore, stenographer; Wallace J. Smith, caseworker; Wayne E. Gilbert, caseworker; and Dallas Hornsby, case supervisor. The photograph was taken at the time of the agency's move from South Main Street to a remodeled church at 109 South State Street, across the street and southeast from the Carnegie library. (Author's collection.)

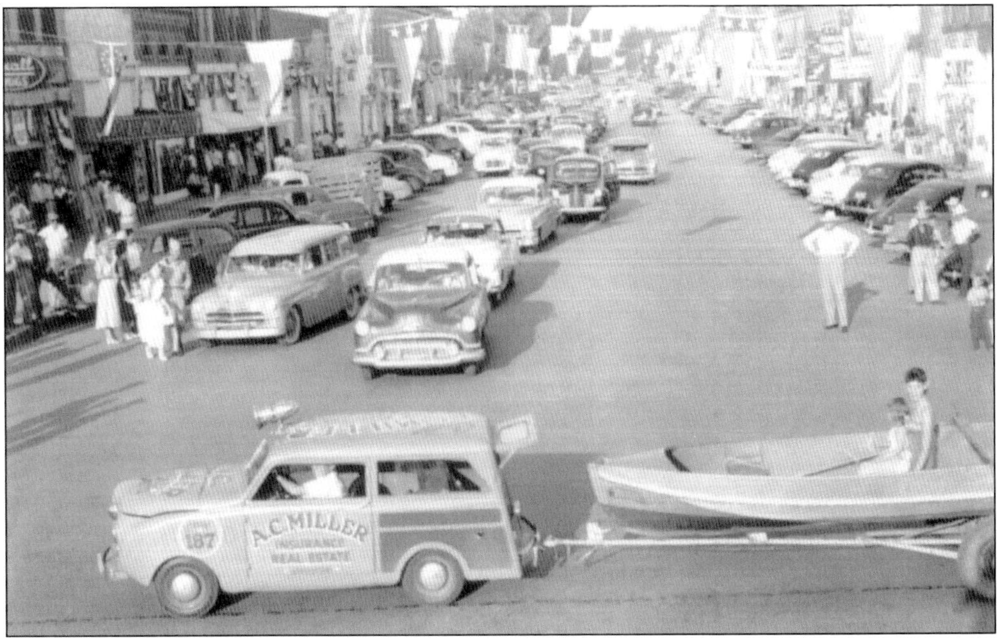

Fort Gibson Lake was still very new when city leaders organized a Miss Lake Wagoner contest. Evelyn Dyer, seated in the boat, was one of the candidates. With her is Linda Dyer, her little sister. The man standing in the street with his hands on his hips is former Wagoner sheriff and chief of police Clay Flowers. (Courtesy of the Cradow Smith collection.)

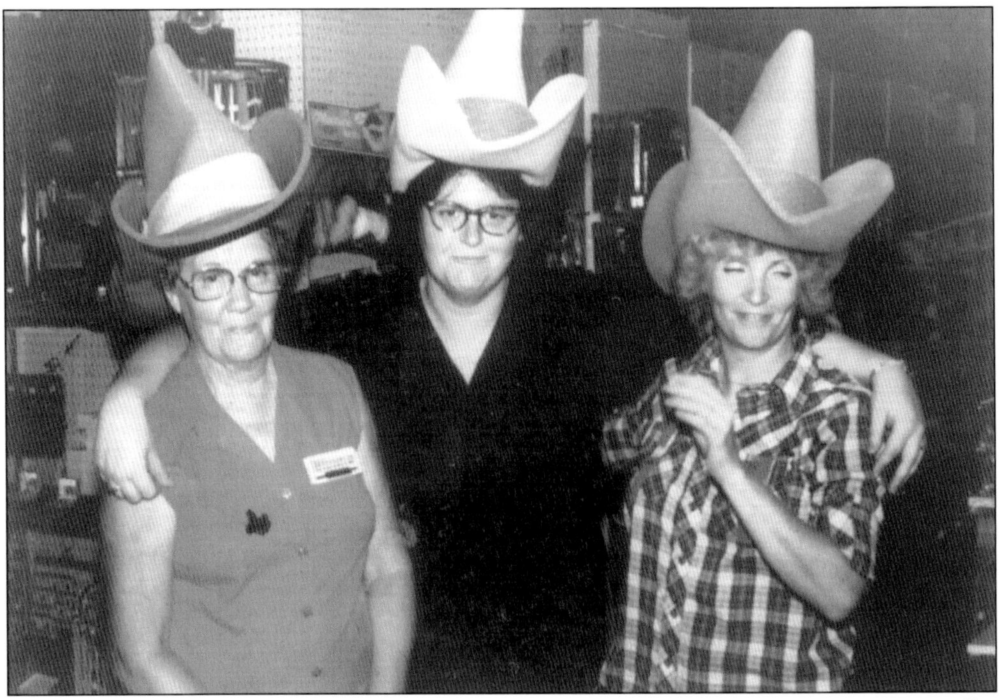

The "girls" at Ben Franklin five-and-dime are, from left to right, Willie Damet, Oneta Castillo, and Pat Carter. (Courtesy of Billie Rice.)

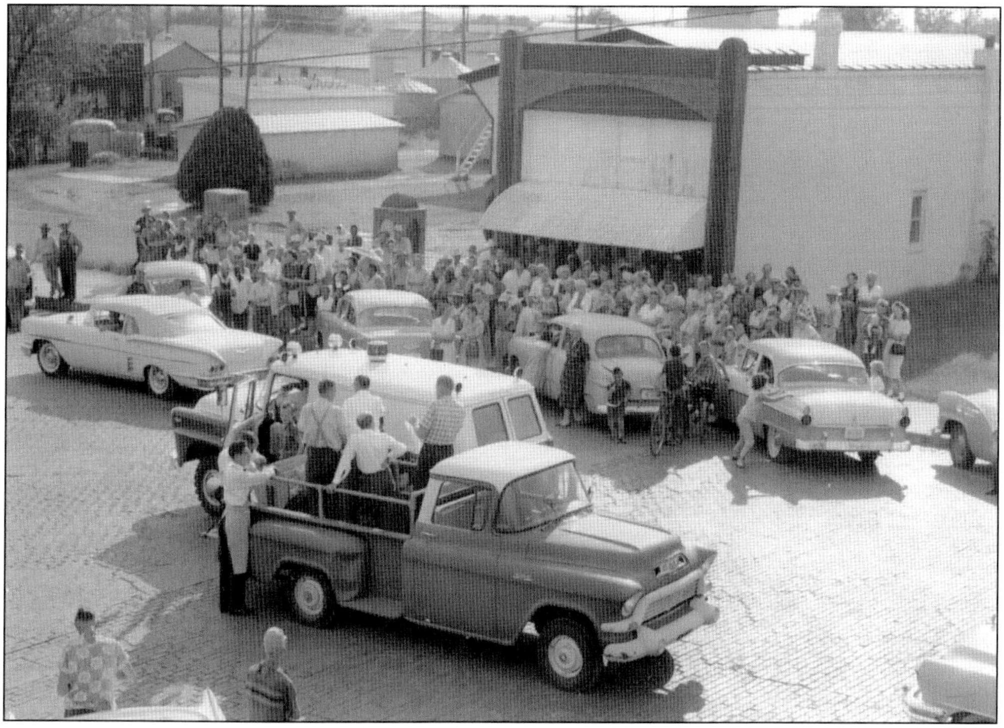

Wagoner Lumber on North Main Street hosted this trade days promotion in the 1950s. Bob Jeffrey was president of the chamber of commerce and organized the Saturday drawings to bring more people to town. (Courtesy of the Cradow Smith collection.)

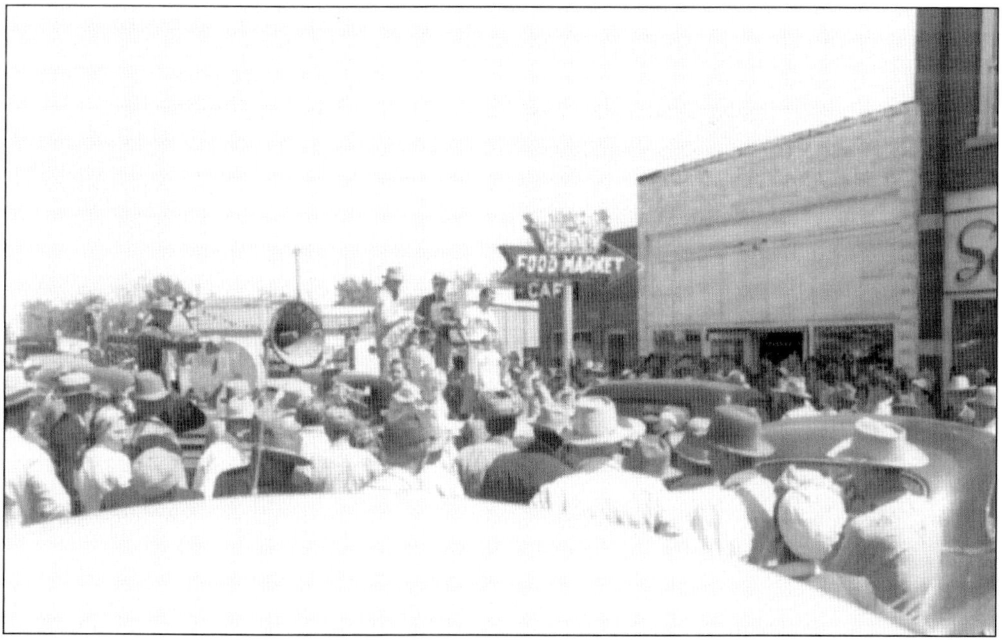

A large crowd has gathered at Don's Food Market, across the street from the courthouse, for a trade days drawing one Saturday afternoon. Don Heathcock owned the store. It later became Jack Smalley's Jack's Food Market. (Courtesy of the Cradow Smith collection.)

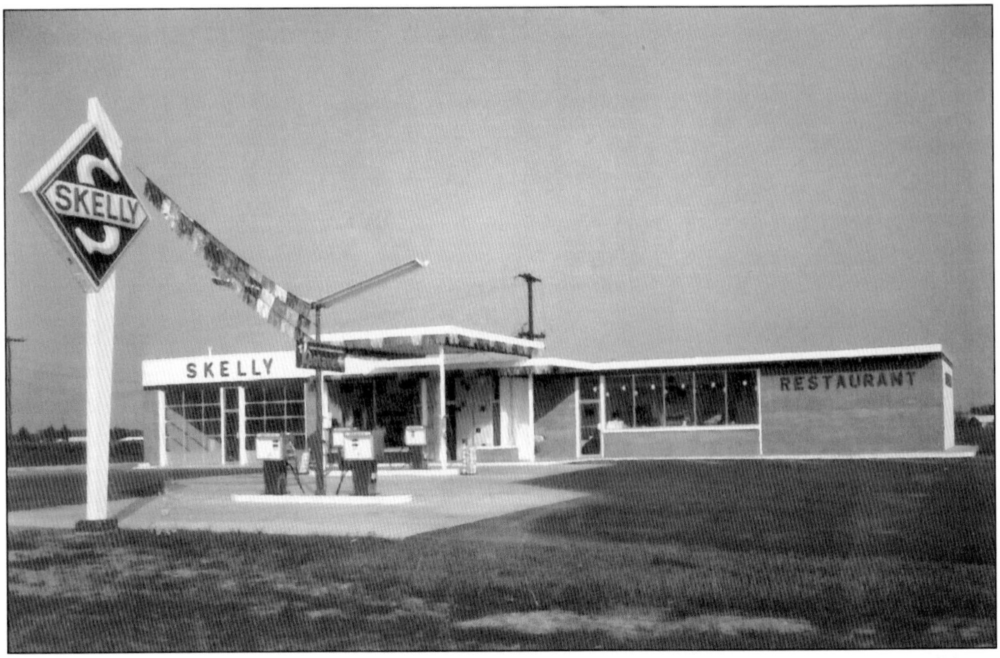

Glen Adams first opened a service station and restaurant on US 69, north of Wagoner, and later moved to the current location just north of the highway at the US 69–US 51 intersection. He eventually phased out the service station and opened a bar in part of the expanded business. (Courtesy of the Cradow Smith collection.)

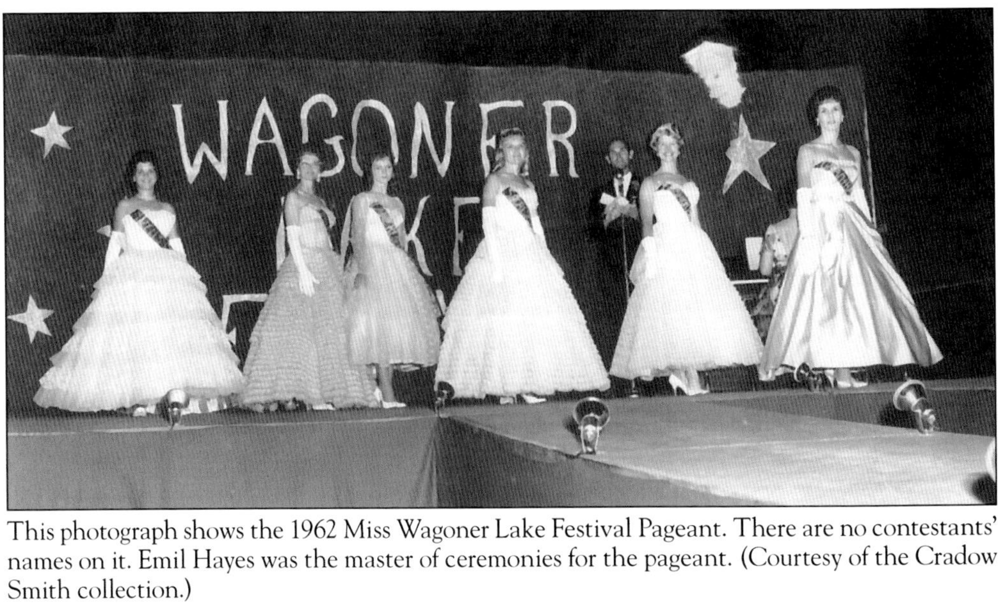

This photograph shows the 1962 Miss Wagoner Lake Festival Pageant. There are no contestants' names on it. Emil Hayes was the master of ceremonies for the pageant. (Courtesy of the Cradow Smith collection.)

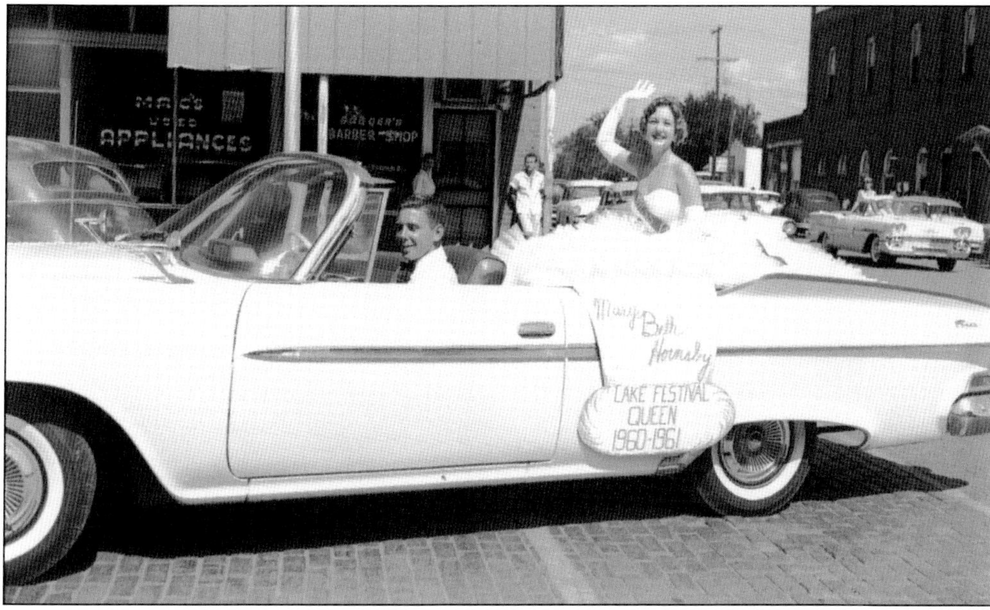

Mary Beth Hornsby was the very first Miss Wagoner Lake Festival. She reigned from 1960 to 1961. The driver for her convertible in the parade is Jack Cochran. (Courtesy of the Cradow Smith collection.)

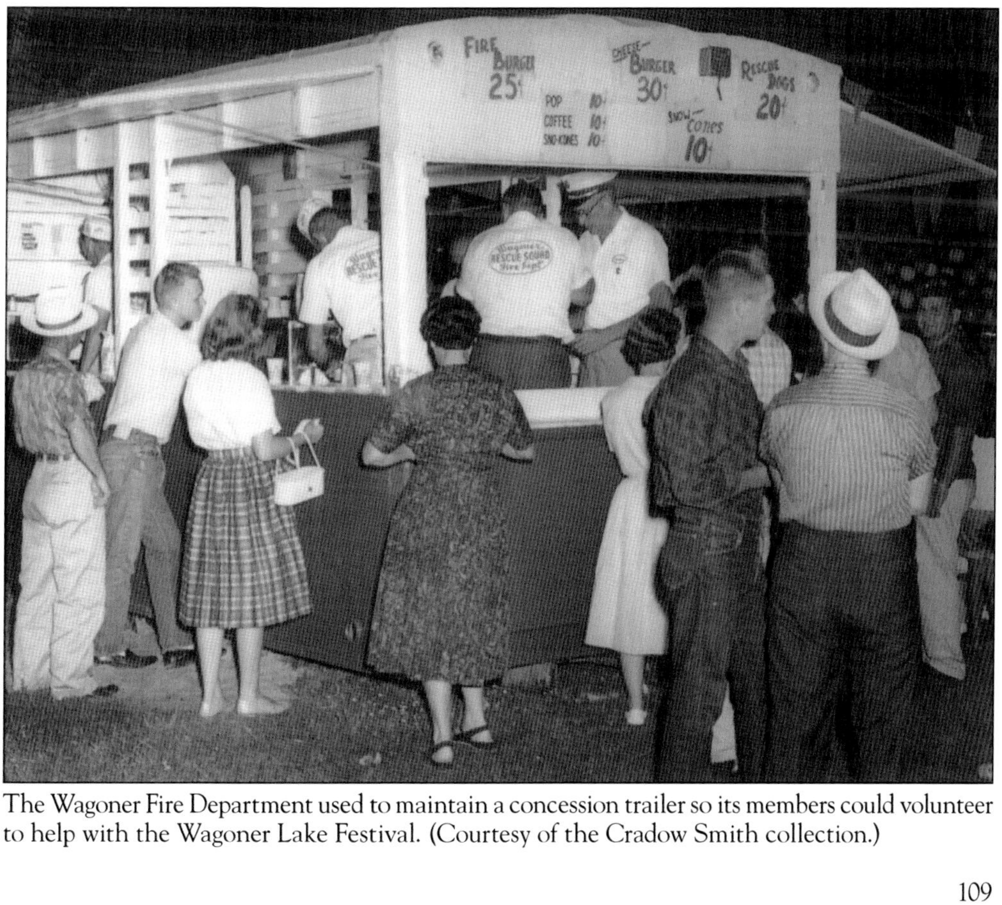

The Wagoner Fire Department used to maintain a concession trailer so its members could volunteer to help with the Wagoner Lake Festival. (Courtesy of the Cradow Smith collection.)

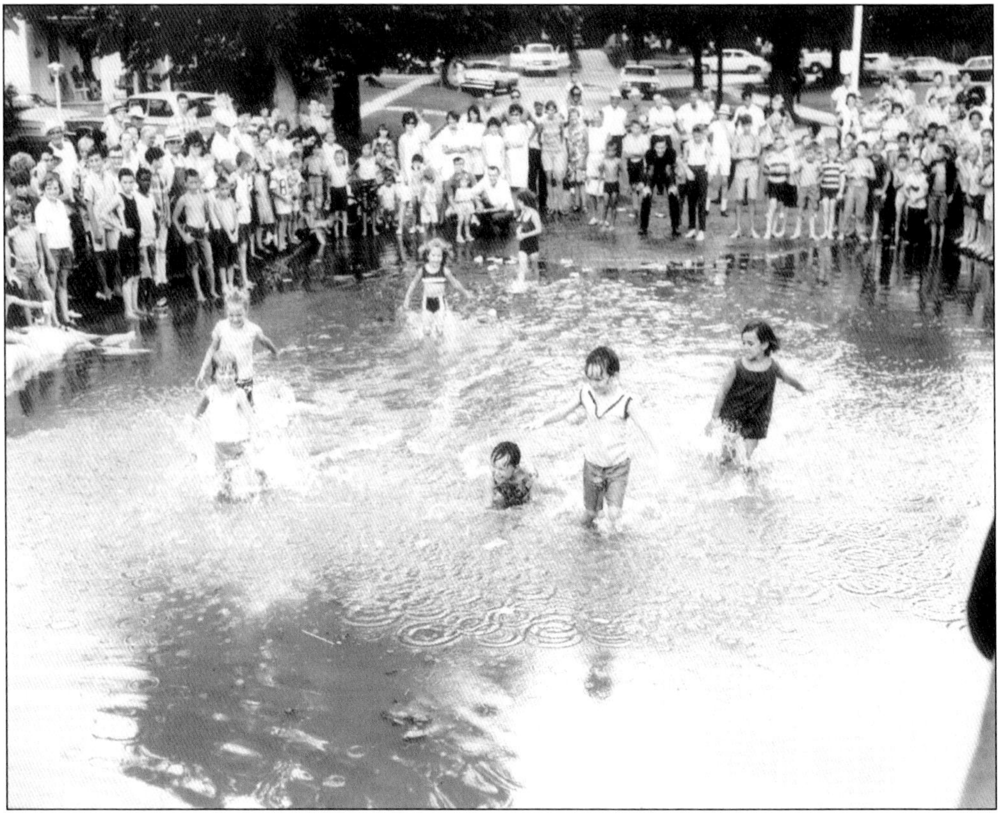

One of the favorite events ever at the Wagoner Lake Festival was the fish scramble. North Casaver Avenue was dammed with sandbags and the fire department pumped water in to create a temporary lake. The state wildlife department turned in tagged fish such as carp, and the youngsters were turned loose to catch the prize fish. A greased pig contest was also held. (Courtesy of the Cradow Smith collection.)

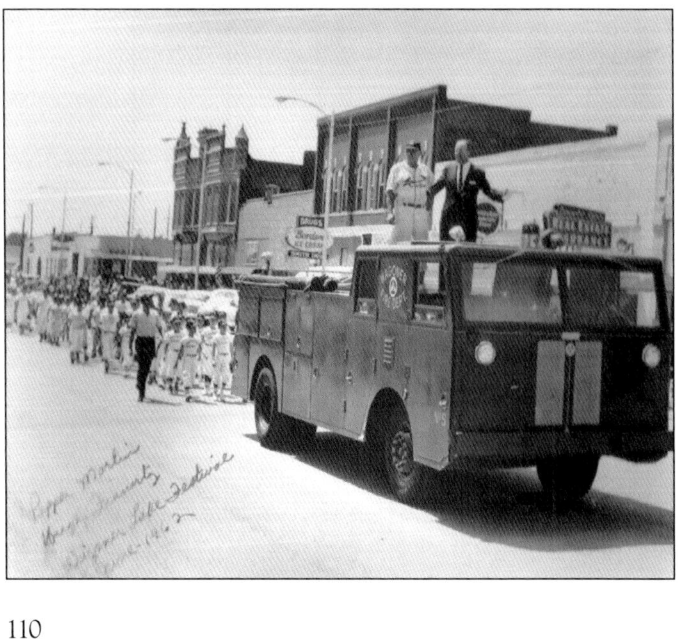

Professional baseball player Pepper Martin and Tulsa sports personality Hugh Finnerty ride atop a Wagoner fire truck for the 1962 Wagoner Lake Festival parade. Martin played for the St. Louis Cardinals. (Courtesy of Sara Posthuma.)

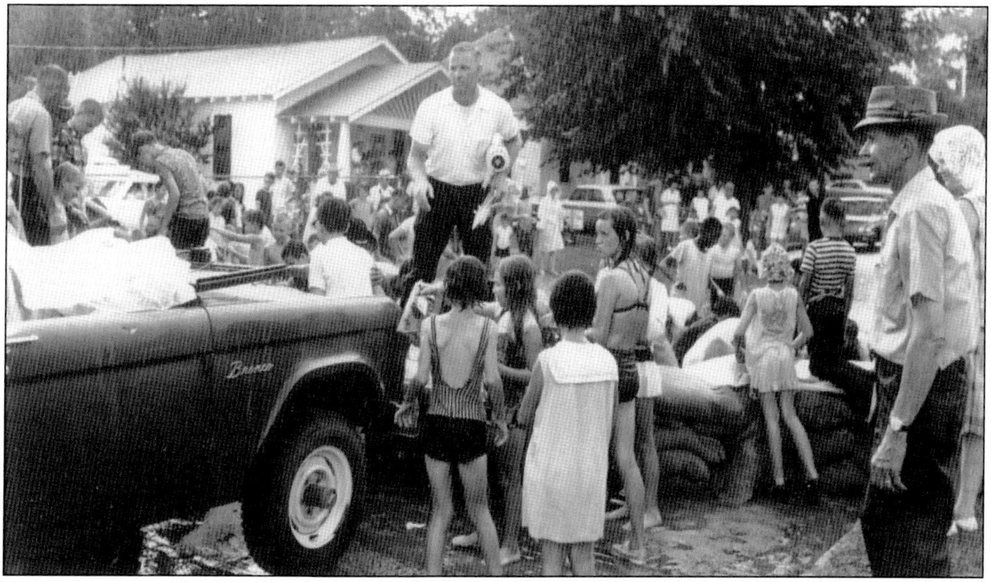

Rance Robison, vocational agriculture teacher, helps get things organized for the Wagoner Lake Festival fish scramble. At right is Johnny Johnson, one of the original organizers of the annual event. (Courtesy of the Cradow Smith collection.)

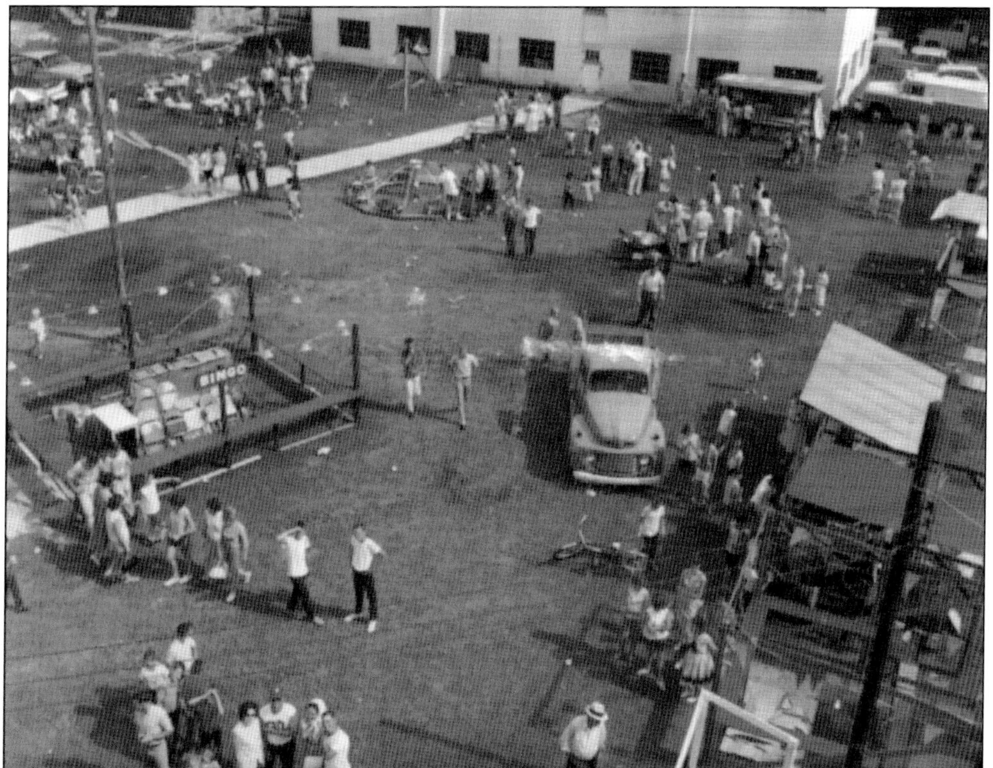

At first, the Wagoner Lake Festival was held on the courthouse lawn and the elementary playground behind the courthouse. There were no other carnivals allowed in Wagoner at the time. (Courtesy of the Cradow Smith collection.)

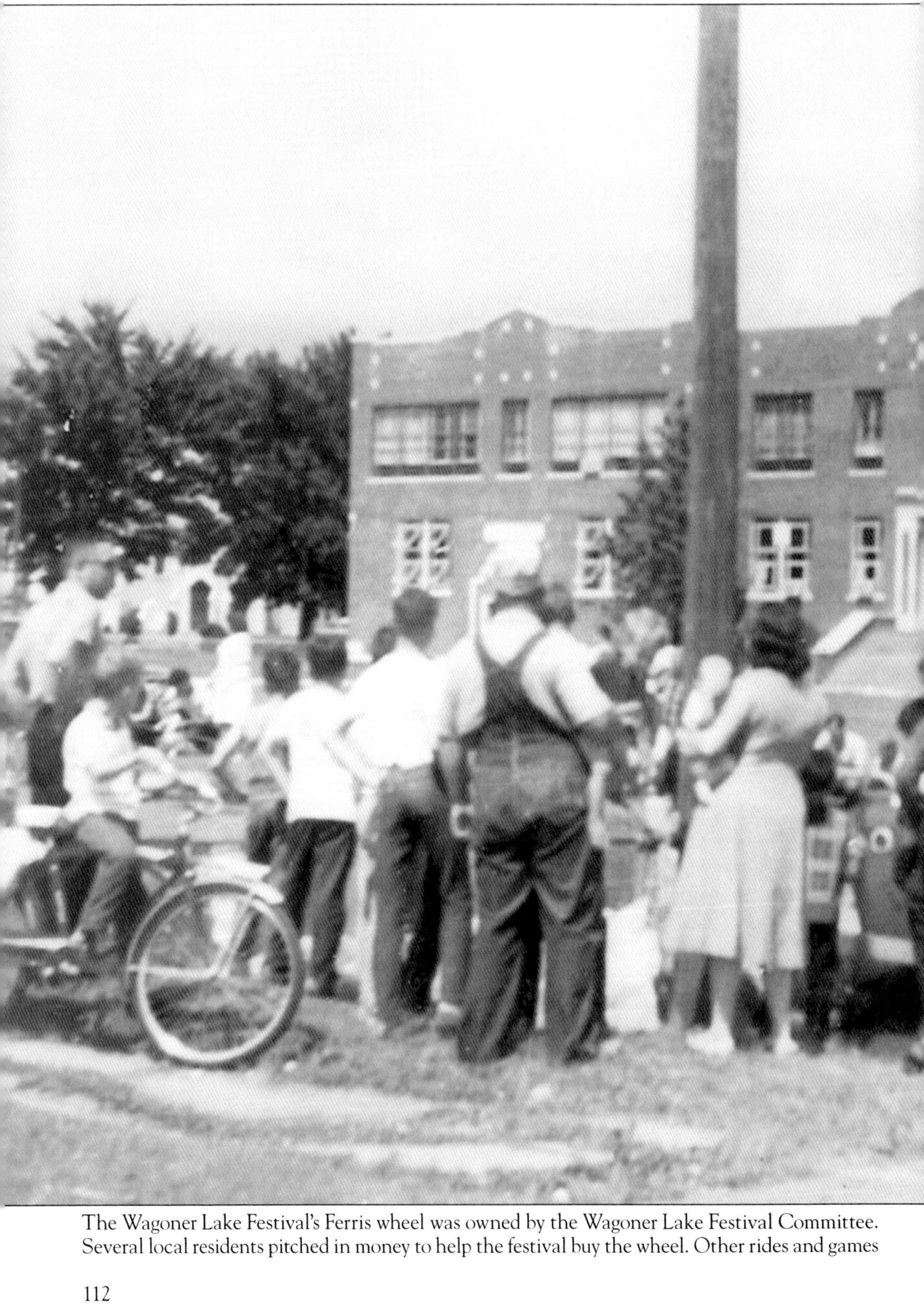

The Wagoner Lake Festival's Ferris wheel was owned by the Wagoner Lake Festival Committee. Several local residents pitched in money to help the festival buy the wheel. Other rides and games

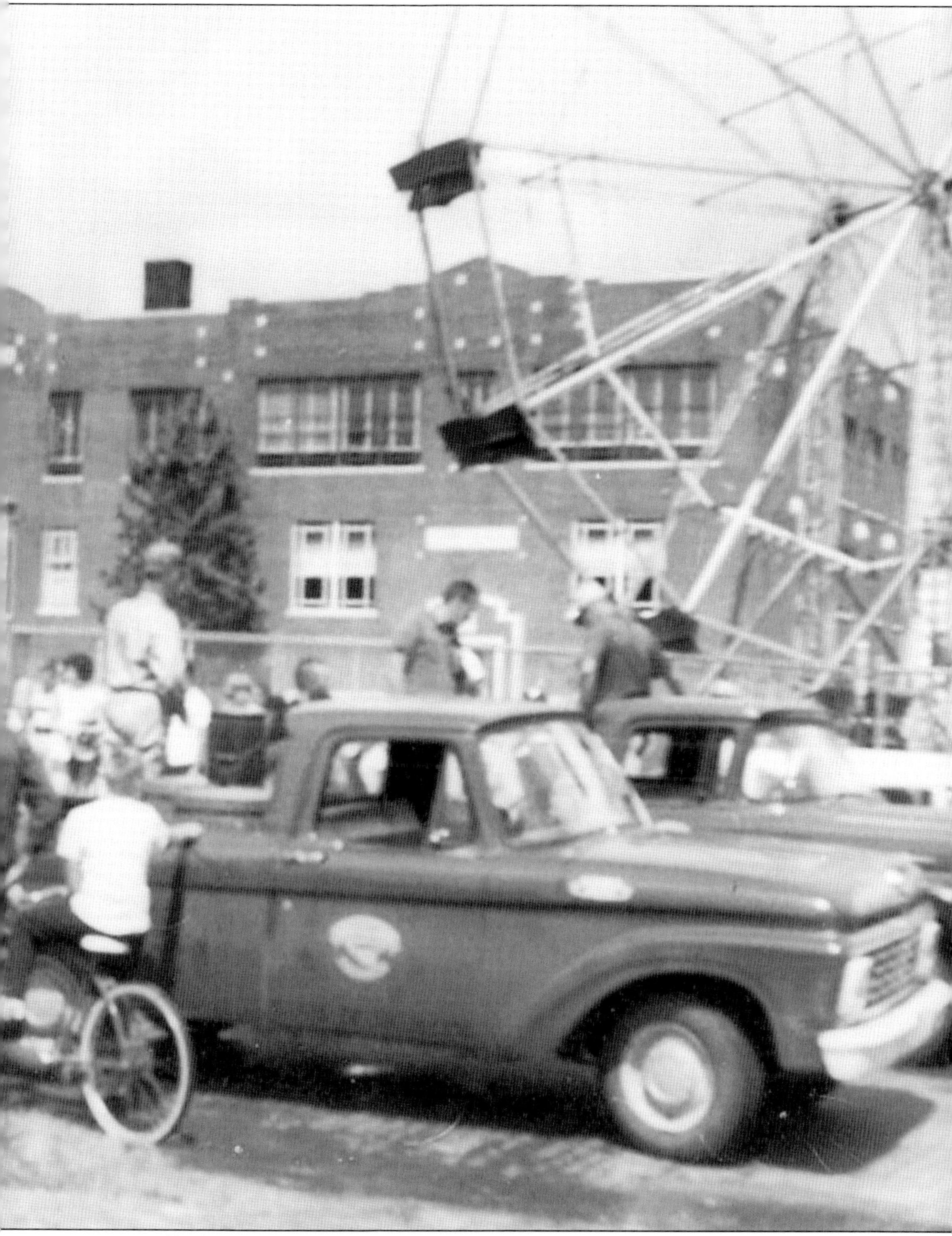

were operated by local businesses and civic groups. The crowd is gathered here for a fish scramble on North Casaver Avenue. (Courtesy of Jerry Hickman.)

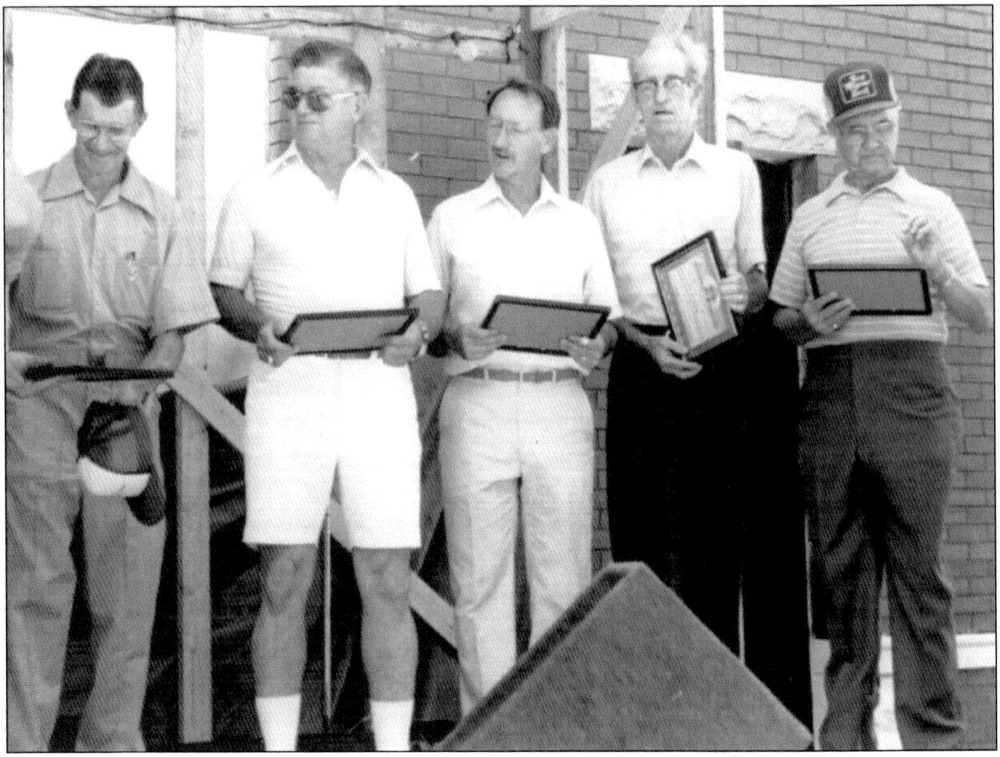

This group was honored at Summerfest for its role in having started the event as the Wagoner Lake Festival. The festival name was changed around 1971. Pictured, from left to right, are Johnny Johnson, Bub Stacy, John Sleeper, Joe Ben Cobb and Pete Stauss. (Author's collection.)

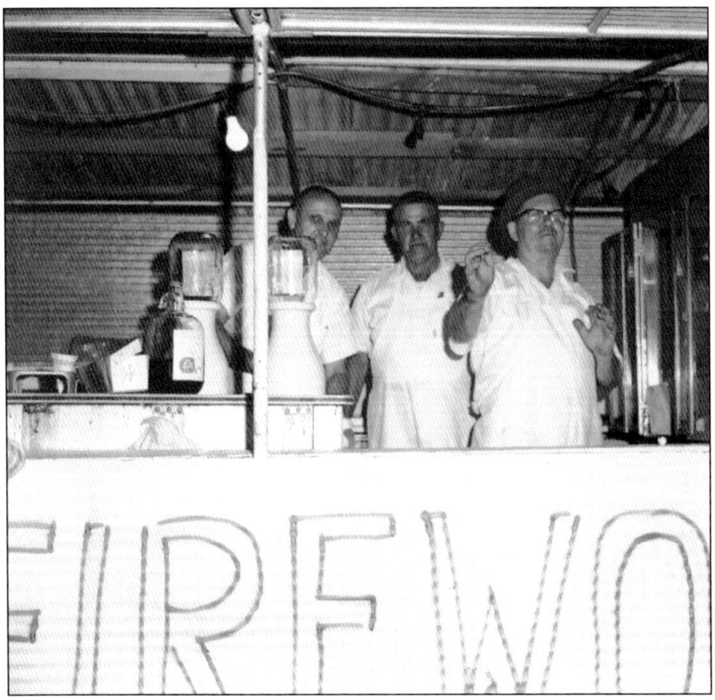

Wagoner Fire Department volunteers operate a fireworks stand at Cherokee Street and Casaver Avenue. (Courtesy of the Cradow Smith collection.)

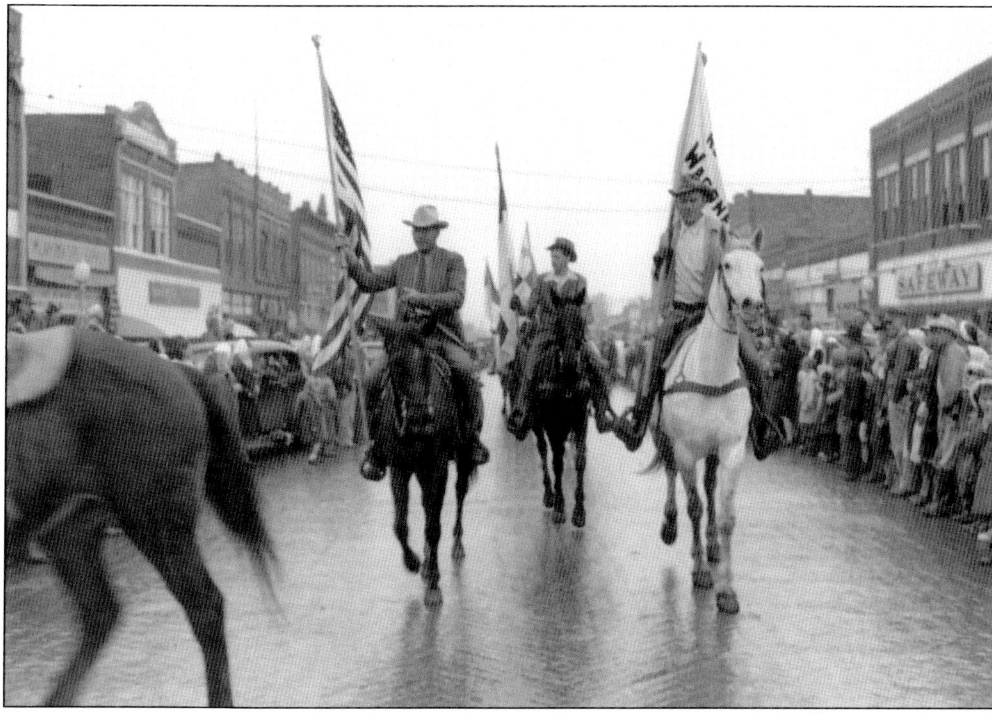

Wagoner's brick streets glisten after a rainfall just before this parade through downtown. The riders, coming north on Main Street, are from the Wagoner Round-up Club. (Author's collection.)

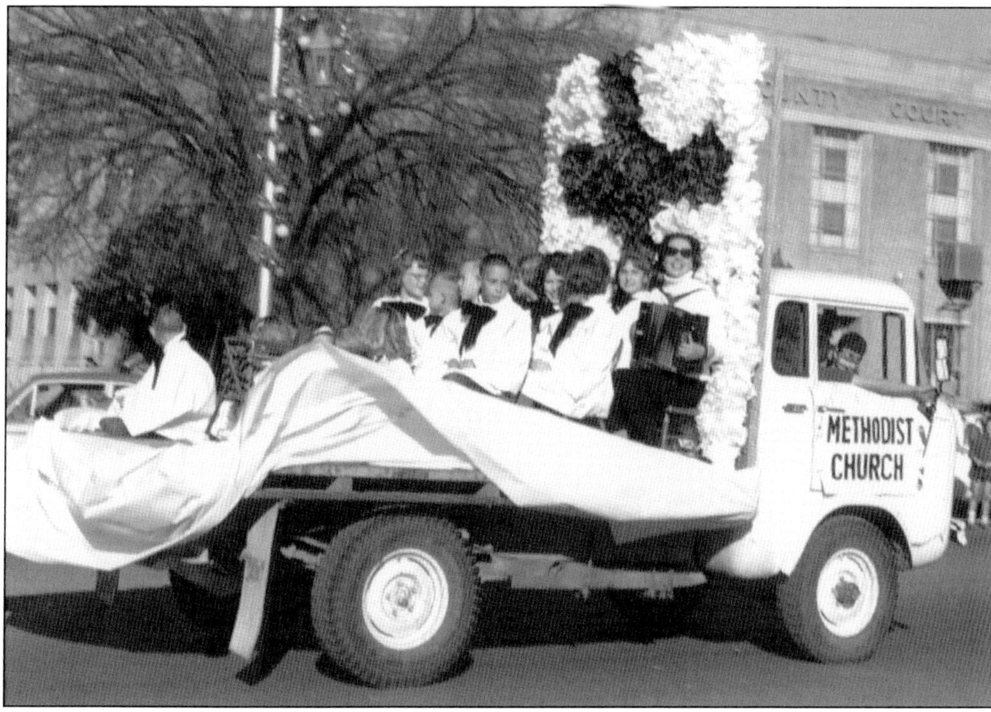

Mary Stacy, beloved choir director at First Methodist Church, rides on the back of a truck in a parade held during the 1950s or 1960s. (Courtesy of the Cradow Smith collection.)

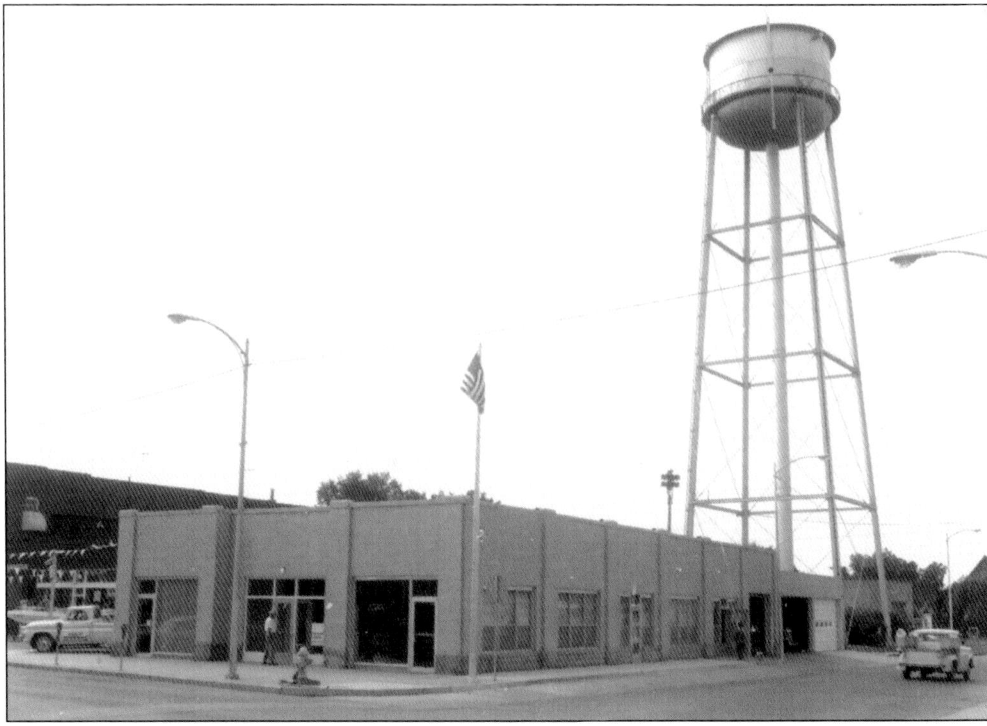

Wagoner City Hall operations had been moved to the old Agricultural Stabilization and Conservation Service offices on Church Street by the time this photograph was taken. The chamber of commerce offices took over the office at the right front of the building. The water tower was later torn down. (Courtesy of the Cradow Smith collection.)

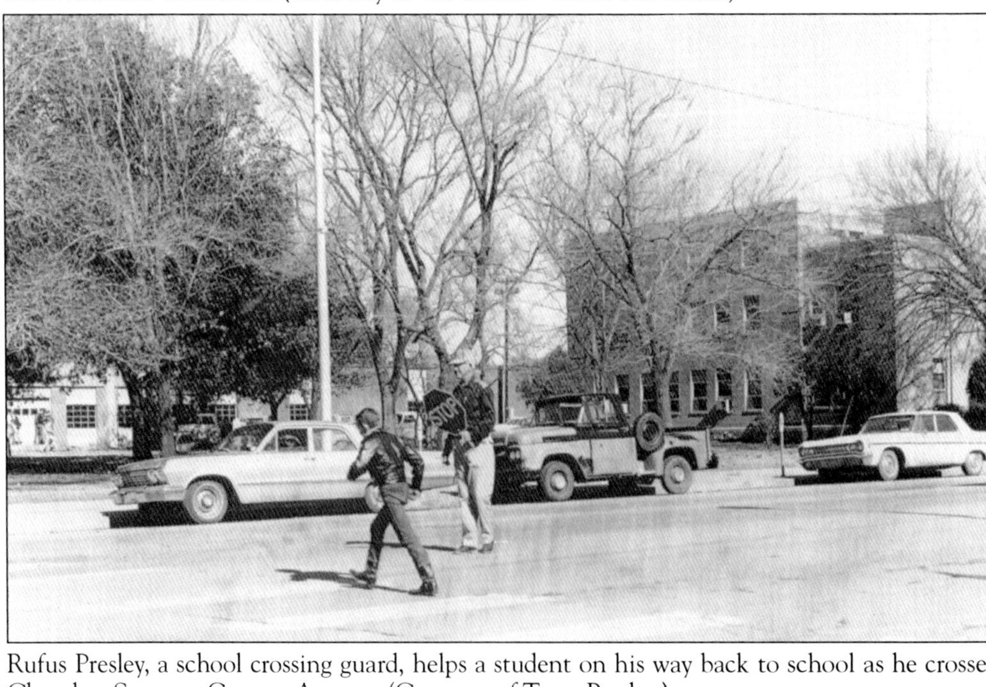

Rufus Presley, a school crossing guard, helps a student on his way back to school as he crosses Cherokee Street at Casaver Avenue. (Courtesy of Terry Presley.)

One of five Wagoner storefronts built by tinsmith Ed Lee in the late 1800s was this one. Carr's Furniture occupied the building for many years. The front was replaced before a fire heavily damaged the building in 1976. (Author's collection.)

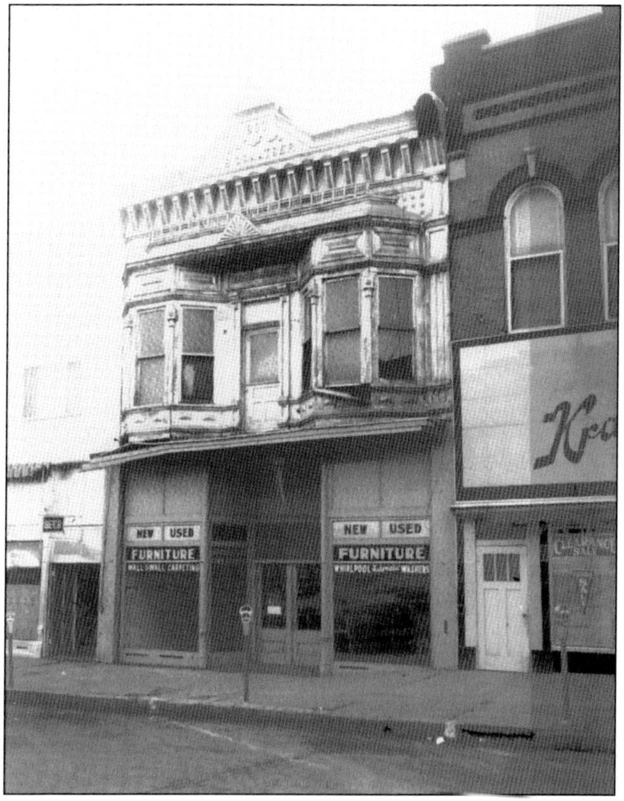

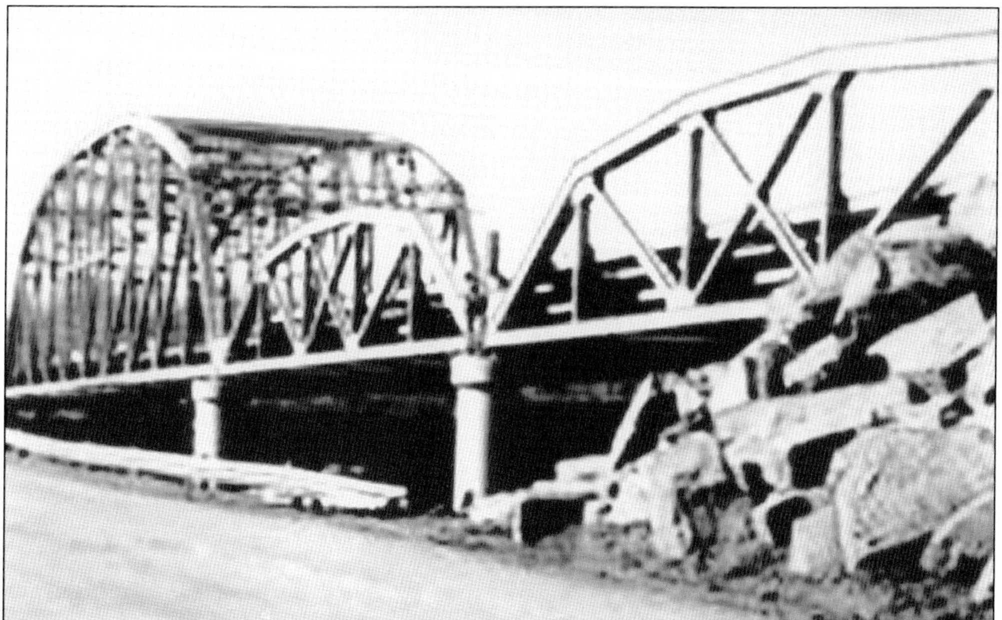

This bridge, built over the Verdigris River west of Wagoner in 1954, was raised to new heights when the McClellan-Kerr Navigation System started. It was imploded when a new bridge was built in 2009. (Author's collection.)

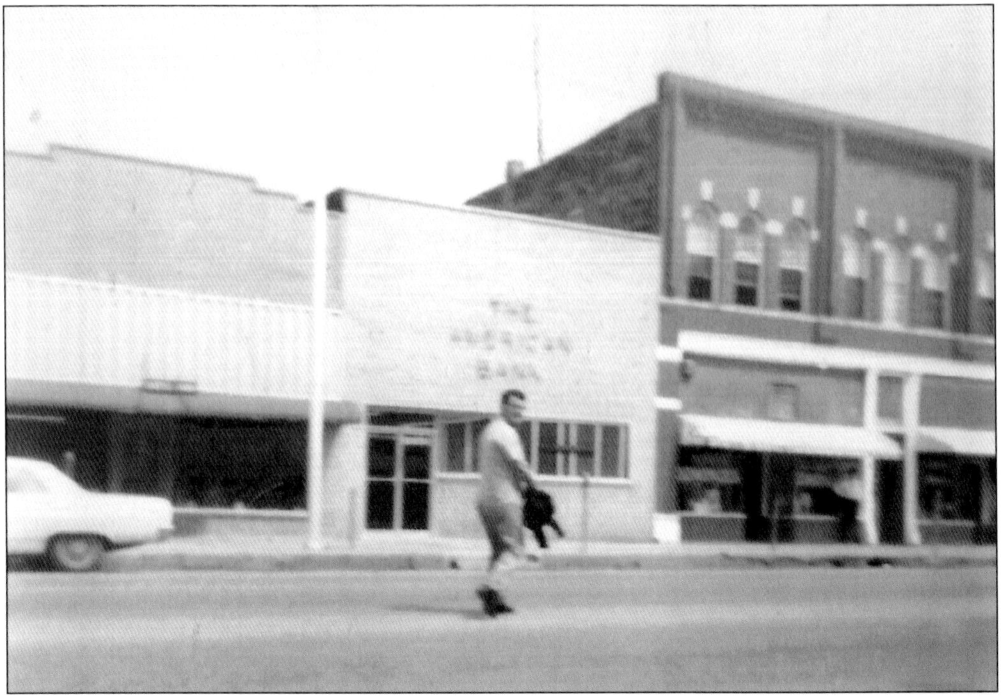

Before American Bank saved the Cobb Building from destruction by remodeling it, the bank was located in this small, one-story building on East Cherokee Street. (Author's collection.)

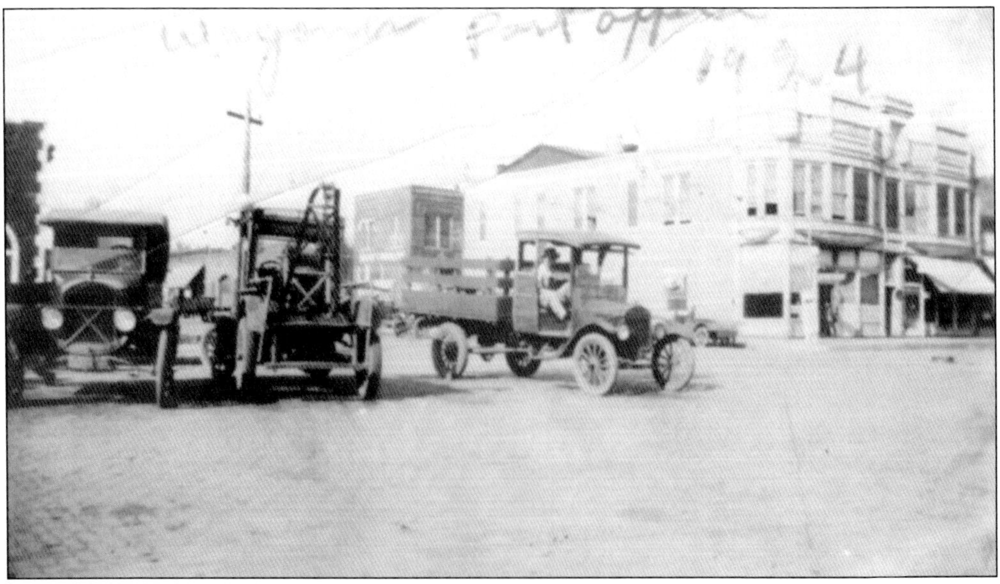

The grand S.S. Cobb Building at Main and Cherokee Streets was about to be razed when the owners of American Bank stepped up and rescued it. Extensive renovations were done and the building is now listed in the National Register of Historic Places. In this 1924 photograph, the building houses the Wagoner Post Office. The government paid $2,100 per year to rent it. (Courtesy of Shirle Lamb Williams.)

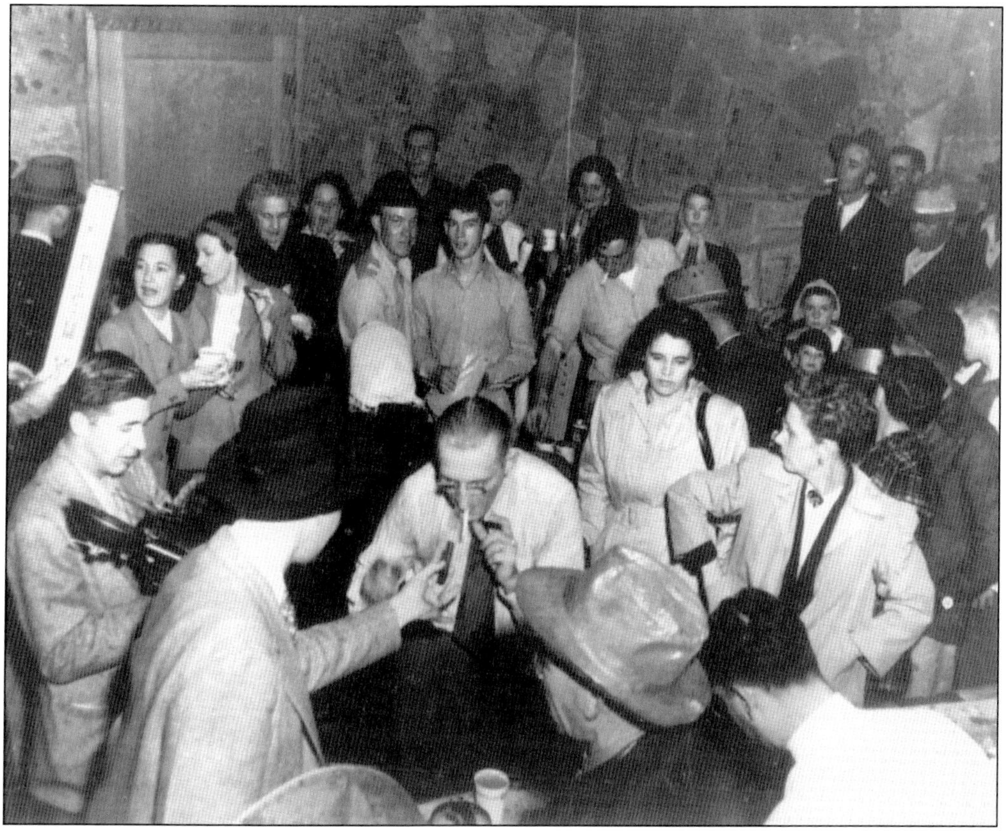

This photograph is believed to be from a celebration in November 1947 celebrating the opening of the "new" US 69, when it was moved from Gertrude to Blake. This event was held in the Community Building. Lillian Adams is just to the right of center with the light coat. Jack Cochran is in the background with black hat. (Author's collection.)

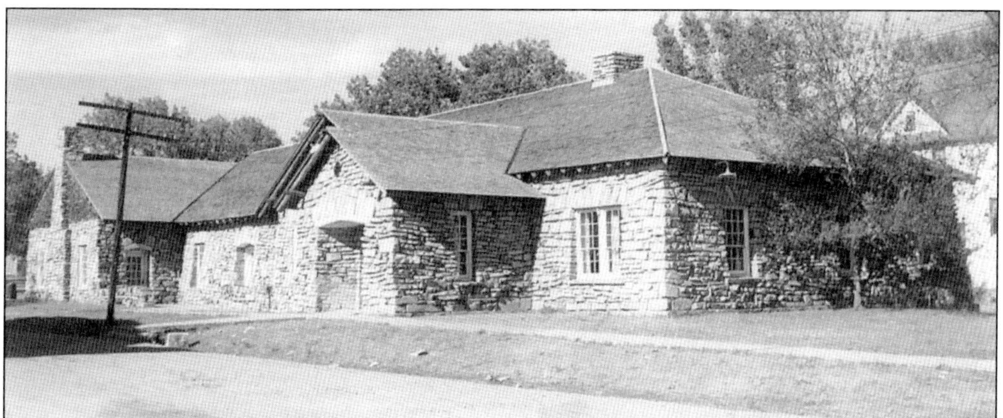

Built in the 1930s by the Works Progress Administration, the Community Building at Jefferson Avenue and Cherokee Street is rented out for a wide variety of events, including birthday parties, family reunions, and square dances. (Author's collection.)

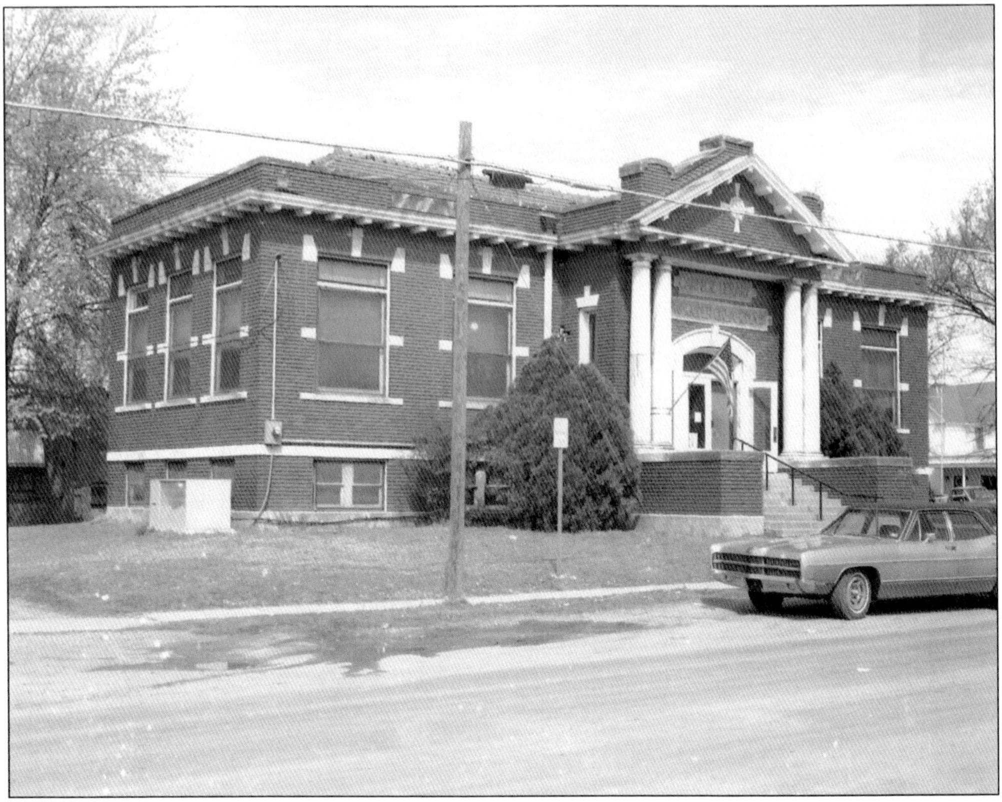

Built with a grant from the Carnegie Corporation in 1913, Wagoner's old library now houses the Three Forks Genealogical Society. (Courtesy of the Cradow Smith collection.)

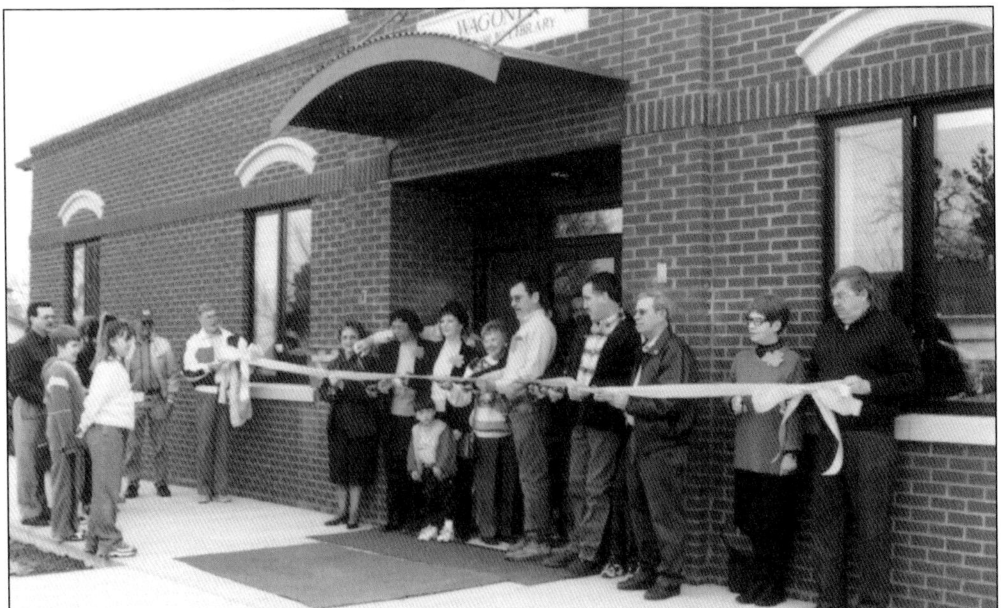

The ribbon cutting for the Wagoner City Library was held in 2001. The facility is at Northeast Second and Main Streets. (Author's collection.)

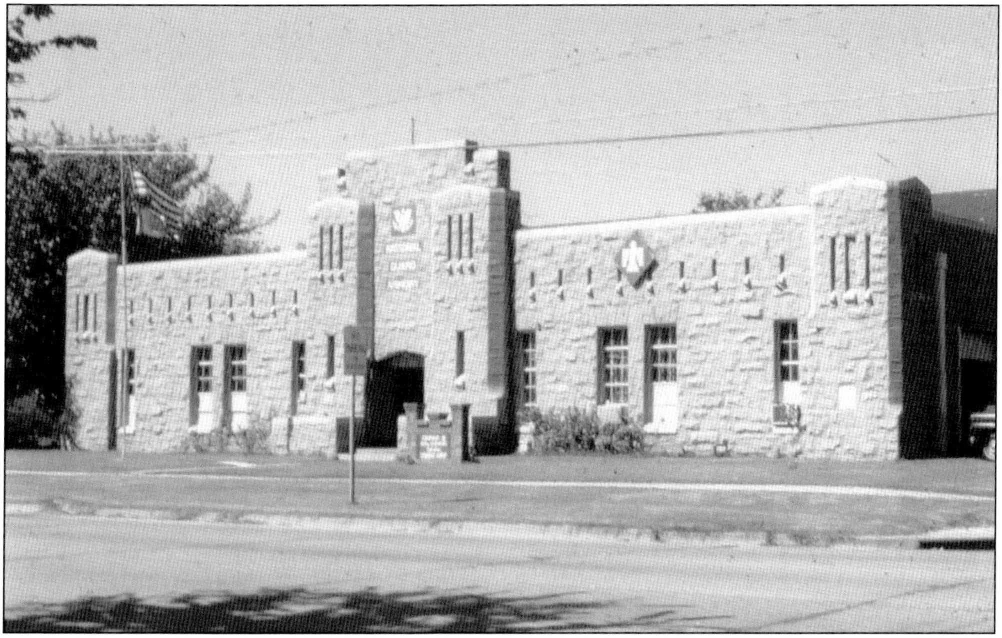

Wagoner's National Guard Armory is now used to store supplies for the Wagoner Public Works Authority. It was built by the Works Progress Administration and for many years housed the prestigious Company C 1st Battalion 279th Infantry Division of the Oklahoma National Guard. (Author's collection.)

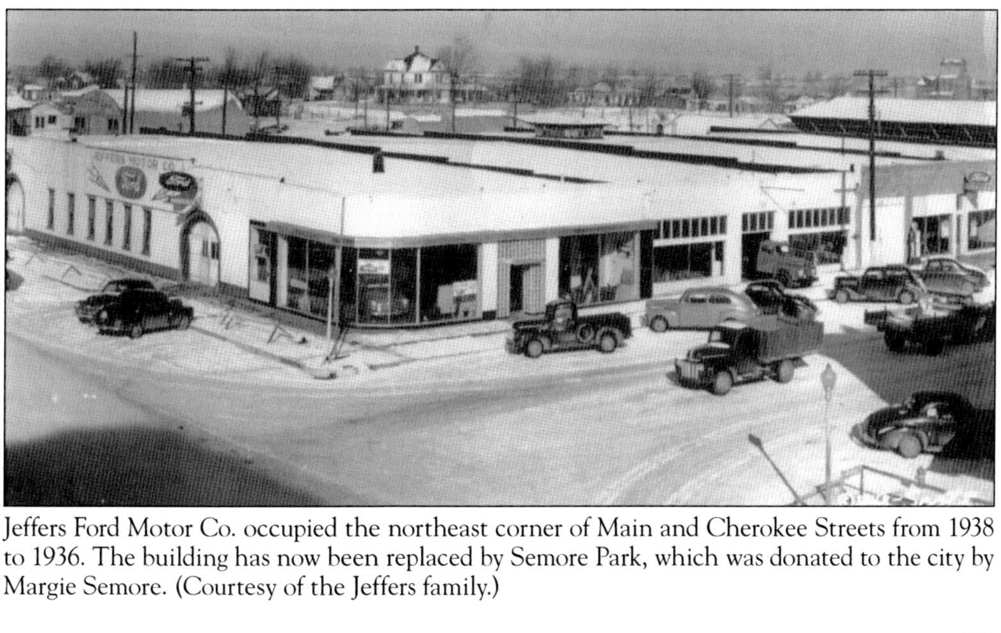

Jeffers Ford Motor Co. occupied the northeast corner of Main and Cherokee Streets from 1938 to 1936. The building has now been replaced by Semore Park, which was donated to the city by Margie Semore. (Courtesy of the Jeffers family.)

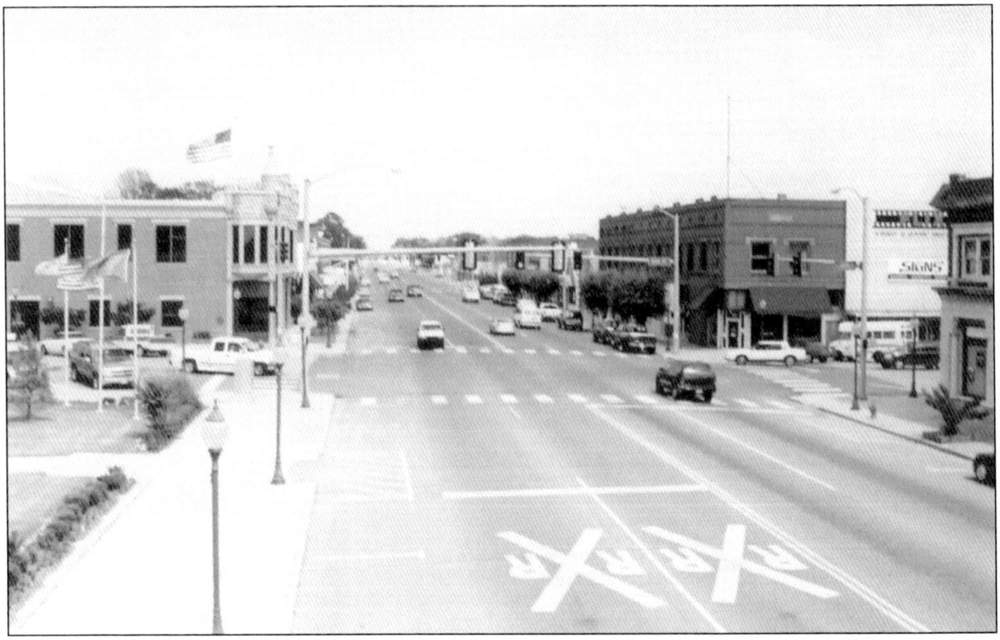

This aerial photograph with a view looking west at Main and Cherokee Streets was taken around 2000. Old-fashioned streetlights give the town a look from the past, while it looks toward the future. (Courtesy of Kenneth Peters.)

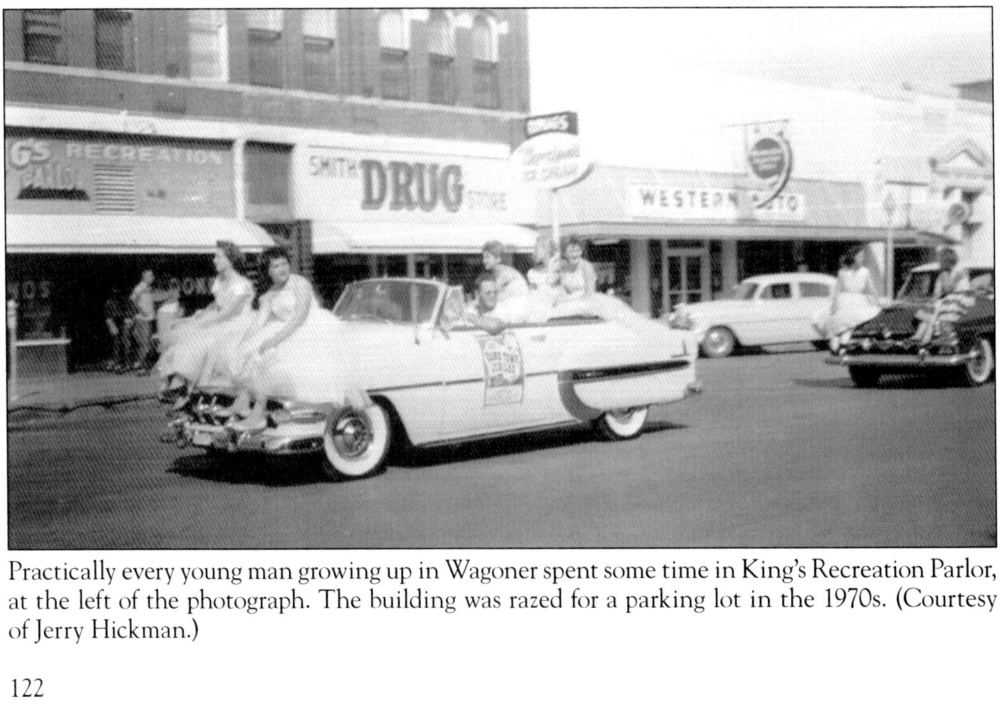

Practically every young man growing up in Wagoner spent some time in King's Recreation Parlor, at the left of the photograph. The building was razed for a parking lot in the 1970s. (Courtesy of Jerry Hickman.)

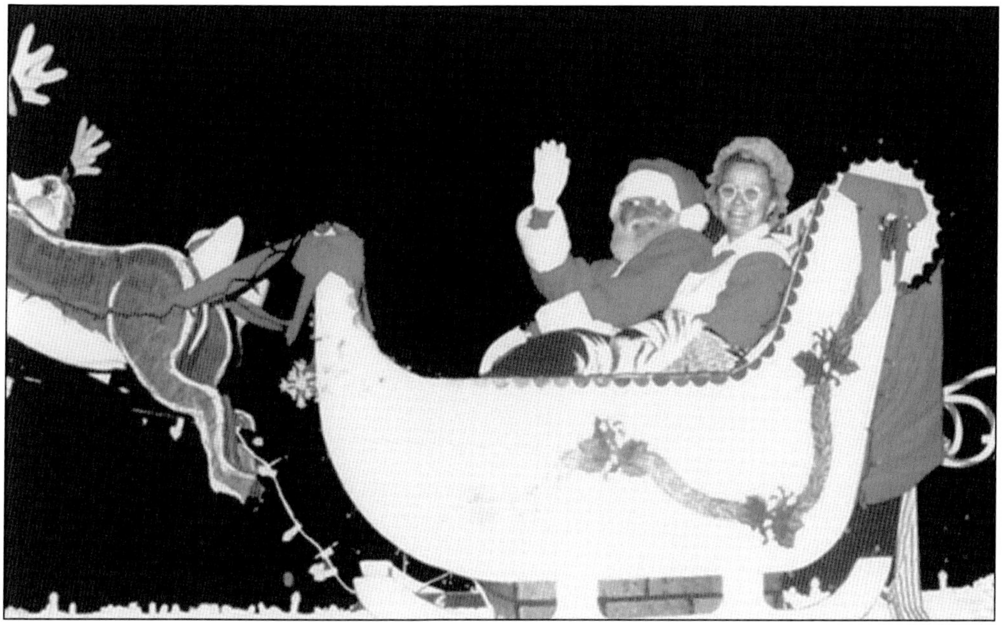

Mrs. Claus always joins Santa for a ride in Wagoner's Christmas parade these days. The city owns the reindeer-driven float and John and Mary Yates play the North Pole couple. (Author's collection.)

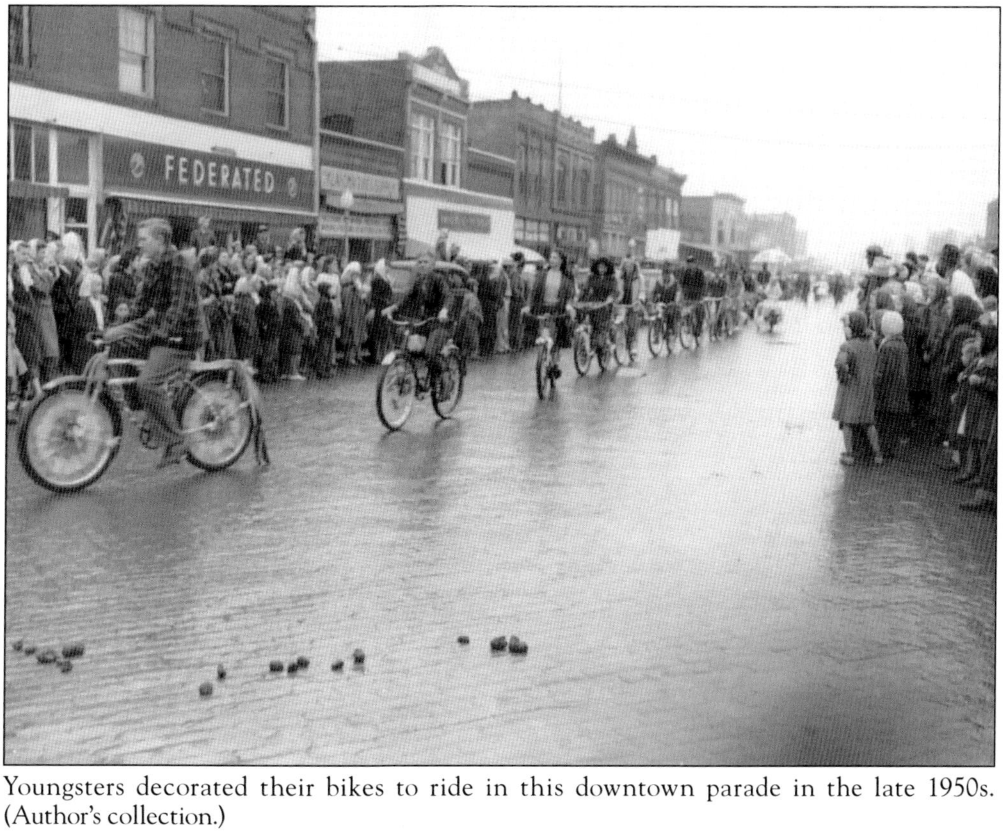

Youngsters decorated their bikes to ride in this downtown parade in the late 1950s. (Author's collection.)

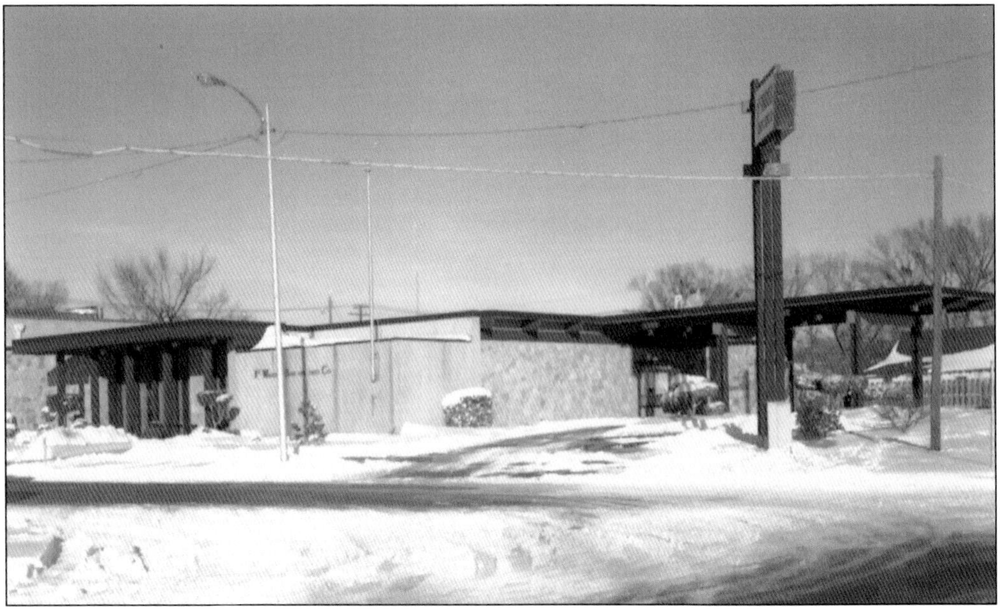

After many years at the heart of Wagoner's downtown, First Bank and Trust Co. built a new facility at Casaver Avenue and Church Street several years ago. The bank is just across from the post office and two doors down from city hall, making it a vital part of downtown. (Courtesy of the Cradow Smith collection.)

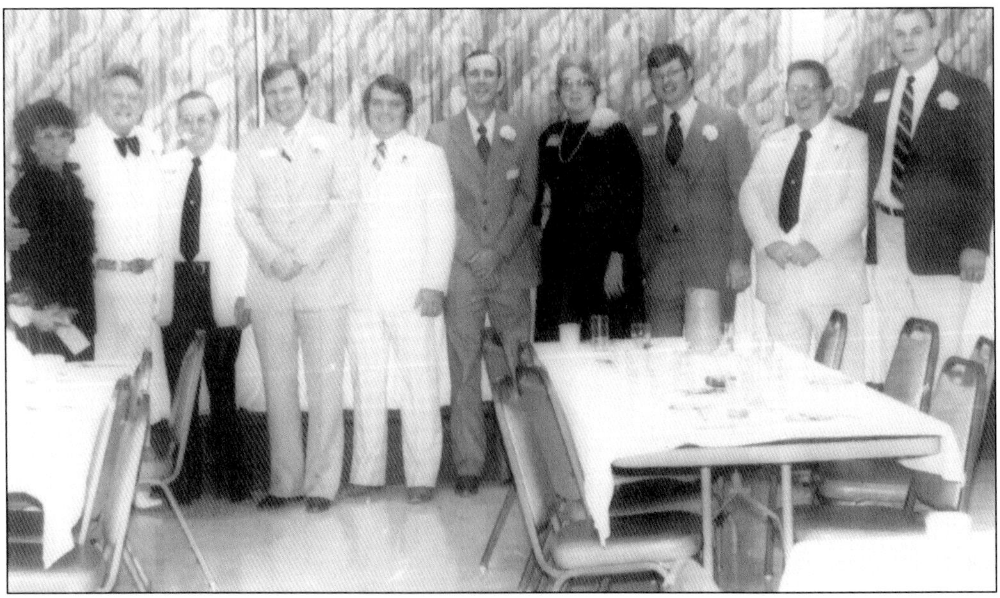

Jerry Clower (second from left), the wonderful country comedian, was guest speaker at a packed Wagoner Chamber of Commerce banquet held at Western Hills State Lodge in the early 1970s. Lucy Mallett, standing next to Clower at far left, was the person with the idea of bringing a big name to the annual banquet. Chamber board members pictured are, from third from left, Jim Sanders, Jess Page, Dr. Robert Hughes, Bob Vanbrunt, Nancy Durham, Dan French, Red Chapman, and Jimmy Williams. (Author's collection.)

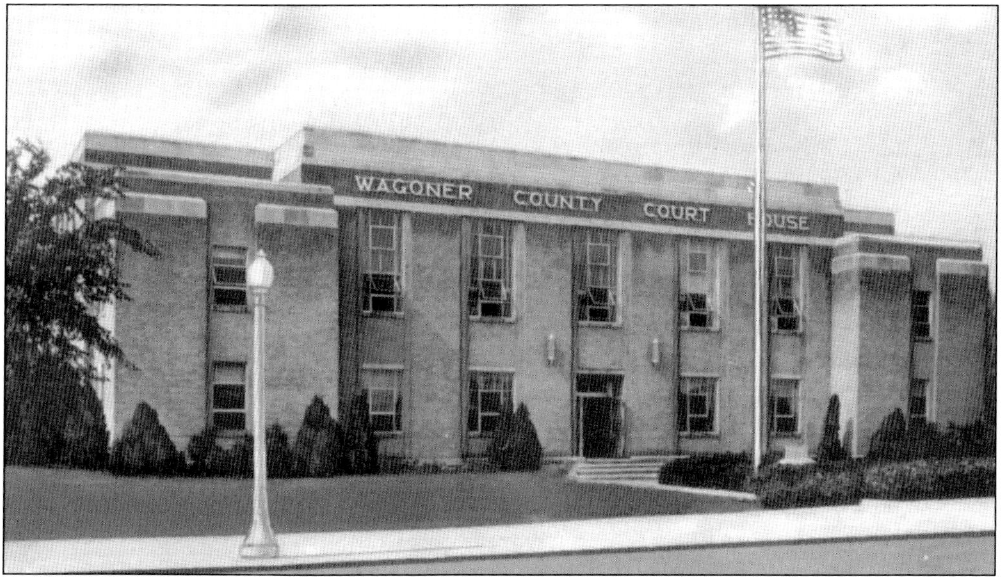

Built by the Works Progress Administration in 1936, the Wagoner County Courthouse outgrew its building a half century later and greatly expanded. (Author's collection.)

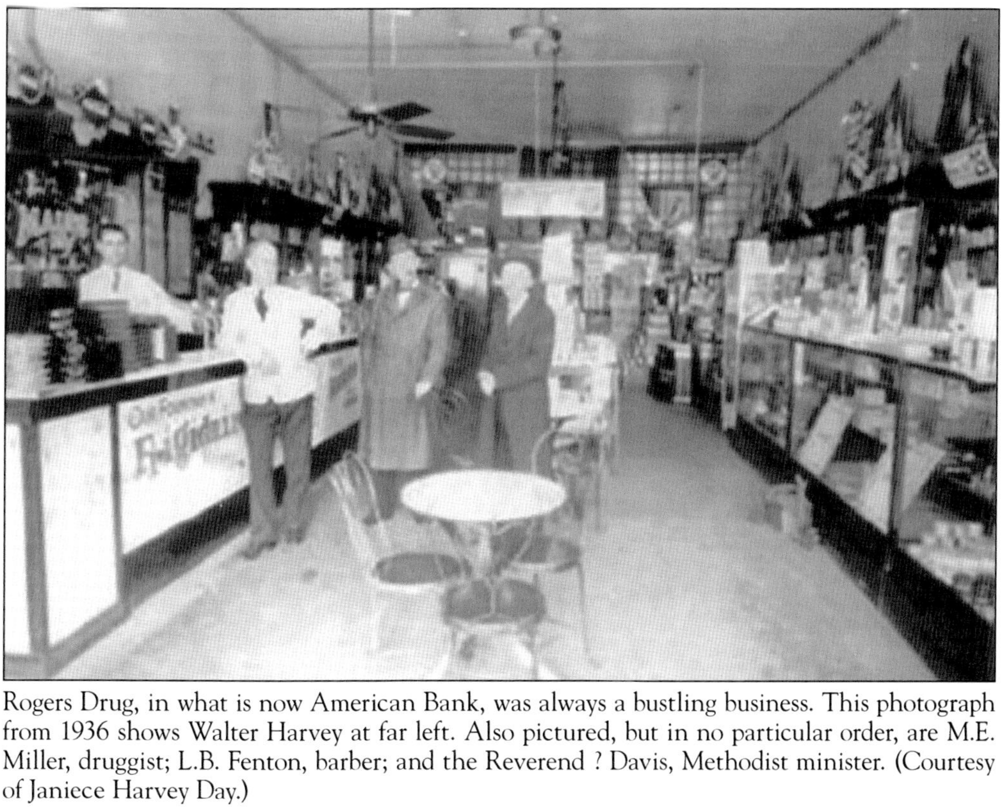

Rogers Drug, in what is now American Bank, was always a bustling business. This photograph from 1936 shows Walter Harvey at far left. Also pictured, but in no particular order, are M.E. Miller, druggist; L.B. Fenton, barber; and the Reverend ? Davis, Methodist minister. (Courtesy of Janiece Harvey Day.)

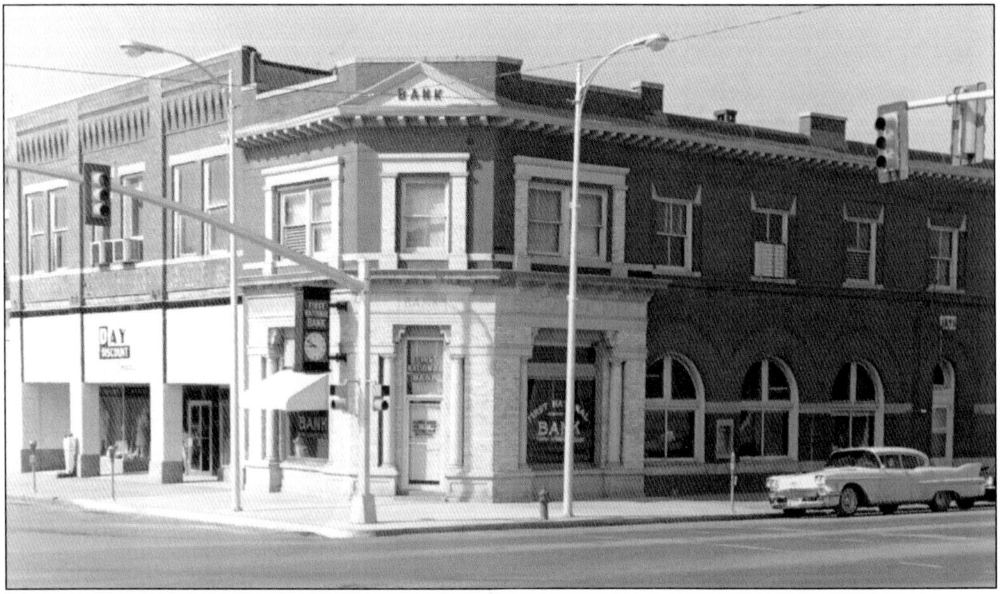

First National Bank became the sixth bank to be chartered in Oklahoma when it opened at Cherokee and Main Streets in 1895. While the bank no longer is located on that corner, the building is occupied by a financial advisor's office. (Courtesy of the Cradow Smith collection.)

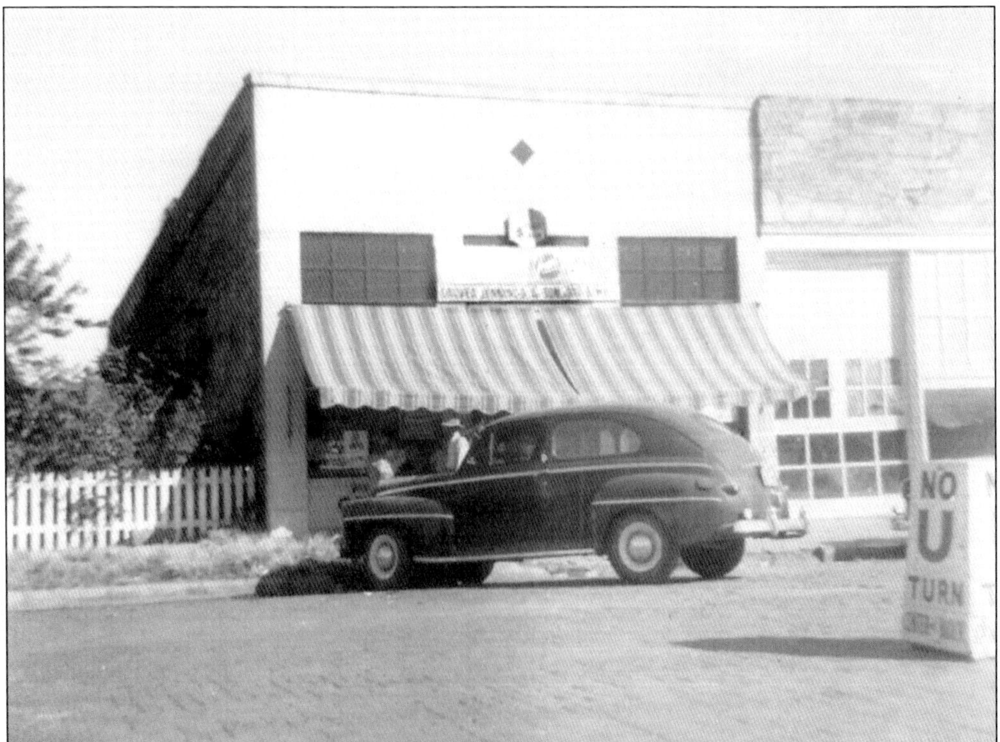

Grover Jennings opened a little grocery store on South Main Street in 1933. When he retired, his son, Ivan, took over. In 2015, a third-generation Jennings, James, operated the store with the help of his mother, Maxine. (Courtesy of James Jennings.)

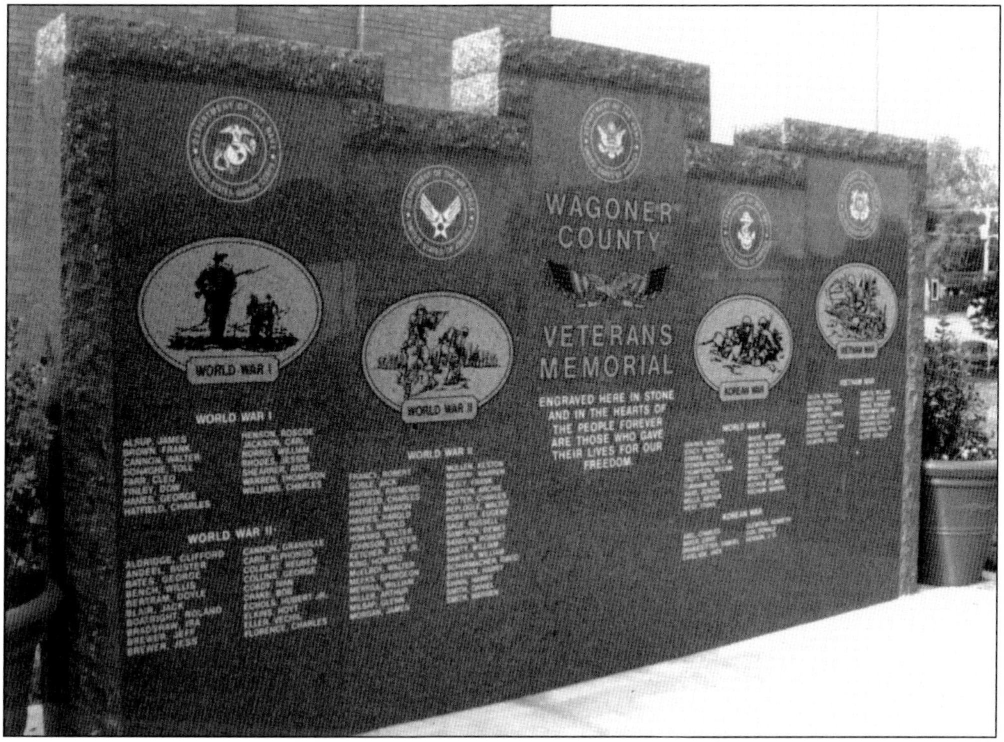

A granite monument on Wagoner's courthouse lawn pays tribute to the county's war dead. Memorial Day and Veterans Day programs are held at the monument each year. (Author's collection.)

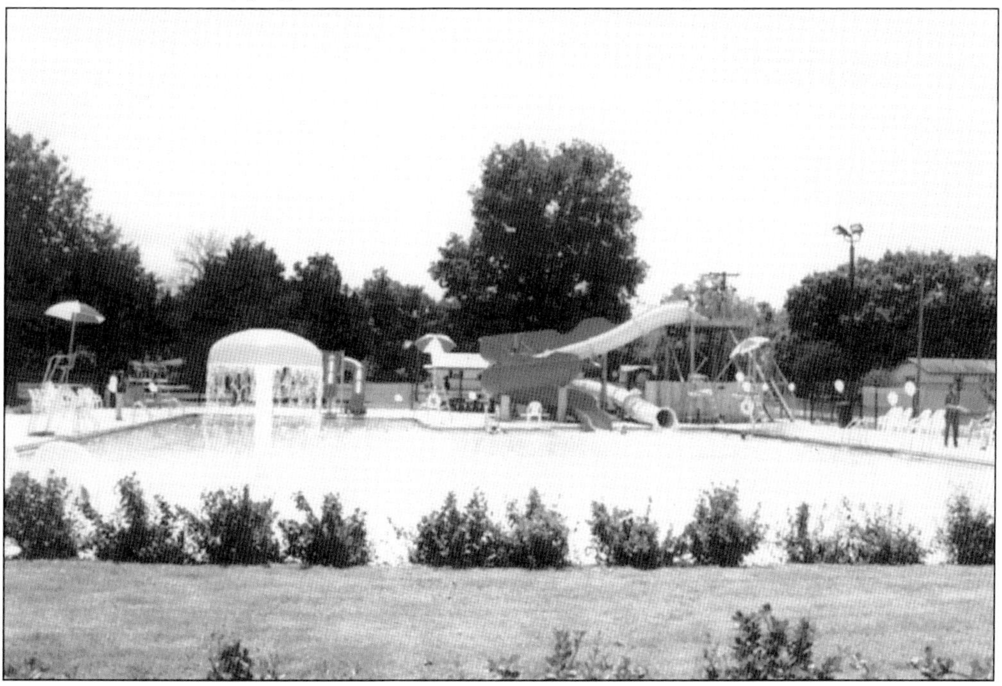

A water park with two slides has been built at Maple Park, and hundreds of children take advantage of the opportunity to cool off there each summer. (Author's collection.)